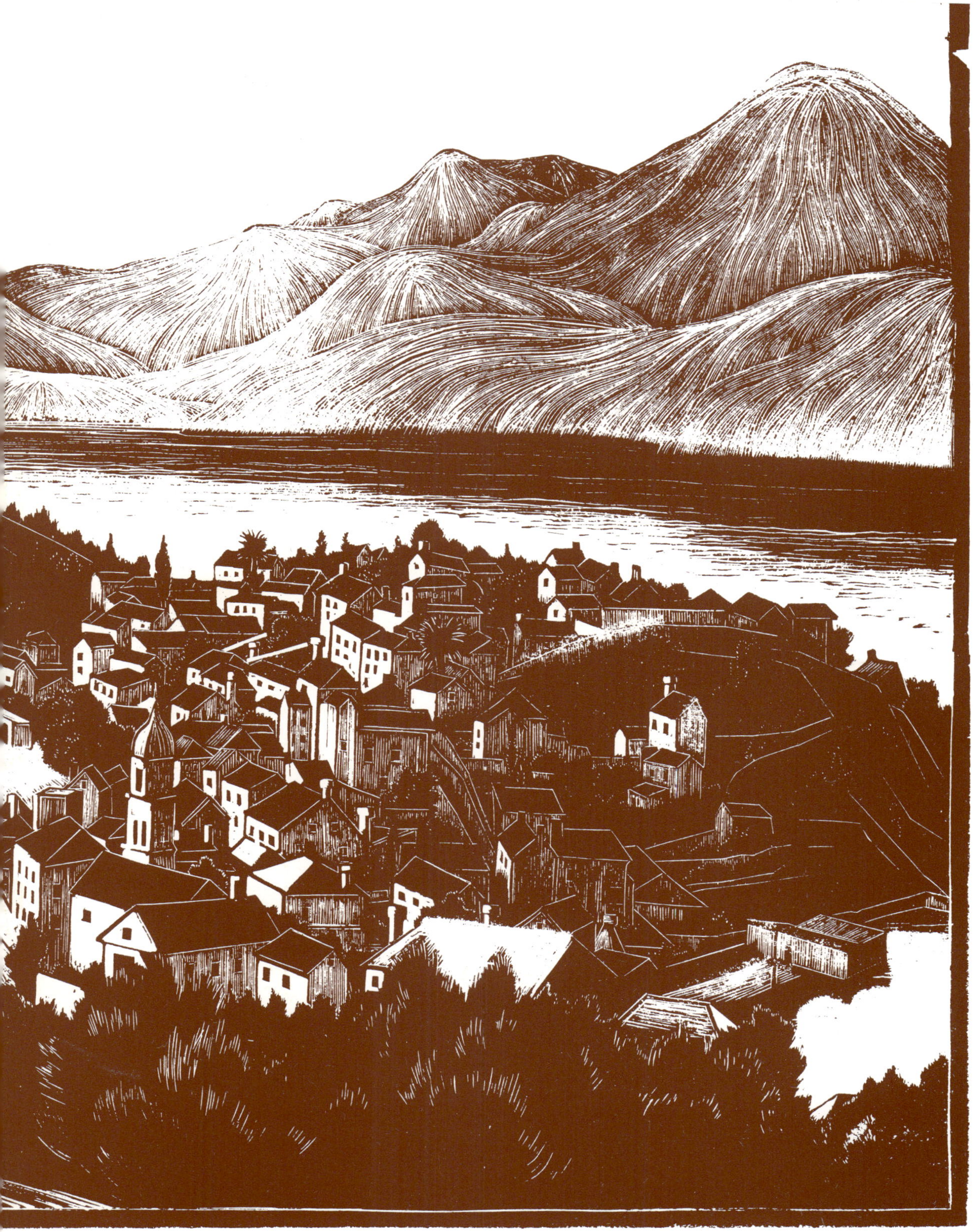

THE WOOD ENGRAVINGS OF

CLARE LEIGHTON

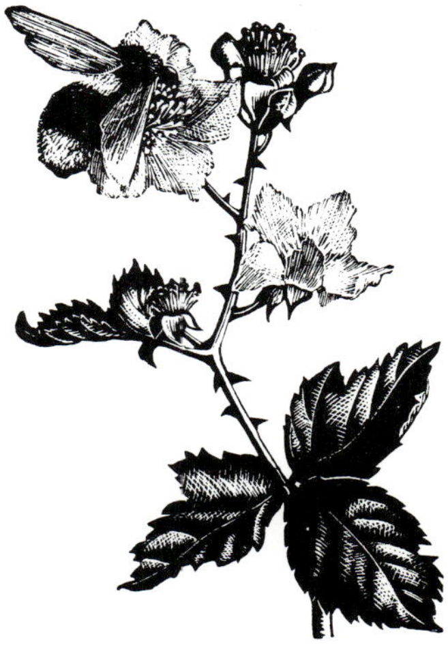

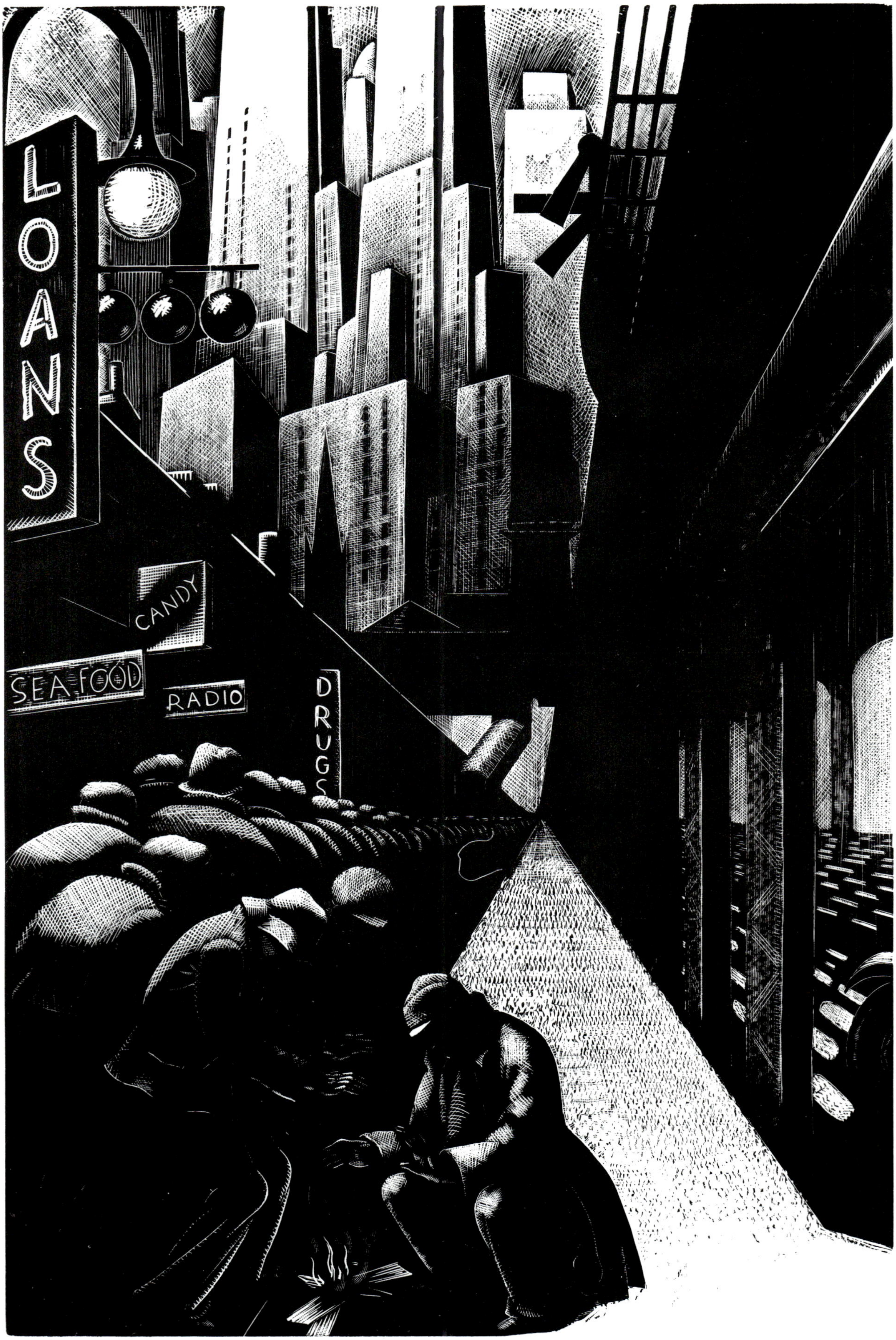
LOANS
CANDY
SEA FOOD
RADIO
DRUGS

THE WOOD ENGRAVINGS OF

CLARE LEIGHTON

SELECTED WITH AN INTRODUCTION BY

PAT JAFFÉ

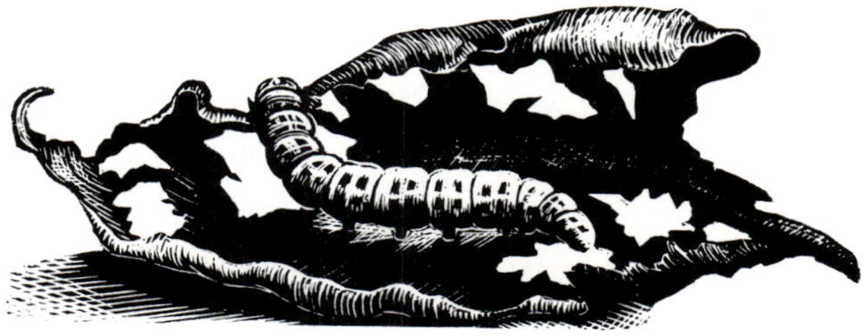

SILENT BOOKS

CAMBRIDGE

DEDICATION

To the children and grandchildren of Evelyn Leighton, appreciative curators of Clare's memory and achievements.

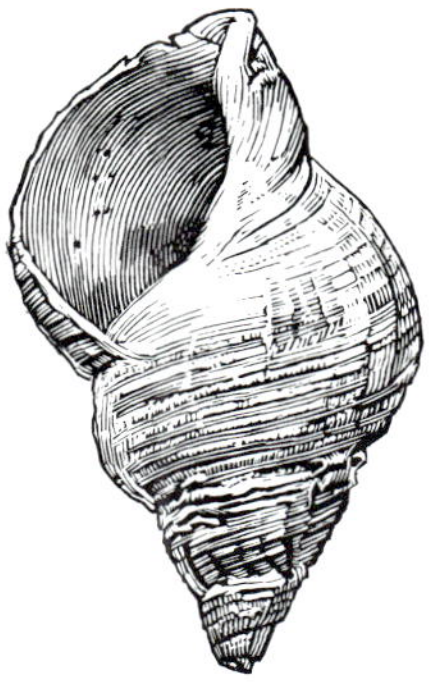

First Published in Great Britain 1992
by Silent Books, Swavesey, Cambridge CB4 5RA

British Library Cataloguing-in-Publication Data
A catalogue record for this book is available from the British Library

Typeset by Goodfellow & Egan
Printed in Great Britain by Redwood Press, Melksham

Half-title: *Bee on Bramble*, 1936 6.3 × 4.1 cms.: 2½ × 1⅝ ins., p. 112 in Clare Leighton, *Country Matters*, London: Victor Gollancz; New York: Macmillan Co., 1937

Tailpiece: *Mouse*, 1923 3.2 × 4.4 cms.: 1¼ × 1¾ ins.

1. (Frontispiece) *Bread Line, New York*, 1931–32 30.5 × 20.3 cms.: 12 × 8 ins.

2. (Facing introduction) *Clare Leighton*, 1931 photograph by Cyril Jenkins for illustration p. 8 in Clare Leighton, *Wood-engraving and Woodcuts*, London: The Studio Ltd.; New York: The Studio Publications Inc., 1932.

CONTENTS

INTRODUCTION 7

THE WOOD ENGRAVINGS 23

BIBLIOGRAPHY 158

ACKNOWLEDGEMENTS

My thanks are due above all to David Leighton who has been instrumental in providing copy for many of the prints here reproduced, and who has put me in the way of much vital information about the life and work of his aunt. In Cambridge the Friends of the Fitzwilliam Museum most perspicaciously acquired two groups of prints and working proofs, one for *Four Hedges*, the other for *Under the Greenwood Tree*, thus complementing the surviving English blocks bequeathed to the Fitzwilliam Museum by the artist. Sheila Munby generously gave me hospitality on return visits to the University after my husband's retirement. In Oxford Timothy Wilson and his staff were helpful even beyond their call of duty in the Ashmolean Museum. With the publishers I am grateful to all those who have made prints available for reproduction here, and to Jean Boon who rushed me to a country auction to acquire one which was otherwise elusive.

Prints whose captions are followed by the letters *D.L.* are reproduced from the collection of David Leighton: those followed by AM are reproduced from volumes in the Rhodes House Library, Oxford courtesy of the Ashmolean Museum, Oxford. Other sources are indicated fully where appropriate. Prints for which no source is indicated are reproduced from the author's collection.

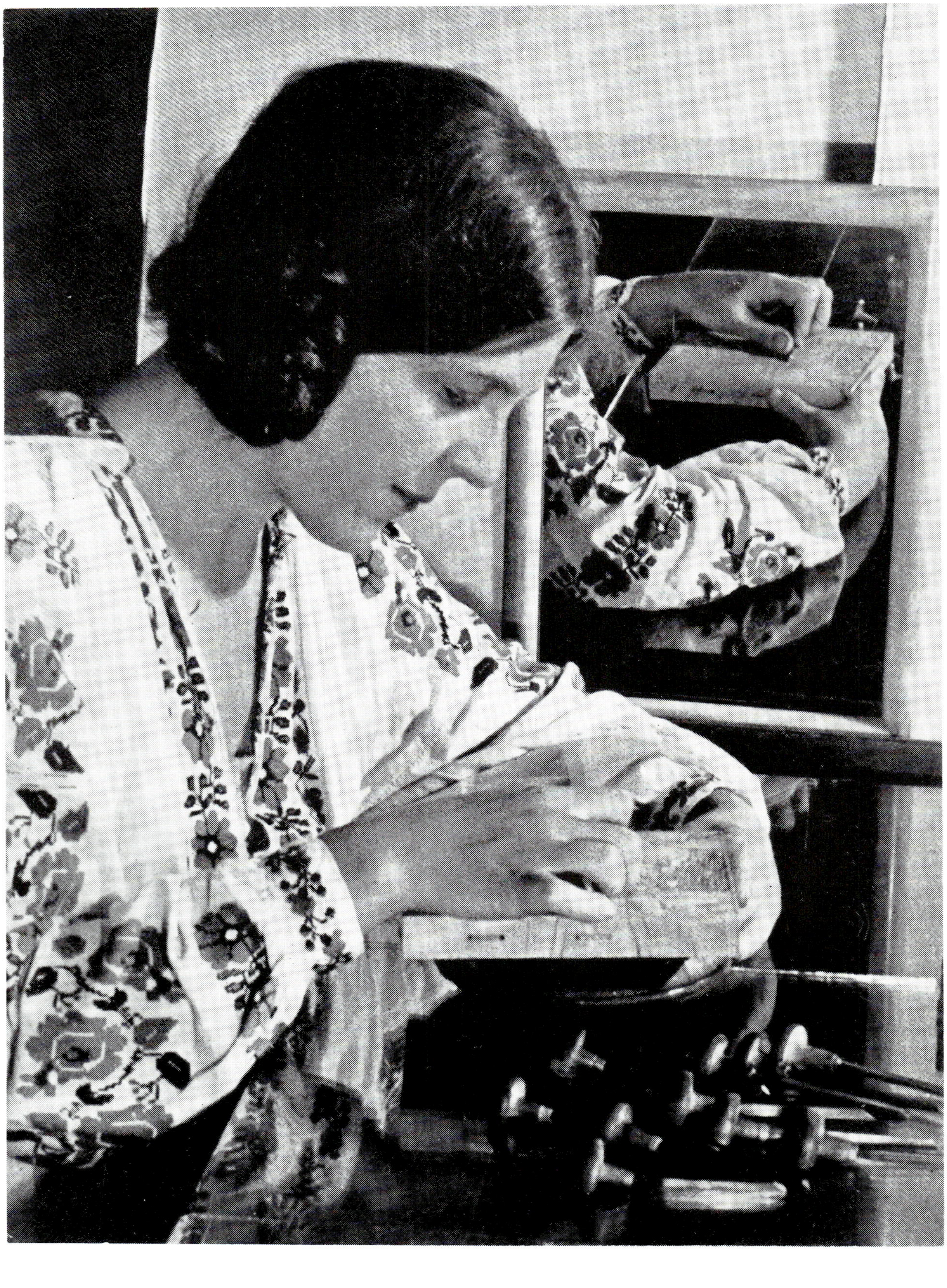

INTRODUCTION

CLARE LEIGHTON, of whose engravings this book is a survey, had qualities which inspired other women: as a rôle model she helped to demolish barriers of prejudice against their practising as artists in the commercial world. Eminent entirely through creative success, her reputation and influence were international and unconfined by feminism. She addressed the matter of wood engraving in a practical rather than a theoretical vein. Blessed with self-confidence, she struck off at one blow, in an essay so short that most writers would have been strait-jacketed by it, the frankest first sentence any amateur is likely to read in a book of instructions: 'Of all media wood-engraving is the one in which there is the least to be taught and the most to be learnt'. Thus opens her 1932 *Wood-Engraving and Woodcuts*, commissioned by C.G. Holmes, general editor of Studio Publications. The second title published of their 'How to do it' manuals, it was a tribute to Clare Leighton's abilities that Holme, a distinguished and very experienced editor, should have asked her to write so early a volume in their new series. When commissioned, she was barely 33. For the first time a woman had been singled out as the most suitable person to instruct amateurs in an art which had, within living memory, been the exclusive province of men. Holme's judgement was impeccable. Clare's instructions, characteristically, are direct and clear. Good craftsman that she was, she told her readers how to learn the skill, rather than how to concoct the content. Her introduction ends with a short paragraph: 'In the following examples I have chosen prints rather as illustrations of varieties of technique than for their interest as works of art. Careful study of these prints through a magnifying glass will give more help than any amount of reading.' Thus, having cautioned against too glib an approach, she turns her pupils loose upon the plates to learn for themselves.

Born on 12 April 1898, Clare Leighton belonged to that generation of women whose world and ways were changed by the women's suffrage movement and two world wars. Her parents, Robert and Marie Leighton, were both energetic creators of popular fiction; he of boys' adventures stories, and she of romantic serials by whose thrills and spills many avid readers were chained to newspapers owned by Lord Northcliffe. With the bravura of her Celtic ancestry Clare's mother dominated the scene. Both parents worked from home, and everyone under the roof must have realised which partner produced the more profitable work. In Clare's own account,

'The entire household revolved around my mother's writing, for it was the large sums of money she earned that supported us. My father's work was not supposed to matter nearly as much, because he earned far less.' It was an upbringing which heightened Clare's imagination, though it restricted her freedom. Her mother's manner was as colourful as her stories: thoroughly nannied in the last years of Victoria's reign, Clare sniffed the remnants of the naughty nineties from beyond the nursery door; then, as a teenager, she aspired to Edwardian elegance, crocheting lace trim for underwear, before escaping from family tentacles into a rather starker post-war world.

Her elder brother, Roland, had nicknamed her 'The Bystander'. This name was perpetuated by Marie Leighton in *Boy of my Heart*, Roland's biography published anonymously when Clare was only eighteen. There Clare's role was represented as exclusively that of 'Bystander'. One is given the impression of a quiet, observant girl 'taking things all in, as she always did'. Her artistic abilities were totally ignored by her mother, although her portrait drawing of Roland in uniform was to decorate the front dust cover of the book. He was undisguisedly his mother's favourite, and the biography was prompted by his death in 1915, a casualty of trench warfare. There is scant reference in the book to the two younger children. It is easy to deduce that Clare and her younger brother Evelyn must have been forced to develop strongly independent characters. They had to surmount that assumption of their own inadequacy to console, implicit in Mrs. Leighton's ceaseless grieving. Evelyn survived as a naval cadet at Osborne. Clare, though repressed as a child, and not even granted much chance of education, developed her art, and built a dynamic, creative world of her own.

During the First World War the Leightons moved to a small cottage in Sussex where Clare, while servants and money were in short supply, was expected to help at home. Opportunely organising the household, she set time aside for her own interests and bicycled regularly to the Brighton School of Art. Her serious studies had begun. After the Armistice, when her parents moved back to London, she was able to register at the Slade to study painting under Sir Henry Tonks. Yet her mother continued to curtail her liberty; even after she was 21 and already in employment, her comings and goings were monitored censoriously. Not surprisingly the daughter cast about for means of earning sufficient funds to buy her independence. Book illustration seemed promising, so she enrolled in Noel Rooke's course at the Central School. Rooke was an inspiring teacher, particularly when it came to wood engraving. His enthusiasm for the technique was contagious. His 'ecstasy entered into me' she recalled years later, and his analogies appealed to her greatly. 'A drawing is to a print' he declared 'very much what speech is to literature.' Her family background did at least give her a clear realisation of what that meant: in wood engraving she had found the medium which focused all her abilities and understanding. She was twenty-four, and suddenly her artistic confidence blossomed. Inopportunely her parents moved to Bishop's Stortford. The little country town provided 'a somewhat uneventful existence . . . There was, however, one weekly excitement in our lives . . . Bishop's Stortford had a thriving livestock market, which took place each Thursday.' Here Clare studied subjects for several of her earliest published prints including not only *The Calf Auction* (plate 5), but also *The Malthouse* (plate 3), astonishingly only the second block she engraved. We do not know whether Marie ever took notice of it, but it certainly impressed Clare's friends as well as her artistic uncle Jack Leighton and his socialist sister Sarah. Eric Gill, once a neighbour in Sussex, bought an impression of *The Malthouse*; uncle Jack set about finding her a bed-sitting room in Bloomsbury; and aunt Sarah urged her to take a portfolio to show to the editor of *The New Leader*, the socialist literary and philosophical magazine. All these responses to the print were of crucial importance in her life and career. Gill, in his enthusiasm, arranged her first small exhibition; uncle Jack effected her escape from home to the freedom of 'a tiny room four floors up' in Heathcote Street, Bloomsbury; and the editor, H.N. Brailsford, accepting *The Malthouse* for publication in April 1924, was enchanted by the artist as well as the work.

These were days of achievement and metamorphosis for Clare. Brailsford, believing passionately in a new world order, and sure that it could only be achieved provided that the most creative intellects in the socialist movement rallied to the cause, was using all his editorial wiles to turn *The New Leader* into a publication of literary and artistic distinction. On the literary front there were occasional contributions from Shaw, reviews by E.M. Forster, the serialisation of a book by H.G. Wells, poems by Frances Cornford, and science features by Julian Huxley. In addition every issue had some artistic content, reproductions of drawings, lithographs or woodcuts from such artists as Jack Yeats, Muirhead Bone or Käthe Kollwitz. It was a prestigious contributors' list to join. *The Malthouse* was only the first of nine of her wood engravings to be published by Brailsford, and her reputation as a new young talent rapidly spread. Hilaire Belloc, chancing to read an issue of *The New Leader*, came upon a reproduction of *The Calf Auction*, engraved in 1924. He was so delighted by its vigour that he brought Clare's work to the attention of J.C. Squire, editor of *The London Mercury*, the leading literary and artistic magazine with a wide circulation throughout Britain and North America. In August 1925 *The London Mercury* honoured Clare Leighton's new skill by reproducing *The Malthouse, The Calf Auction*, and *Barges* (plate 4), introduced with a two-page eulogy by Belloc himself, written in glowing, even heroic, terms. She could not have been launched more enthusiastically. Squire followed this first selection of prints with a second, published in March 1926: *Breaking up the Barge* (plate 6), *Toulon Washerwoman*, and *The Washing Boat*. This time the artist was thought to need no introduction, and the prints stand on their merit, without review. Clare Leighton had found a medium which suited her artistically and ideologically, and one which was to reach a wide audience through the most respected monthly magazine of its day.

Socialist aunt Sarah, who had delighted in Clare's meeting such a leading thinker as Brailsford, must have felt great satisfaction when, in the summer of 1927, he moved from Battersea to a flat in Belsize Park Gardens, Hampstead and found, just around the corner, new accommodation for Clare, whose Bloomsbury room had become too cramped. From then on they shared much, including a housekeeper and foreign holidays. Despite an age discrepancy of 25 years, and Brailsford's separated alcoholic wife who refused to divorce him, their liaison was to last twelve years. Brailsford's multitude of friends and colleagues, and his wide-ranging interests afforded Clare the society and education she had earlier been denied: her mother had not only afforded her scant attention, but deemed spasmodic attendance at a few unremarkable girls' schools sufficient for a mere daughter. After Clare moved to Hampstead the pace of recognition, acclamation and commissions quickened.

Between 1923 and her move to 27 Belsize Square in 1927, Clare and her uncle Jack had made sketching trips to France (plates 11 and 12) and to the Balkans (plates 13–16). Although she had remarkable success with occasional landscapes (plates 14 and 16), her preferred subjects centred on working people. *Mussel Gatherers: Toulon* (plate 11) is a direct development from such English agricultural subjects as *Milking* (plate 10), the ponderous stoop of labourers in the foreground animating a quiet landscape setting. Comparable in scale to the earlier English ones, these new prints are still conceived as single works framed in black – an old practice which made the finished engraving far easier to print, and was probably advocated by Rooke. Despite the frame, Clare had begun, in the French, Italian and Yugoslav subjects, to release her actors into the air and space of their surroundings. No longer are figures anchored to foreground earth with only a peep of blank white for sky at the top of the print. In *Mussel Gatherers: Toulon* the silver sea sparkles beyond clogs and rolled trousers, wafting an atmosphere around and behind the working men. In *Umbrella Menders: Toulon* (plate 12) sunlight itself dazzles upon the ground, glancing off the figures in a fleeting but animating fashion. Independence of style as well as of spirit continued to develop after the move to Hampstead.

Through Brailsford she found an American agent who arranged exhibitions for her, and a lecture tour. Clare came back to England with 'enough illustrating contracts to occupy me for several years'. Thus she added to Thomas Hardy's *The Return of the Native* (plates 19a–20b), Joseph Auslander's *Letters to Women* (21a–21d), and Thornton Wilder's *The Bridge of San Luis Rey* (plates 22a–23b). Further commissions were triggered so that, instead of being obliged to illustrate her father's books as she had first planned when joining Rooke's class, she rapidly became an internationally renowned illustrator. The American visit also inspired large single prints: in *Boston Cod* (plate 24), where she catches the cold slither of fish and bodies heaving on the wharf, the exhilaration of a new subject is evident; or again, the searing cold of men clearing snow, set against the sheer majesty of 20s skyscrapers, is brilliantly suggested in *Snow Shovellers: New York* (plate 25).

In the spring and summer of 1928, working on her favourite commission, *The Return of the Native*, she set out to study Hardy's Wessex landscape at first hand. This entailed finding lodgings in Dorset and exploring Egdon Heath, the Cerne Abbas giant, Stonehenge, and many deep winding rural lanes. She engraved over 61 blocks for the book, striving above all to capture in them a sense of place and moment. Increasingly she made the images her own, dispensing with precise form, but concentrating on composition and atmosphere, freeing herself from the conventions of Rooke's English school of engraving. Although Brailsford understood her feeling 'that Hardy's spirit has entered into you', her delight in the countryside, and her absorbed concentration on the illustrations must have kept her away from London longer than he, in the free moments of his own busy summer schedule, could bear. In September he persuaded her to holiday with him in the Dordogne and the Pyrenees. She was exhausted with overwork, and although, as we know from accounts she gave in *Sometime . . . Never*, the whole holiday meant much to her, very little graphic work commemorates it. Brailsford, increasingly devoted, had just dedicated to her *Olives of Endless Age*, 'a big book on the idea of International Unity – political and economic'. Now he became 'extraordinarily solicitous', and began to worry about her health. A private retreat seemed to offer the best hope of keeping and cosseting

Clare. On 28 June 1929 he sent off a cheque in payment for a plot of land on the chalky slopes of the Chilterns, above Monks Risborough. He gave the plot to Clare, and together they built a house and cultivated the garden which would eventually inspire Clare's most perennially popular *Four Hedges* (plates 55–60).

Even before that, in the growing security of her relationship with Brailsford, and the primaeval satisfaction of possessing a plot of countryside of her own, Clare moved energetically into new projects. Belloc turned his admiration of her work into a limited edition volume of 42 of her most successful prints, *Woodcuts: examples of the work of Clare Leighton*, published by Longmans in 1930 (plates 3–19a, 22a and b, 24, 25 and 31). At the same time she produced, much in the style of Gwen Raverat whom she had met and admired, six serene English views as advertisements for the London Omnibus Company (plates 26–31), each of which is charmingly patterned, unstressed, and filled with beguiling sunlight: too agreeable, they lack that originality and bite of which she was so capable. In later life she admitted 'The portrayal of this English world seemed unable to satisfy. I needed to escape into something new and unknown.' Escapist literature was not the answer. She had tried that, working throughout 1930 on twelve large, dramatic engravings to illustrate Emily Brontë's *Wuthering Heights* (plates 33–38). In them she had caught the obsessive force of the novel: powerful, lone figures are depicted against a bleak landscape, Heathcliff strides through the snow (plate 33), or hammers his head against a tree in grief at Cathy's death (plate 35). Compelling and live, they show her experimenting with new techniques: a multiple tool is used to relieve the stark contrast of black and white, making grey shadows on the snow, or creating the gloom of rolling moors, surrounding the graveyard as Heathcliff digs frantically by lantern light (plate 37). Fictional melodrama having provided no lasting satisfaction, in October 1930, while Brailsford was touring in India, and their house in the Chilterns was being built, Clare again sailed for the United States. She spent time in New York and California then, in the early months of 1931, made a trip to Ottawa to study lumberjacks. By this time Brailsford too had travelled to the United States, and Clare joined him in New York so that they could sail back on the same ship in March. It was as though each had indulged in a final independent tour before setting up home together.

At the new house Clare had, for the first time, a studio of her own, and settled down to produce such great engravings as *Bread Line, New York* (plate 1), and the *Lumber Camp* series (plates 39–43). The North American trip had refreshed her for England. Germs of ideas for a new book must soon have begun to work in her imagination. No doubt her innate curiosity took her about the Buckinghamshire countryside as a respite from the intense concentration on engraving. Bicycling into scenes which gave her new inspiration, she began to formulate *The Farmer's Year* (plates 44–48) in the summer of 1931. The work is a brilliant innovation. As in a slide lecture, each powerful print is accompanied by a complementary text. For the first time she was author as well as engraver and, in the written work particularly, one sees Brailsford's influence developing those qualities of vision which he had first admired in the early engravings. The scenes depicted transcend the parochial, emphasising the universal and essential nature of agricultural work. Brailsford's strong Marxist beliefs placed him far from the world approved by Clare's mother. One is tempted to speculate on the strength of the reactionary tendencies stimulated by Marie Leighton. When she was a girl Clare had often been denigrated by Mrs. Leighton. Once she had overheard her mother conversing with an admirer: '"Funny," my mother was saying to Mr. Bowles, "Funny how one can produce such an utterly unimaginative daughter. Clare has neither looks nor charm. The looks don't matter, for some of the world's sirens have been the most hideous of women. But charm is a necessity. What do you suppose happened to make her so dull?"' Since such scornful unkindness could hardly endear the mother to the daughter, it is no surprise that Clare reacted strongly against her mother's genteel pretensions and snobbish disregard of the working classes. She was certainly drawn to the socialist ideals promoted by Brailsford in *The New Leader*, and Brailsford himself lavished love and praise upon her personally, glorying in her talents and her beauty. It is no surprise that he became her inspiration, and encouraged her to champion the working man. Since she wrote the text herself, her independent wit was able to express itself for the first time. The deliberate bathos of many of her analogies saves her from the exaggerated drama of much of her father's writing, the sentimental mawkishness of much of her mother's, and the sententiousness of Brailsford's. One relishes *The Sages* (plate 48a) outside the village pub, 'their knobbly hands resting on the top of their sticks like pink toads', and one can never again see a startled half-shorn sheep with fleece stripped from head and neck, without agreeing that she 'looks like a frumpish old lady in a feather boa'. By such asides, the reader is beguiled into willing acceptance of the author's views. It takes art to hide art under the guise of simplicity, and she had that natural gift. *The Farmer's Year*, so successful that it ran to three English impressions and an American edition in the space of three months, initiated a trend, provoking a rash of agricultural memoirs illustrated with wood engravings:

Faber and Faber were first to follow, publishing a new, 1934 edition of A.G. Street's *Farmer's Glory* with engravings by Gwen Raverat. The symbiosis of rural idyll and wood engraving, still valid today, had been proclaimed.

Clare Leighton's reputation had increased steadily in the United States as well as in Europe, and her circle of friends included many influential authors and critics. Martin Hardie, the eminent print-maker curator at the Victoria and Albert Museum, not only admired, but encouraged and collected her work. Among the prints which he bequeathed to the Ashmolean Museum, Oxford is the first state of *January: Lambing* (plate 44) inscribed 'To Martin Hardie, because he liked it', and a final state of *September: Apple-Picking* (plate 46) inscribed 'To Martin Hardie, in friendliness from Clare Leighton', so we may assume that he was consulted during the gestation of much of *The Farmer's Year*. His own devotion to the early work of Samuel Palmer may well have funnelled that influence into several of the designs, for those gravid, hummocked curves of countryside and beasts, typical of Palmer, are particularly noticeable in the suite of twelve major prints. The strength of Hardie's influence is evident from *The Net Menders* (plate 49) of 1933, commissioned by the Woodcut Society of Kansas City. Their friendly relationship continued throughout the making of *Four Hedges*: the Ashmolean has a note from Clare Leighton to Mrs. Hardie, enclosing a few superb impressions of newly engraved blocks, which explains that they are sent 'so that there should be no appearance of favouritism towards the Hardie family'. *Mullein Caterpillar* (decoration on title page) is one of them.

That Clare now felt more secure when setting figures in a landscape can be seen in her illustrations to Constance Holme's *The Trumpet in the Dust* (plates 50–52) and the charming *Corsican Laundress* (plate 54). Brailsford had been ordered by his doctor to take a rest cure in the Austrian Tyrol, and he had travelled there with Clare in February 1934. Unfortunately no sooner had they arrived than civil strife broke out in Vienna between fascists and socialists. Clare persuaded Brailsford to travel on to Corsica where they spent the remainder of their holiday peacefully, returning to England in March. Clare, who was already deep in her new project, writing and illustrating *Four Hedges*, centring her life on the Buckinghamshire garden, reported wistfully 'My year is out of focus, for I have returned from Corsica, where rose and iris bloomed in the hot damp air of March'. The book, published in 1935, has always had a wide success. It is her happiest and most confidential, as well as confident, written with the enthusiasm of alert delight: 'Our senses feel each change of the weather and watch the great arc of the sky from horizon to horizon for signs. The keyboard of experience expands.' Throughout its 157 pages there are only two openings showing nothing but text. She engraved an astonishing 87 blocks, six of which are full page. The cutting is crisp and deft. The fine drawing of plants and people shows, because the backgrounds are cleared, to best effect. Gone are the shadows and sombre reflections on the hardship of workers implicit in *The Farmer's Year*. This is nature on a domestic scale, and told intimately. Appropriately she dedicated it to Brailsford.

The book came out in October 1935 and, although Clare was probably in London for the launch, she must have sailed almost immediately for the United States, landing in New York on 27 October. She stayed in the United States until the early months of 1936, fulfilling another lecture tour organised by Brailsford's agent, Feakins. Brailsford, too, was in the United States, his fifth lecture tour since 1928. During the tour, and for the entire summer Clare worked on another volume of critical assessment for The Studio, *Wood Engravings of the 1930s*, which was to come out in both cloth and paper editions as their special winter number for 1936. After her intense concentration on *Four Hedges*, she must have found it very refreshing to study a wide variety of other artists' work. She chose prints from many parts of the world, North and South America, Europe including eastern European countries, and the Soviet Union. Again Brailsford's wide interests and travels influenced the scope of the work. In itself it is an unattractive book, the reproductions being unpleasantly over-inked and the text set too wide and dense to be read easily. Not an aesthetic book, it is a carefully studied one, proclaiming wood engraving 'a fitting medium for an intellectual age'. Despite an element of workers' polemic, Clare remained staunchly independent in her judgements. She singled out Gertrude Hermes for her highest approval in both design and technique, making this pronouncement: 'One of the best ways to discover whether a picture is well designed is to turn it upside down, that one may perceive the pattern unhampered by thoughts of what it may represent: Gertrude Hermes stands this severe test.' Far from the credo of a book illustrator, what she is talking about here is the over-all quality of design to be sought in an individual print. It is in a later chapter that she admits 'no artist could live on the proceeds of the sale of his prints. Economic pressure drives all of them into illustration'. Clare Leighton was writing from experience.

The one development which brightened the 1930s for printmakers was the foundation of Print Societies in the United States. Clare Leighton had already had several commissions from such groups (plates 49, 53 and 54) and described their rise as 'a healthy development . . . These clubs buy the complete edition of an artist's block and distribute the prints at regular intervals to their members'. In 1937 The Woodcut Society of Kansas City issued *Winnowers, Majorca* (plate 69) in which a dream-like exoticism is created through a stylised reiteration of rhythmic patterns, the swing of the winnowers counteracted by the curves of the countryside, the two kept in perpetual motion by the circle of the grinding mill, turned by its long, horse-drawn shaft. Very different from an English agricultural scene, this print demonstrates her ability to suggest the very quality of light, here scintillating and bouncing even on rough surfaces while the shadows are black and impenetrable. In creating a great variety of textures, she again uses – on the stones of a little low wall, and on the grinding mill – a multiple tool. The rest of the engraving seems to have been achieved with a fine spitsticker. They are simple means, but the print shows complete technical mastery, and confidence in design. Would she challenge us to turn it upside down?

The phenomenal success of *Four Hedges* prompted Clare and her publisher, Gollancz, to plan a companion volume, *Country Matters* (plates 61–68). In detailing village life in the Chiltern Hills and Buckinghamshire, she tried, as she explained in the Preface to the American edition, 'to capture . . . the quiet of the hills and the simplicity of elemental thought'. The subjects are fascinating, the engravings are beautiful, but replacing the personal narrative of *Four Hedges* and the monumentality of *The Farmer's Year* there is paternalism which sometimes verges on the coy, and must in large part account for this book's failing to match the success of the other two. This time the text lacks bite; again England had ceased to satisfy. Clare's interests were once more abroad. Fascism, which had taken hold in Europe since the Depression, was on the increase, and Brailsford, as a journalist and committed socialist, was involved in refuting arguments of sympathisers, and rousing the left to vigilance. In December 1936 he had written in the popular Sunday paper, *Reynold's News*, 'The question that confronts us is whether we have the manhood to defend ourselves. The alternative is to sit still and await the signal for self-destruction.' In April 1937 he and Clare travelled to the Pyrenees. He remained there with her for two weeks and then, after receiving news that Jane, his wife, had died, Brailsford abandoned Clare and crossed the border into Spain. He was 63 and bitterly disappointed that the International Brigade, formed to support the Republicans, had imposed an age limit of 40 on volunteers. However, he remained determined to help, and intended to use all the informed rhetoric that his journalistic reputation could air. He was keen to collect information with which to recruit volunteers and raise funds for the Brigade. It was in his nature to be obsessive, and his current obsession was the Socialist cause. Yet at the same time he was torn with doubt and dismay, realising that Stalin's brutality had turned the Revolution in Russia into 'a bloody tyranny ruled by terror and lies'. Faced with the threats posed by Hitler and Mussolini, Brailsford became frantic and depressed by turns. Not only does he not appear to have offered to marry Clare now that he was at last free, but was progressively more difficult to live with, even becoming violent on occasion. Moreover he expounded the horrors to come so cogently that the dreadful experiences of the First World War must have been recalled all too vividly to Clare. She was driven to leave. Late in December 1938 she saw Brailsford off from Waterloo station on a journalistic assignment in North Africa and then, as she had secretly arranged, herself caught another boat train, the first stage of her lone voyage to the United States.

She was depressed, and in a state of exhausted confusion: 'Had I, in my escape from life, grown unbalanced?' she wrote. 'Was I seeing things and feeling things that were the fabrication of an exhausted brain?' Her mind was in ferment, with hosts of unresolved memories and unrealised dreams inextricably interwoven. When she arrived in the United States, friends wisely advised her to exorcise her conflicts of recollection, imagination and emotion by writing them out. She had already discussed the concept of a new book with a composer friend before leaving England, and began *Sometime . . . Never* very soon after landing in New York on 6 January 1939: the Macmillan Company published it there in October, and Gollancz published it in London, using the American setting of the text with a slightly differently spaced lay-out for the plates, in time for Christmas. The illustrations are drawings dashed off in soft graphite. The book is dedicated jointly to two friends, the English composer and the imaginative enthusiast who had offered her support and asylum in her home in Baltimore. No key is offered to help the reader differentiate between fantasy and reality. The structure is musical rather than logical or chronological: themes recur, as in a symphony, transformed. To the poetical among her friends, it was an innovation. To most people it was an amazingly frank meditation to have published, one which drew attention to a new voice in America, and proclaimed that she had come to stay.

Having unburdened herself in *Sometime . . . Never*, Clare Leighton was ready to begin life again. Although equipped only with a suitcase, a typewriter and a paint-box when she sailed, she soon had a chunk of England to work on in the United States – illustrations to the most endearing of

Thomas Hardy's shorter novels, *Under the Greenwood Tree* (plates 70–73). The engravings, nostalgic for England and young love, are beautifully adapted to the tone of the tale, as well as to the lay-out of the book. She worked intensely, combining economy and skill to produce 62 blocks. In the Fitzwilliam Museum, Cambridge there is a set of first states, corrected proofs and prints for the headpieces and tail pieces which clearly show her working methods. Proofs are printed on what appears to be crisp, hard lavatory paper, and corrections are made in chinese white. Such paper is an excellent non-absorbent material, allowing the finest brush point to touch in small details experimentally before further irrevocable cutting on the actual blocks. The use of such readily available, cheap paper demonstrates that adaptability which was to keep Clare Leighton independent, employed, and assimilated in the United States throughout the second half of her life.

Under the Greenwood Tree was published by the Macmillan Company in 1940, both in London and New York, to mark the centenary of Hardy's birth. In June Colby College, Maine, which had already begun to amass a special Hardy collection, awarded her a Doctorate of Fine Art in recognition of her achievement. Other commissions were more specifically American. Her reputation as a gardener had preceded her: Putnams commissioned illustrations for Elsie Symington's *By Light of Sun* (plate 74), 'the first record of the spiritual ascendancy of a gardener that has been written in our times'. The engravings in *Four Hedges* were realistic depictions based on personal observations; for Elsie Symington Clare produced images of the spiritual state described in each of the three parts of the book. They are not among her most characteristic successes, but pleased public and publishers: other gardening books followed. Bertha Damon had already written one best seller for Simon and Schuster, *Grandma called it Carnal*; she now produced a punchy, well-written sequel, *A Sense of Humus* which Clare was commissioned to illustrate. She must have enjoyed the read, but was not offered sufficient pay to allow her to immerse herself in the work for long, and merely sketched seven pleasant coloured drawings, while employing her engraving tools for slower and better-paid work. In 1941 she was commissioned by another of the excellent print clubs and produced for them a very American subject, *Cotton Pickers* (plate 75). Its strong play of curves produces a design which could easily withstand her own upside-down test, but one which has sufficient pathos and feeling to require no justification through abstract analysis. When, in 1951, the Print Club of Rochester issued a catalogue on the occasion of its twentieth anniversary, this engraving was chosen for reproduction on the front cover.

Perhaps this very print inspired Clare Leighton to write her first thoroughly American book. She had been attracted south from Baltimore by the lure of agricultural methods which still linked individual workers to the soil. Once settled in Chapel Hill, North Carolina, she began to travel around, much as she had in the Chiltern Hills, exploring the countryside and sampling the lives of the people working there. The result, published by Macmillan in 1942, was *Southern Harvest* (plates 76–78). In the introduction to the Gollancz 1943 London edition she wrote 'the true character of a people is to be found in its workers, and especially in the workers upon the earth, for it is here that man is up against the eternal, and it is here that he demonstrates his values and his worth'. In the South she made friends with whites and blacks alike, viewing homes, leisure pursuits and working practices with unprejudiced sympathy untouched by paternalism. The soft graphite line of the nostalgic illustrations to *Sometime . . . Never* has given way to crisp, decisive images, the engraving tool clarifying and emphasising people and pursuits she had studied in real life. In *Apple Butter* (plate 76) the working swing of the figures and the toss of the apple trees combine in the rhythms of rural life just as they had for English labourers in *The Farmer's Year*. Harold Latham of Macmillan's wrote to her: 'I think perhaps the text is the best text you have ever written. Certainly it is the best from the standpoint of American sales. I have had an independent Southern advisor read it to make sure it does not offend the Southern point of view, and I have been reassured on that point. And incidentally this South advisor liked the book.' The publication was a success.

Finding the South deeply sympathetic, she had struck a chord which evoked a response in harmony. Working on *Southern Harvest*, she had left Baltimore in the winter of 1941. As from the first semester of the academic year 1942–43 she was appointed a visiting lecturer in the Department of Art and Aesthetics at Duke University, Durham, North Carolina. Here she soon became involved in one of the longest lasting projects of her entire career, illustrations to *The Frank C. Brown Collection of North Carolina Folklore*, eventually published in 7 volumes between 1952 and 1964. Professor Frank C. Brown had taught in the English Department at Duke since 1909 and, as founder of the North Carolina Folklore Society, had collected a wealth of native ballads, folk customs and traditions. Plans to publish the material had already been made before he died in 1943. When Newman White succeeded him as general editor of the project, he asked Clare Leighton to make complementary wood engravings to accompany – rather than illustrate – the whole: 'he proposed that they should be "designed" in the main as pictures of various folklore types and activities rather than as specific illustrations or individual bits of folklore'. The project was very much to Clare's taste, and her sympathies with the indigenous people were expressed in such powerful engravings as *The Baptizing* (plate 99) or *Dragging Nets* (plate 101), while *Mountain Haystacks* (plate 104c) and *Wind and Pine* (plate 105a) show how congenial she found the landscape of the Appalachian Mountains. In *Southern Harvest* she had written 'as I approached these mountains, that are the oldest in existence, though I had never before seen them I felt that in coming to them I was coming home . . . I was returning to my own people'. It was the very spirit which enabled her to make new friends and settle agreeably in the United States.

Meanwhile commissions, if not commitments, still kept her in contact with her English public. Allen Lane of Penguin Books ordered twelve blocks for Gilbert White's *Natural History of Selborne* (plates 79a–d), and Studio reissued her *Wood Engraving and Woodcuts*. What probably pleased her most, however, was being asked to illustrate Elizabeth Madox Roberts' *The Time of Man* (plates 80–84), in which the rural labour of country people in the American mountains, of which she was becoming so fond, once more gave her subjects combining elemental life and simple dignity. The success of her sensitive interpretations of the agricultural deep South was recognised in Britain as well as the United States. After the war Wedgwood opportunely and imaginatively commissioned her to design twelve plates depicting the industries of New England (plates 85–96). Now in her early fifties, she was ready to leave North Carolina where the heat often seemed too oppressive. She went with surprisingly little regret: returning troops had sown a seed of discontent among the formerly tranquil mountain folk, making her fear that the glitz of modernity would tarnish the elemental quality she had cherished in them. The Wedgwood project was a refreshing challenge. She had to research in the north-east states for suitable subjects, then present the designs in a circular format. The work took her north, where she eventually settled in Woodbury, Connecticut, planning her ideal house, and having it built from local timber which she selected herself. Here she was to live for the remainder of her days.

The problem of moulding designs full of work people and structures into circles was brilliantly resolved by heaping a pile of implements and tackle in the foreground, thus distancing each scene, allowing a falsely horizontal lower boundary. Within this formula Clare devised a series of variations: *Whaling* (plate 85) rocks mercilessly, the flukes of anchors thrusting upwards at surging waves and slender swooping boat, the circle of the plate keeping the whole in perpetual motion. In *Logging* (plate 89) the zig-zag of floating pine trunks swirl and clash around the margin of the plate, while the eye is brought circling back by the curve of the river bank on the horizon. In contrast, the rotundities of country, wooded and pastured, roll inwards like the circular sweep of the scythe which is the central action of *Farming* (plate 90). Triangular repetitions become the theme in *Ship Building* (plate 92), while horizontal banding is boldly accomplished in *Tobacco Growing* (plate 95), the curve of flower and leaf reconciling the design with the dictates of the circle. Clare worked on the Wedgwood commission for over three years. It was exciting but exacting, with particularly intensive engraving, for the designs had to have neither too rigidly defined a perimeter, nor too ragged a silhouette, drawn details having, ideally, to be balanced in density around the entire circle. As long ago as 1934, when working on *Four Hedges*, she had admitted 'I am unable to work for days after removal to a new place. Is it any wonder that transplanted trees so often die from shock?' Now, though she felt happy in New England, she had to force herself to work and, when the designs for the plates were complete, felt so exhausted that she even resolved to lay her engraving tools aside, as things of the past. In the unpublished notes towards an autobiography made in old age, she recollected: 'Once I had finished the Wedgwoods, I realised I needed to forget wood engraving. It is no wonder that after so many years, I found myself growing exhausted by it. I felt I was running the risk of repeating myself and ceasing to grow.' The comment is extraordinary after a commission which so successfully broke new ground. The thought must reflect an utter lassitude, resulting from her migration north. In Durham she left behind friends who missed her profoundly. She probably felt the wrench equally, and her quixotic reaction against engraving must indicate a subconscious belief that the Wedgwood commission, by luring her north, had uprooted her. The nostalgia syndrome had again set in.

Yet she loved New England: the brilliance of the sun on snow intense with winter cold stimulated her, and in the summers escape from the humid heat took her to Cape Cod. This inspired the fifth and last of her characteristic paeans of delight, her personal account of a particular place, illustrated with wood engravings – *Where Land Meets Sea* (plates 121–127). Perhaps Doubleday had given her the perfect respite from nostalgia, commissioning, soon after her move north, engraved illustrations for the King James version of *The Book of Psalms and the First Psalm of David, The Book of Proverbs, The Book of Ecclesiastes* (plates 118–119). The uplifting power of her illustration to Psalm 18, *He sent from above, he took me, he drew me out of many waters* (plate

119b) has much in common with the grace and strength of her depiction of the magnificent *Blue Fish* (plate 122b). The technique of both is broader and simpler than either *North Carolina Folklore* or the Wedgwood plates: there is much use of negative cross-hatching, long swinging or swirling parallel lines, or pebble-dash picking with the point of a graver. In fact the structure and textures are more painterly, and tell one that her creative attention had now focused on colour and the stroking and stippling effects achieved with a hog's hair brush. The concepts are simpler, broader, bolder. She was now in her mid fifties and, in common with the majority of mankind, probably found her eyesight changing. Close, detailed work may have become more difficult, making her exacting standards harder to attain. Yet such was Clare Leighton's resilience and adaptable creativity that, in the late 1950s, she accepted a commission to design and make for the Cathedral of Worcester, Massachusetts, thirty-three windows based on the life of St. Paul. Other commissions for stained glass followed, giving her opportunity to design on a breadth and scale impossible in tiny engravings. For the rest of her life she saw prints as domestic, winter work, powerful in content perhaps, but in no way innovative. She illustrated thus several poetic compendiums edited by Helen Plotz: *Imagination's Other Place* (plates 128 and 129) may stand as representative. H.R. Williamson's *The Flowering Hawthorn* (plates 130–132) inspired eight strong though simple engravings. Her swansong as author and engraver was, appropriately, commissioned by a literary and artistic foundation, The Book Club of California. *Growing New Roots* (plates 133–137) comprises an essay first published by the immigrant Clare Leighton in *Common Ground* in the summer of 1944, accompanied by 15 new engravings to celebrate the 1976 bicentennial of the founding of her adopted nation.

She died in Connecticut on 3 November 1989, remembered with affection and admiration by family, friends and admirers on both sides of the Atlantic.

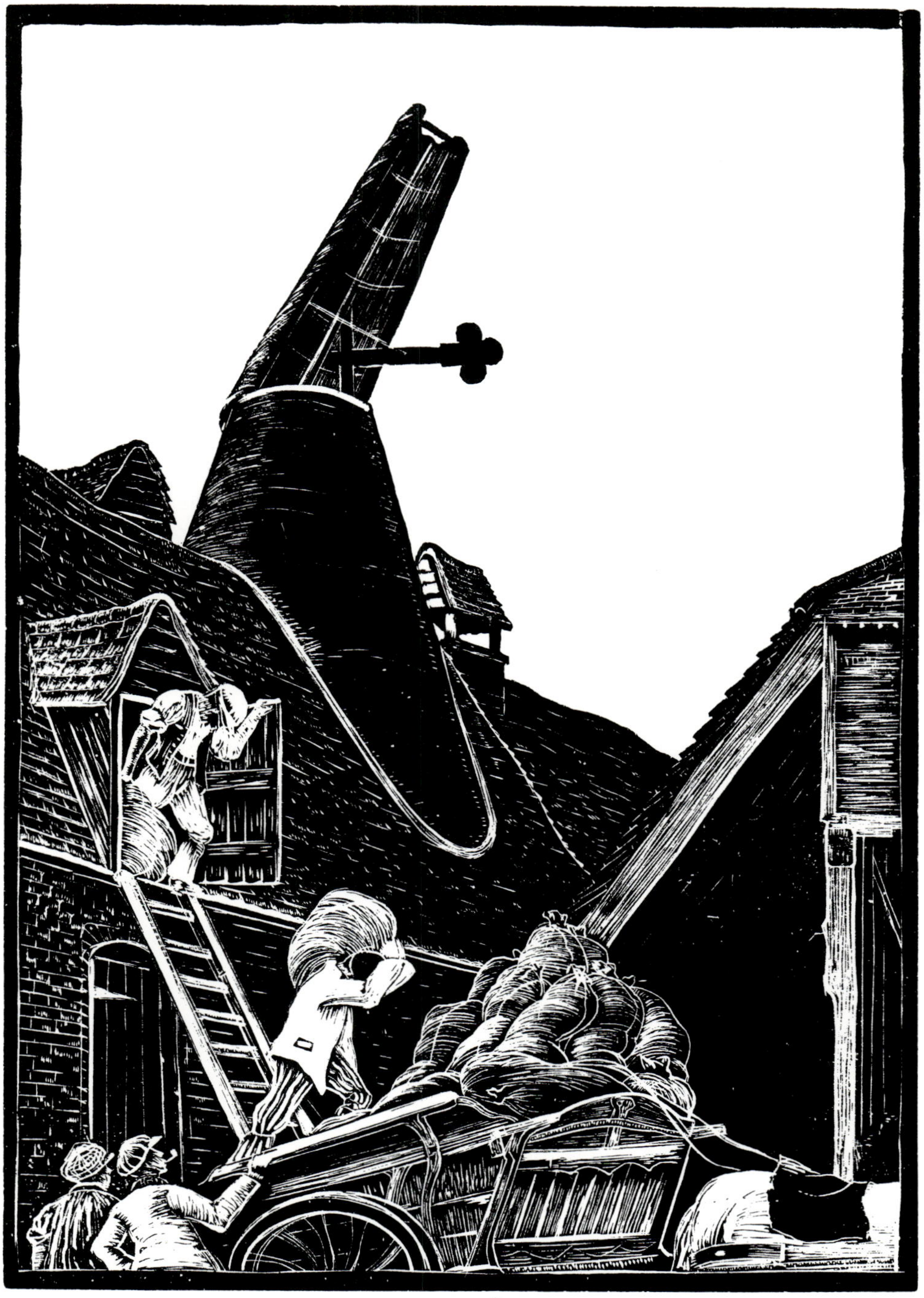

3. *The Malthouse*, 1923 17.8 × 12.5 cms.: 7 × 4 $^{15}/_{16}$ ins. repr. *The New Leader*, April 1924, and *The London Mercury*, August 1925 (with review by Hilaire Belloc).

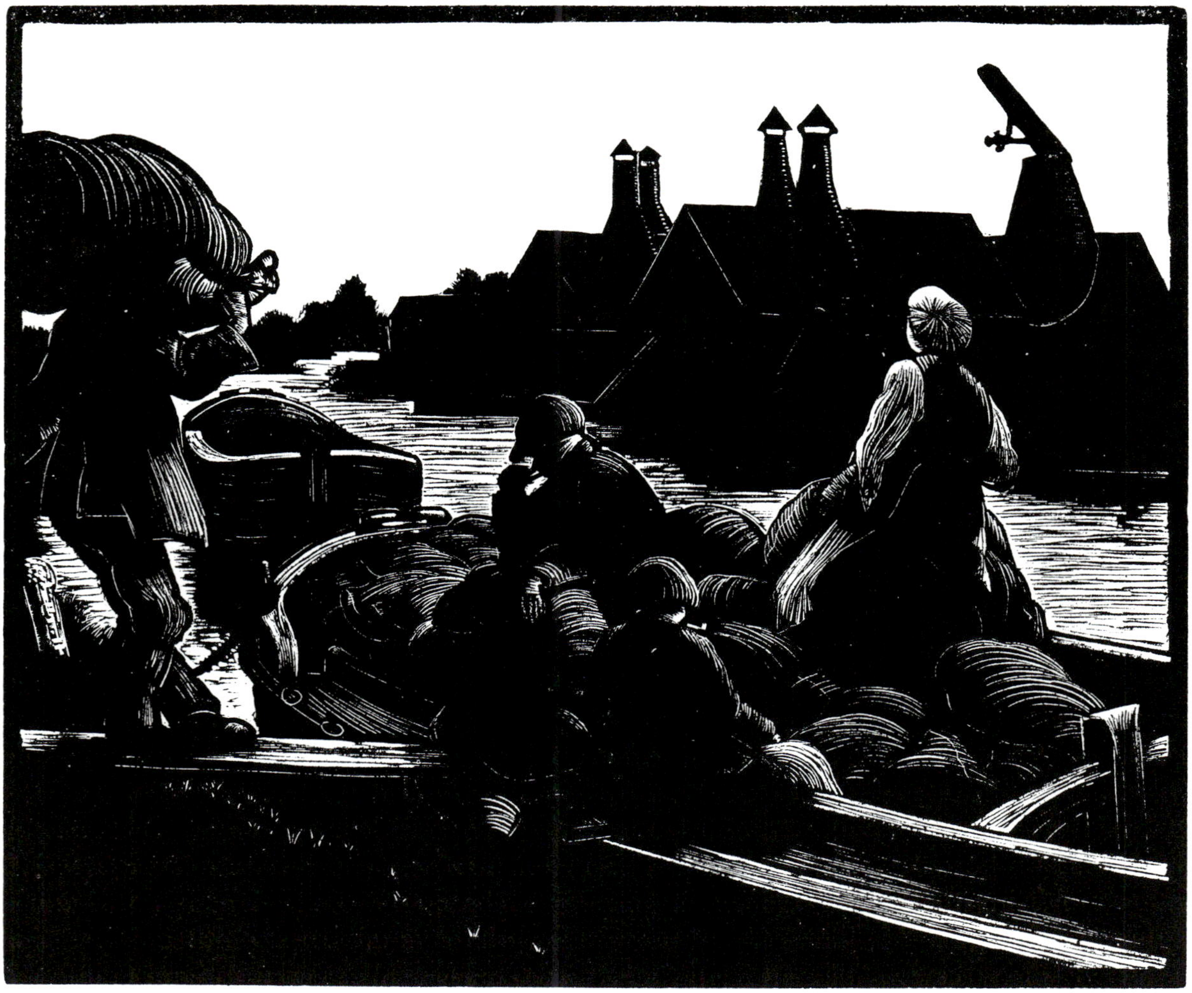

4. *Barges*, 1924 13.2 × 15.7 cms.: 5³⁄₁₆ × 6³⁄₁₆ ins. repr. *The London Mercury*, August 1925 (with review by Hilaire Belloc).

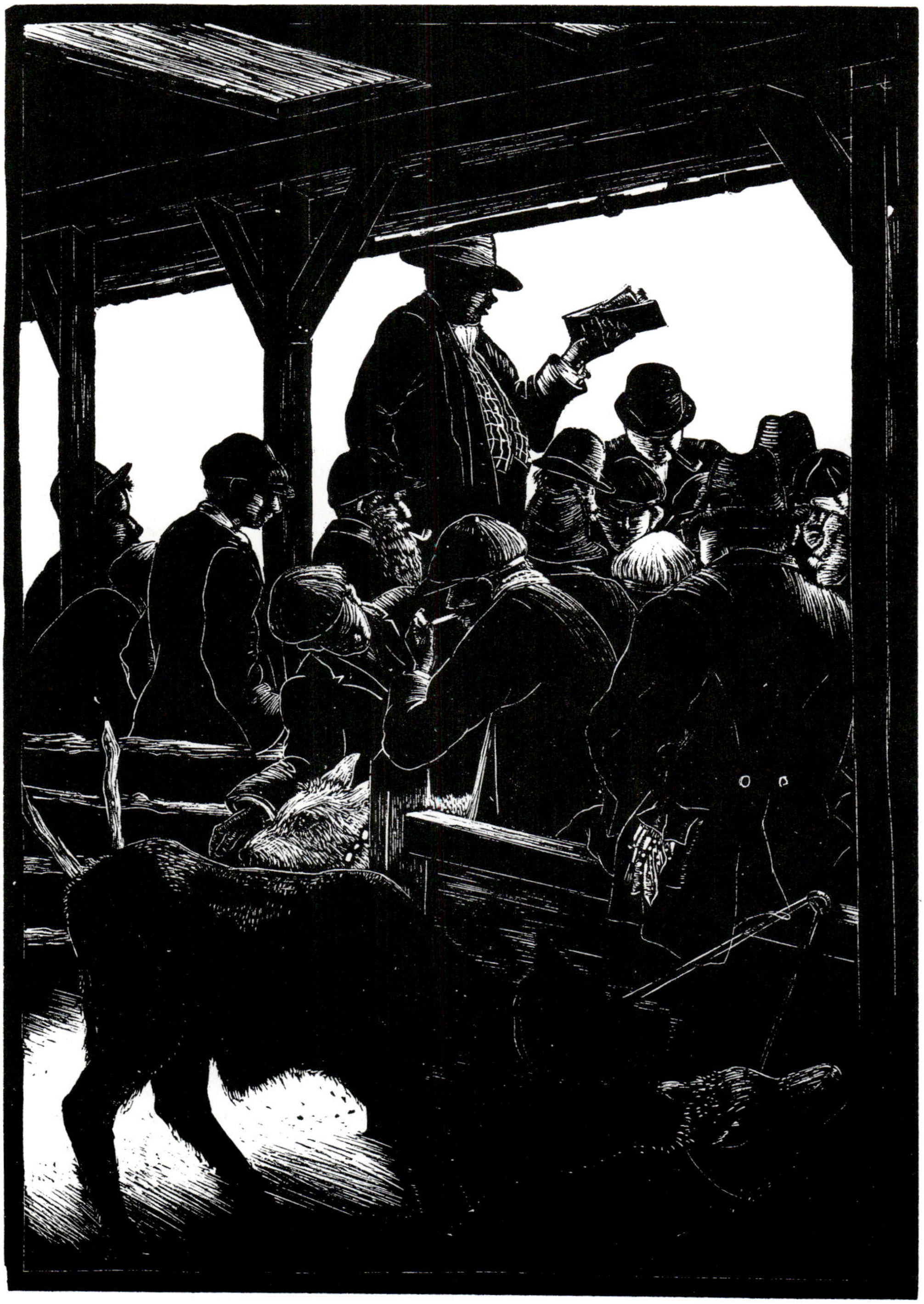

5. *The Calf Auction*, 1924 18.7 × 13.2 cms.: 7⅜ × 5³⁄₁₆ ins. repr. *The New Leader* and *The London Mercury*, August 1925 (with review by Hilaire Belloc).

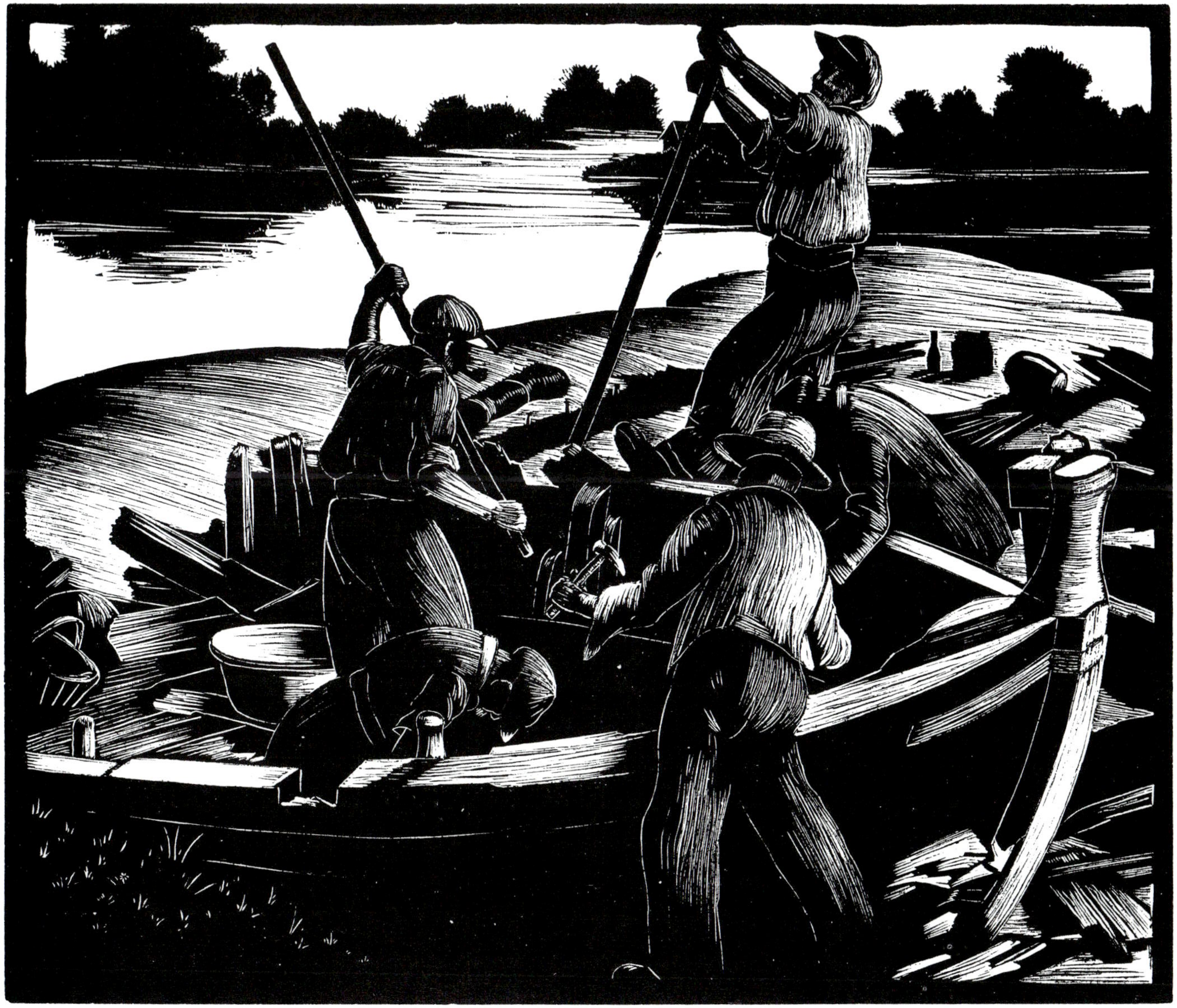

6. *Breaking up the Barge*, 1925 15.3 × 17.8 cms.: 6 × 7 ins. commissioned for *The New Leader Book*, 1926; repr. *The London Mercury*, March 1926

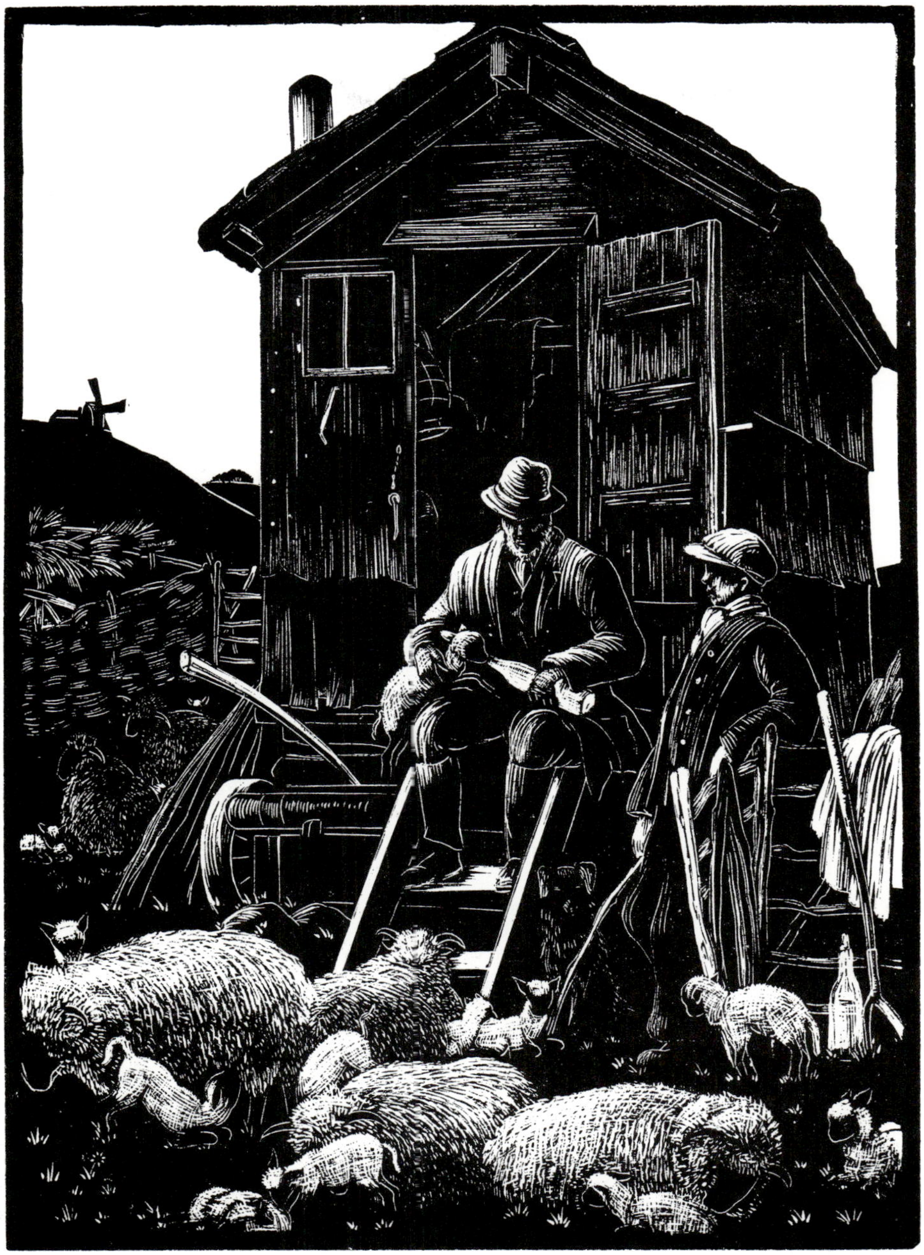

7. *Lambing*, 1926 16.5 × 12.1 cms.: 6½ × 4¾ ins. commissioned for *The Forum*

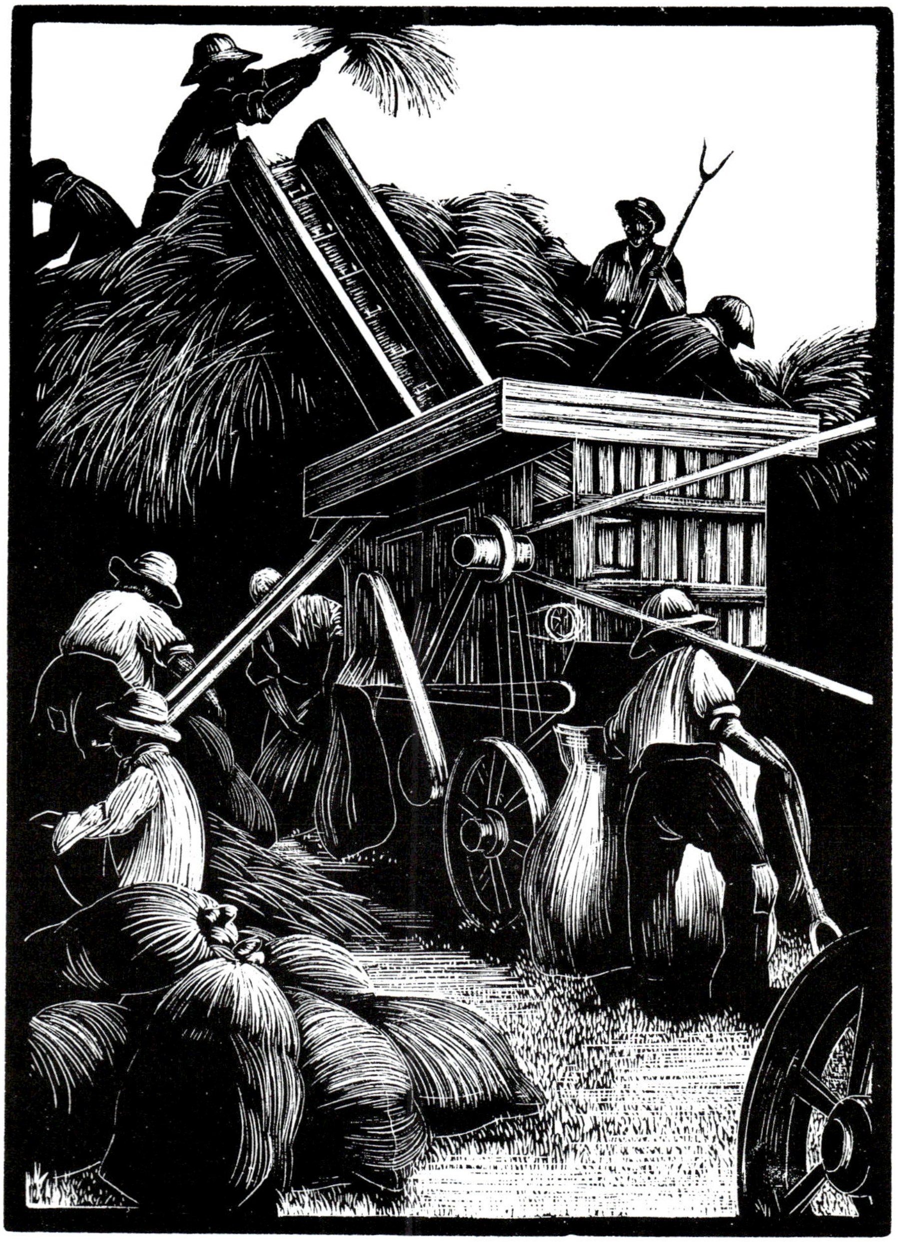

8. *Threshing*, 1926 16.5 × 11.8 cms.: 6¹⁄₁₂ × 4⁵⁄₈ ins. commissioned for *The Forum*

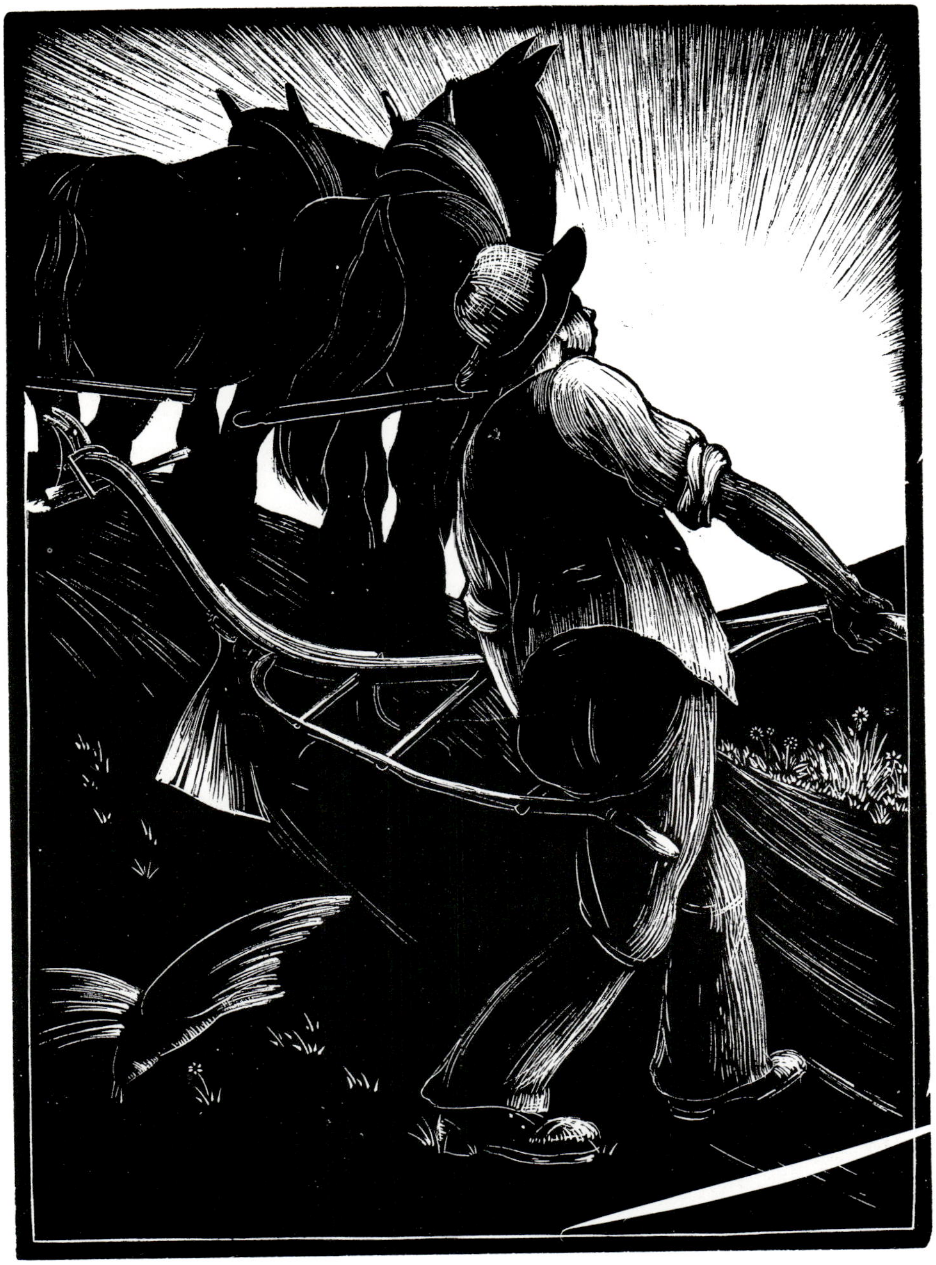

9. *Turning the Plough*, 1926 16.5 × 11.1 cms.: 6½ × 4⅜ ins. commissioned for *The Forum*

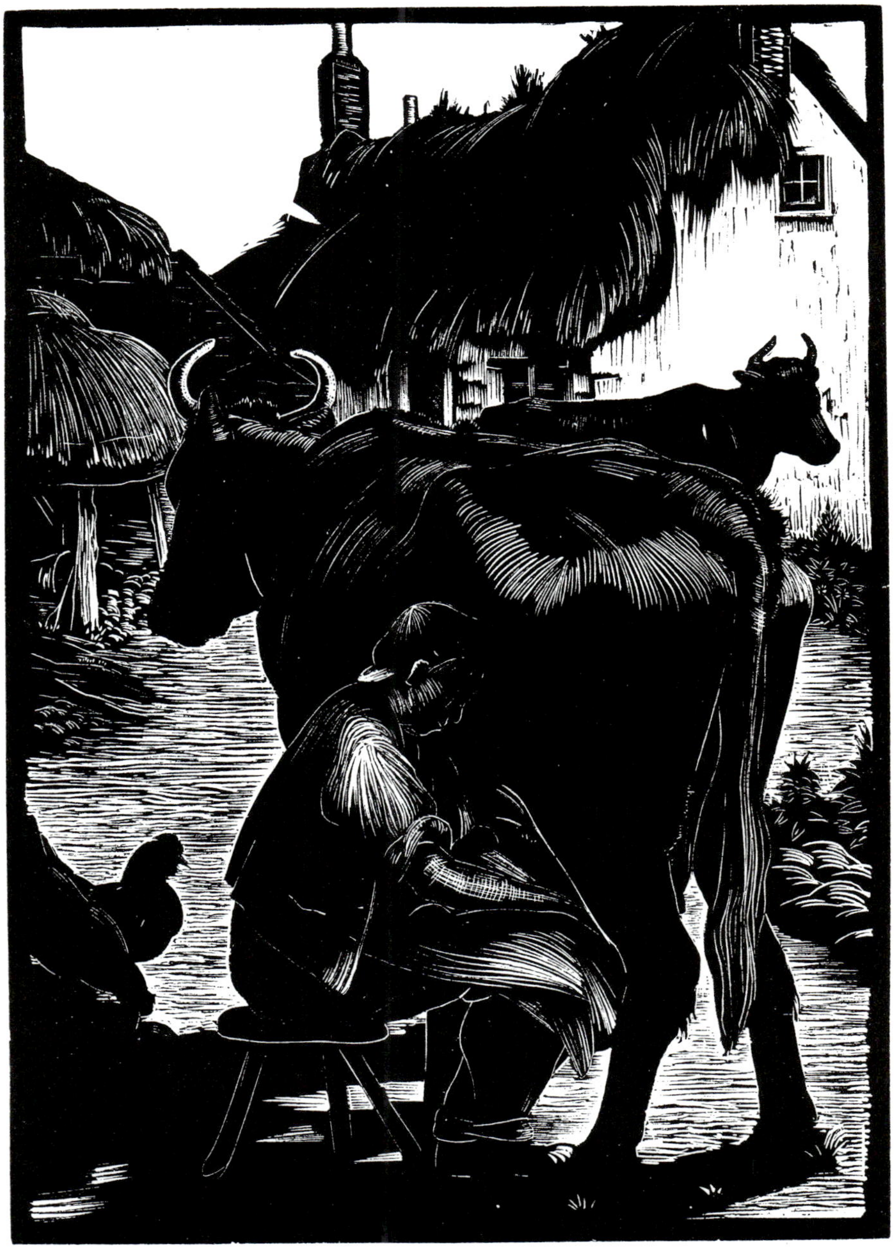

10. *Milking*, 1926 16.5 × 11.8 cms.: 6½ × 4⅝ ins. commissioned for *The Forum*

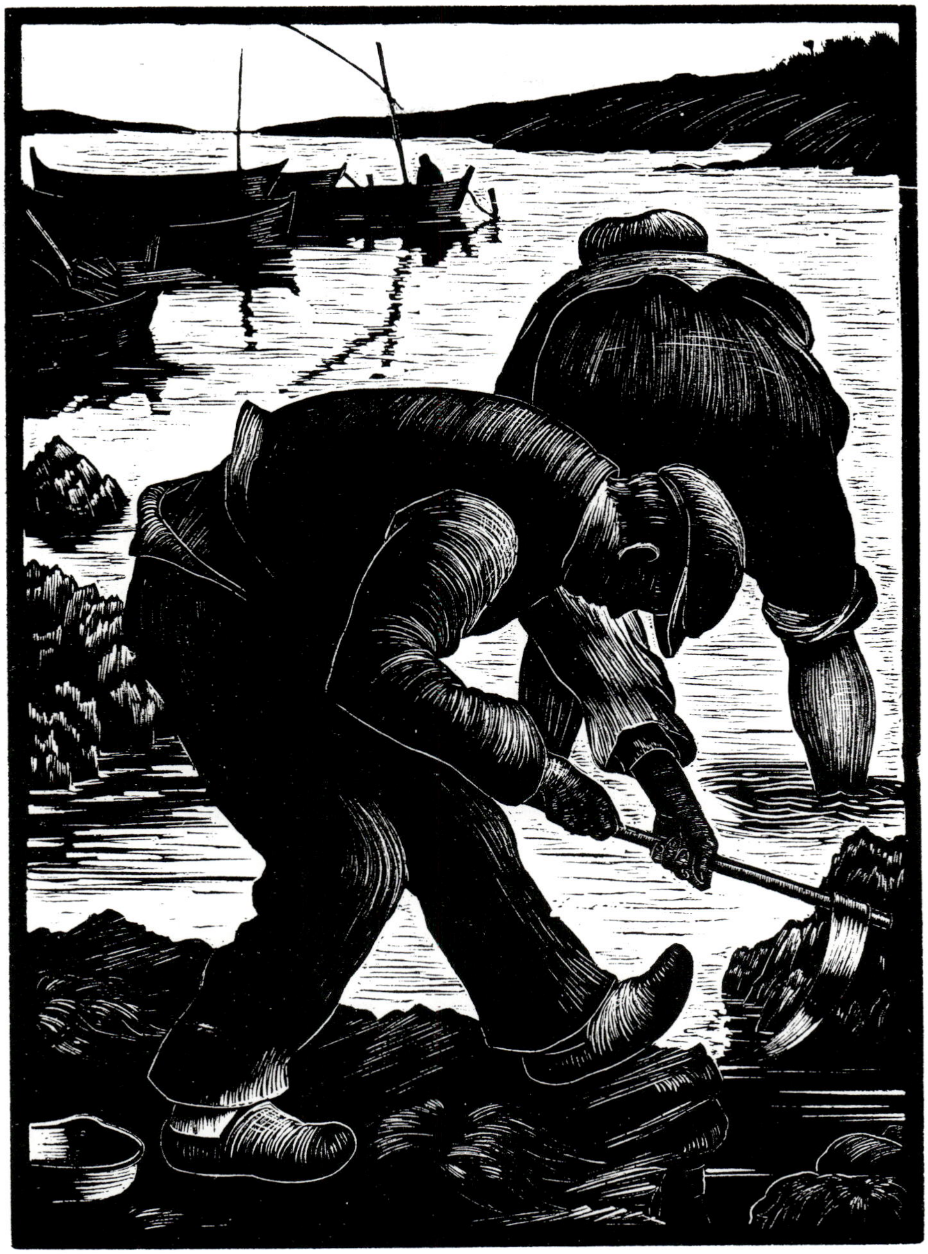

11. *Mussel Gatherers: Toulon*, 1926 16.4 × 12.1 cms.: 6⁷⁄₁₆ × 4¾ ins.

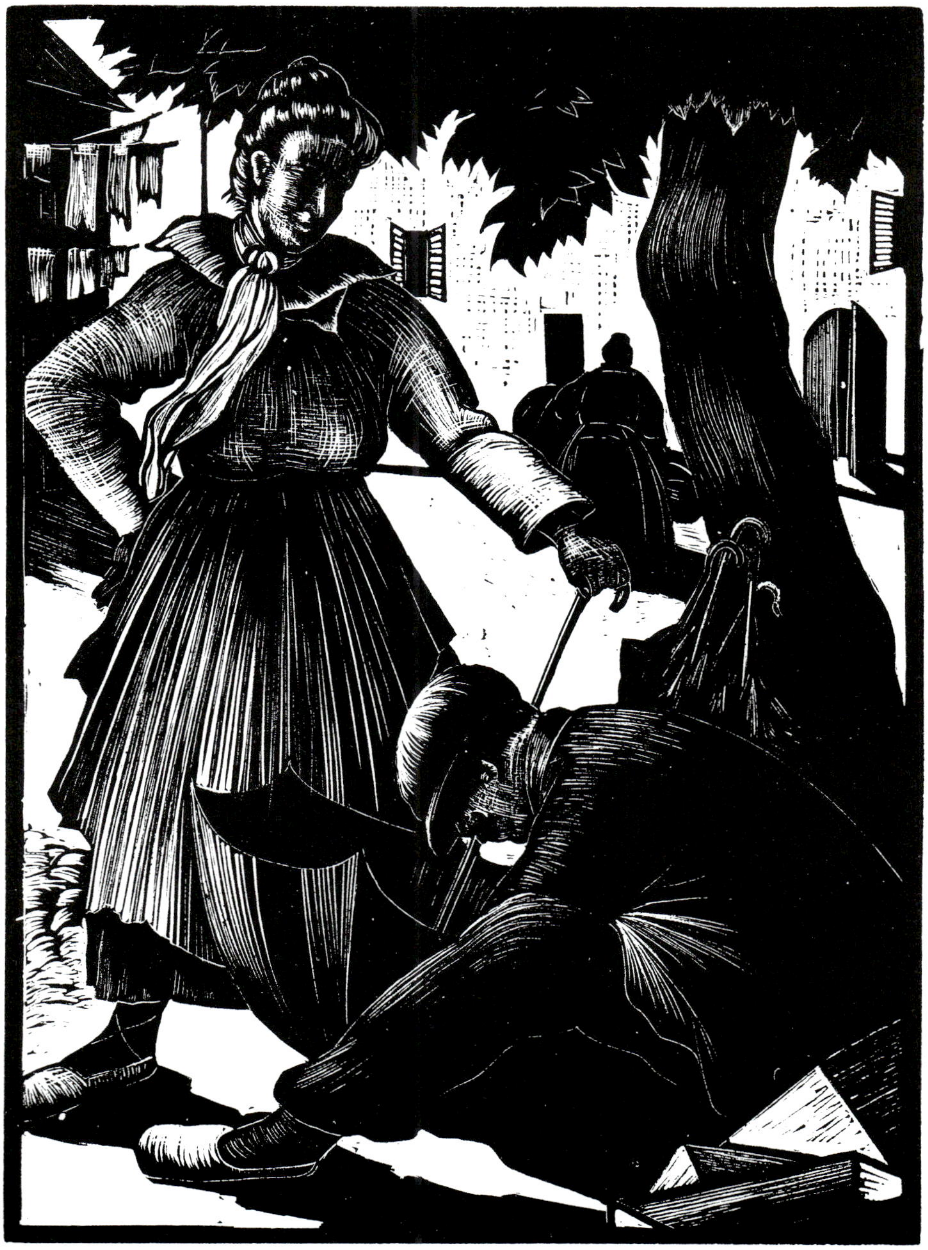

12. *Umbrella Menders: Toulon*, 1926 16.5 × 12.2 cms.: 6½ × 4¹³⁄₁₆ ins.

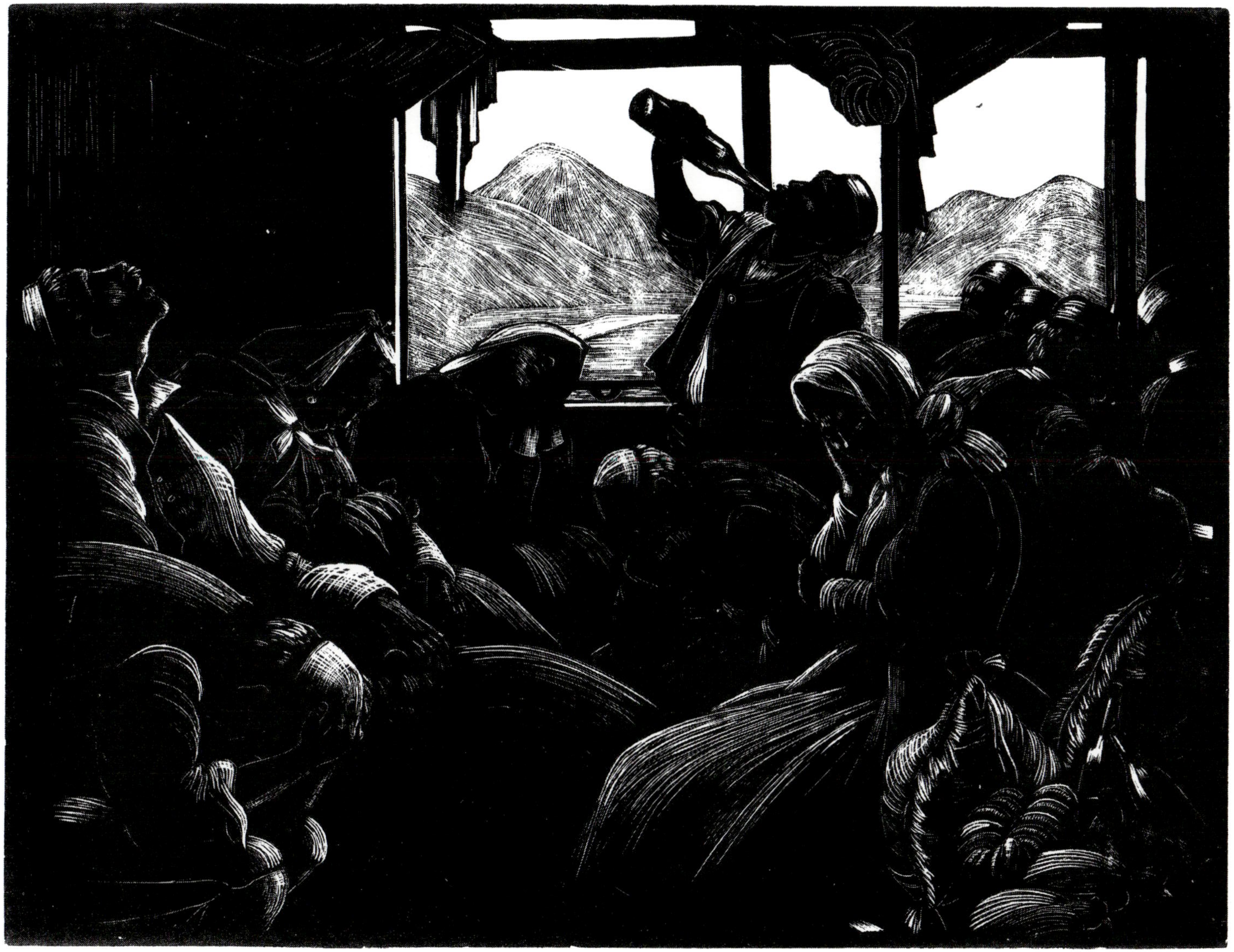

13. *Dawn in the Train to Mostar*, 1926 14.6 × 19.1 cms.: 5¾ × 7½ ins. (repr. from an impression in the Department of Western Art, Ashmolean Museum, Oxford, signed and numbered 36/75. From the Martin Hardie Gift.)

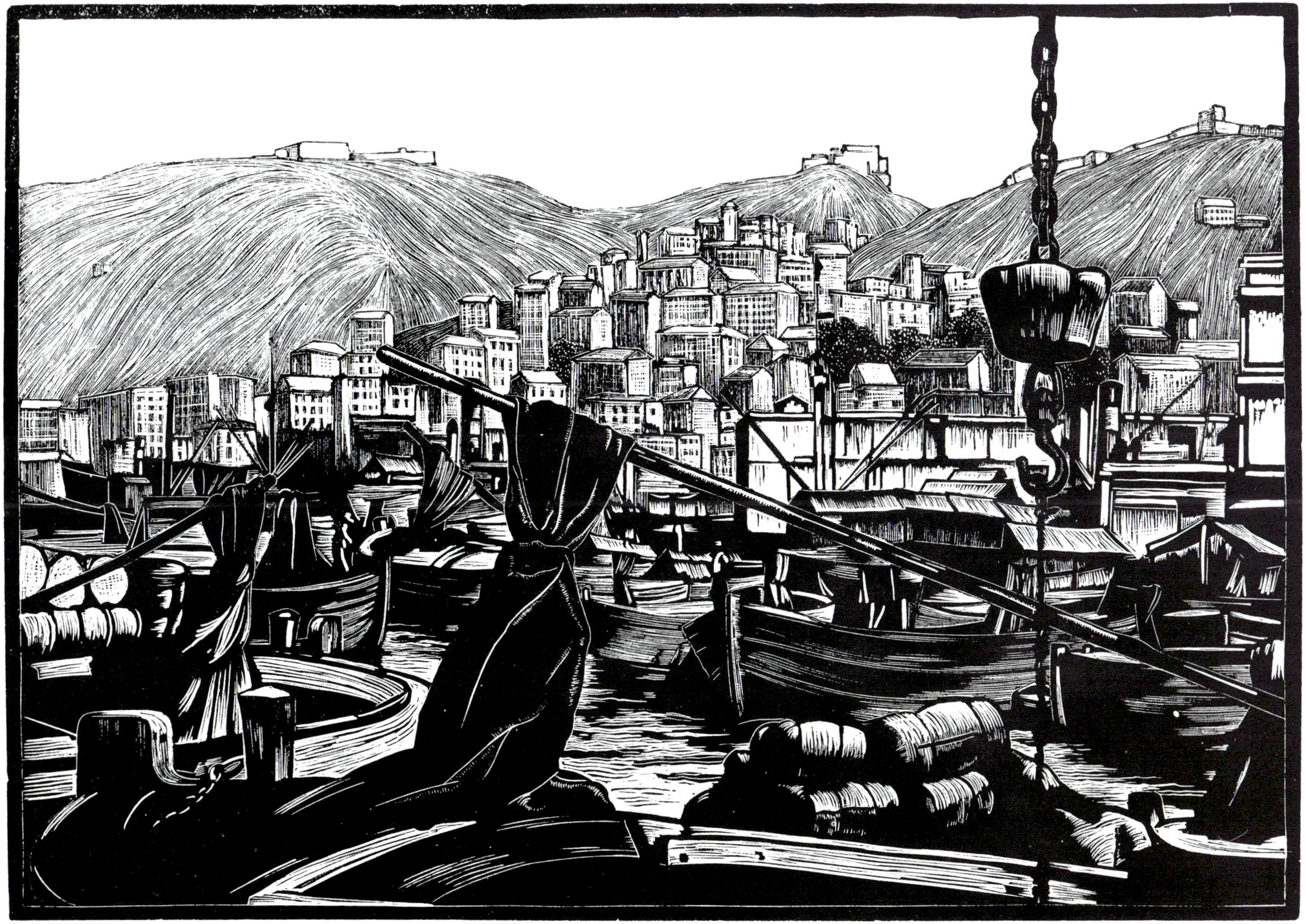

14. *Genoa*, 1927 15.3 × 21.6 cms.: 6 × 8½ ins.

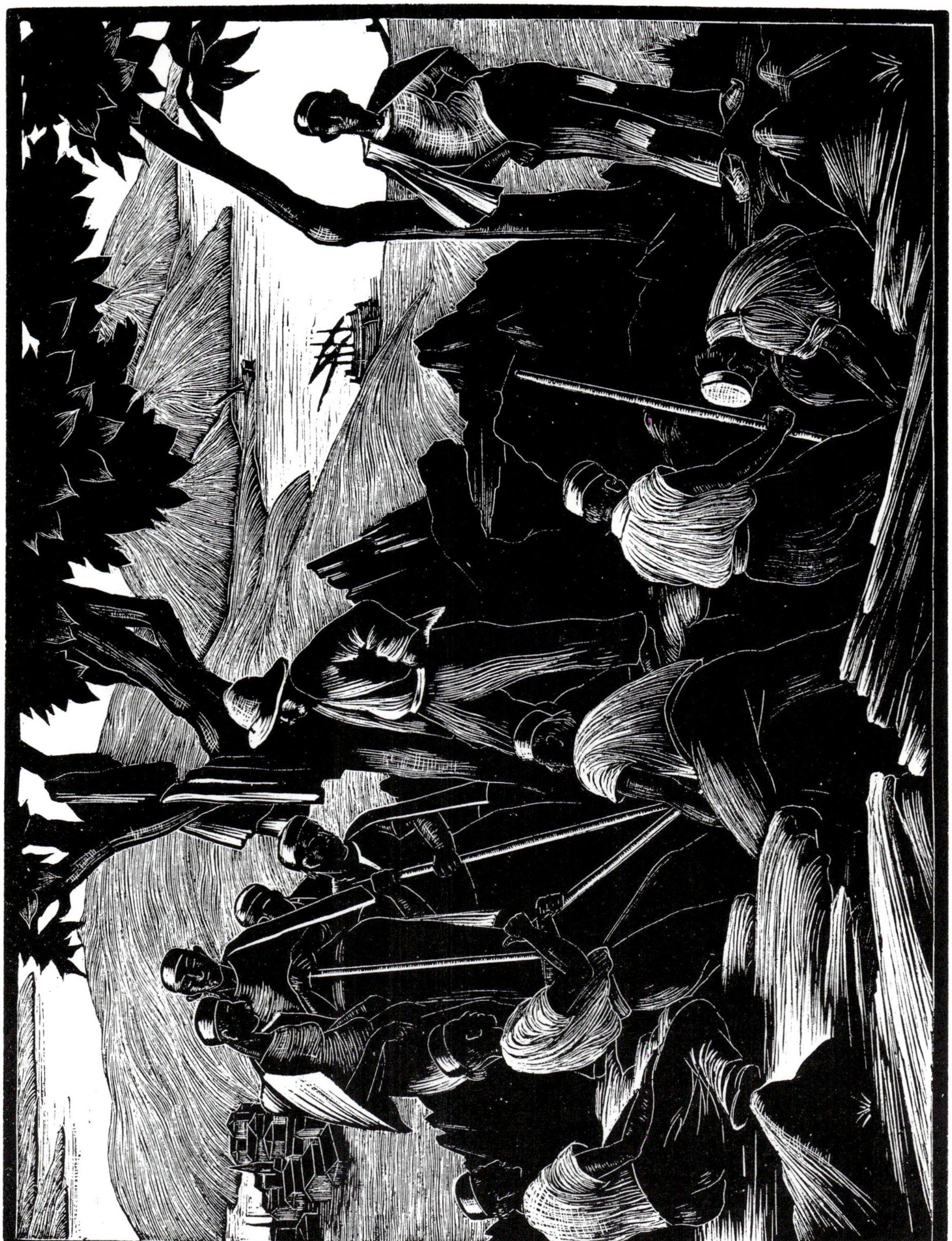

15. *Roadmakers: Dalmatia*, 1927 15.3 × 20.3 cms.: 6 × 8 ins.

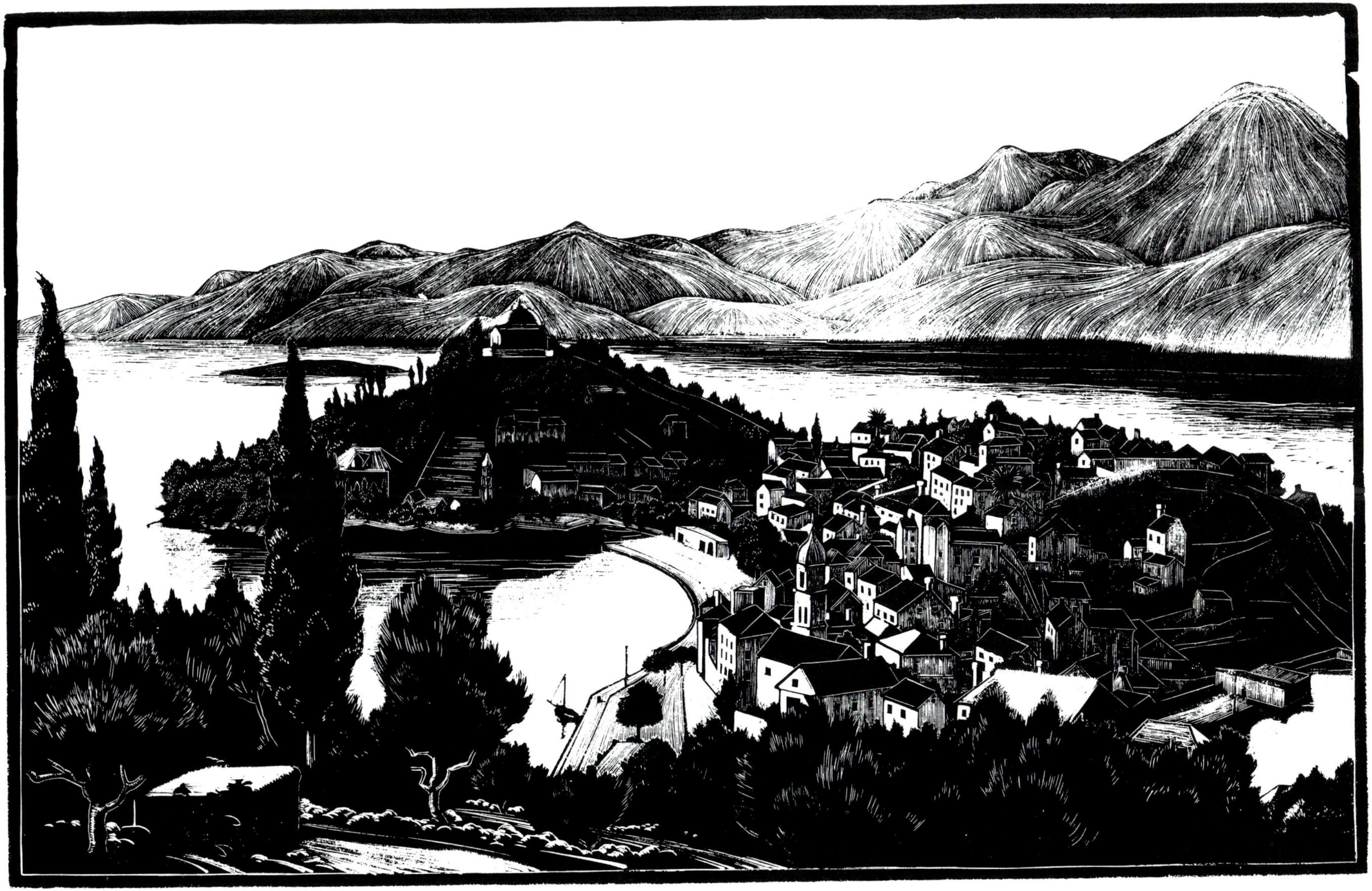

16. *Cavtat*, 1927 19.8 × 30.8 cms.: 7¹³⁄₁₆ × 12⅛ ins.

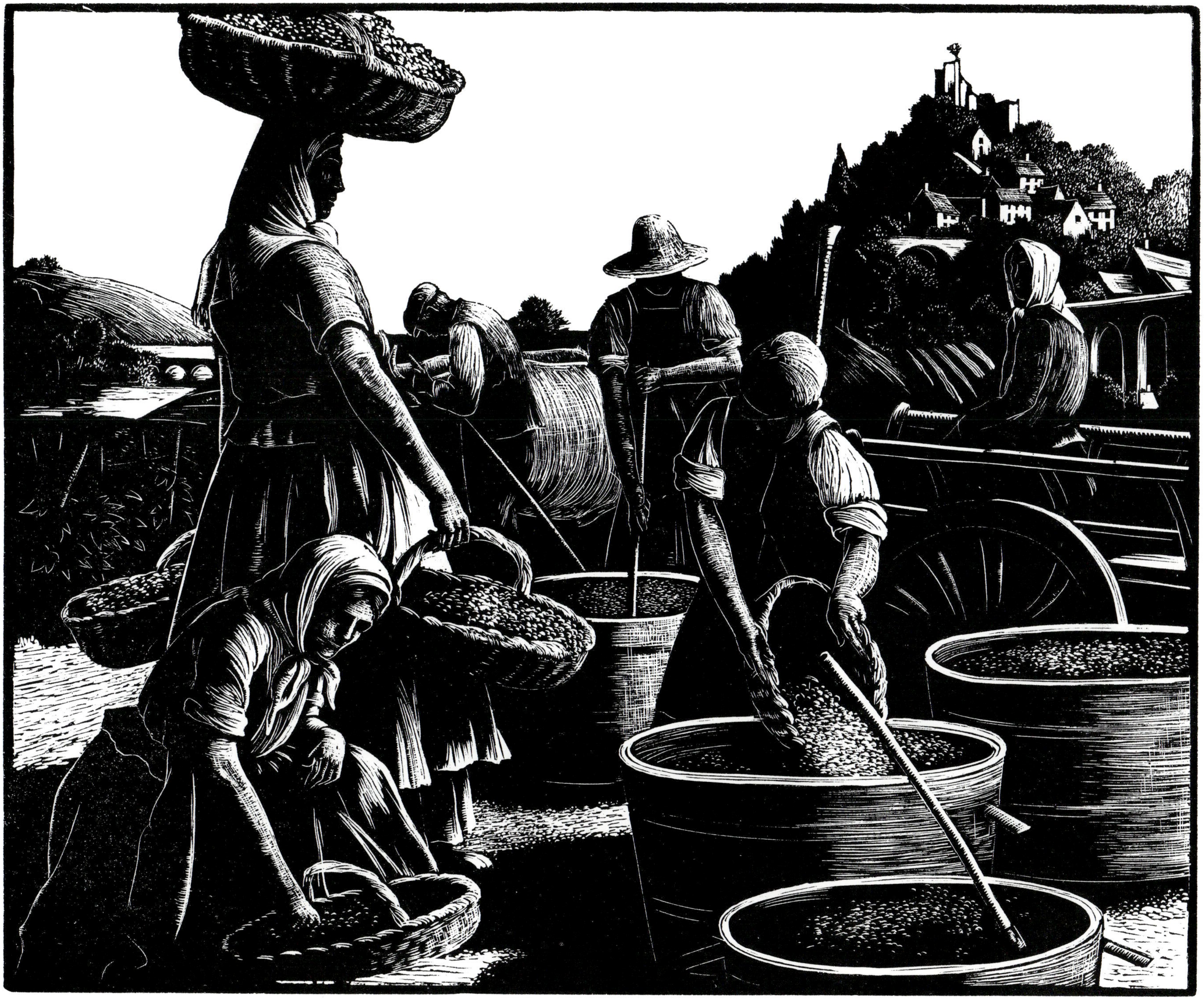

17. *The Grape Harvest*, 1928 18.9 × 22.7 cms.: 7⁷⁄₁₆ × 8¹⁵⁄₁₆ ins.

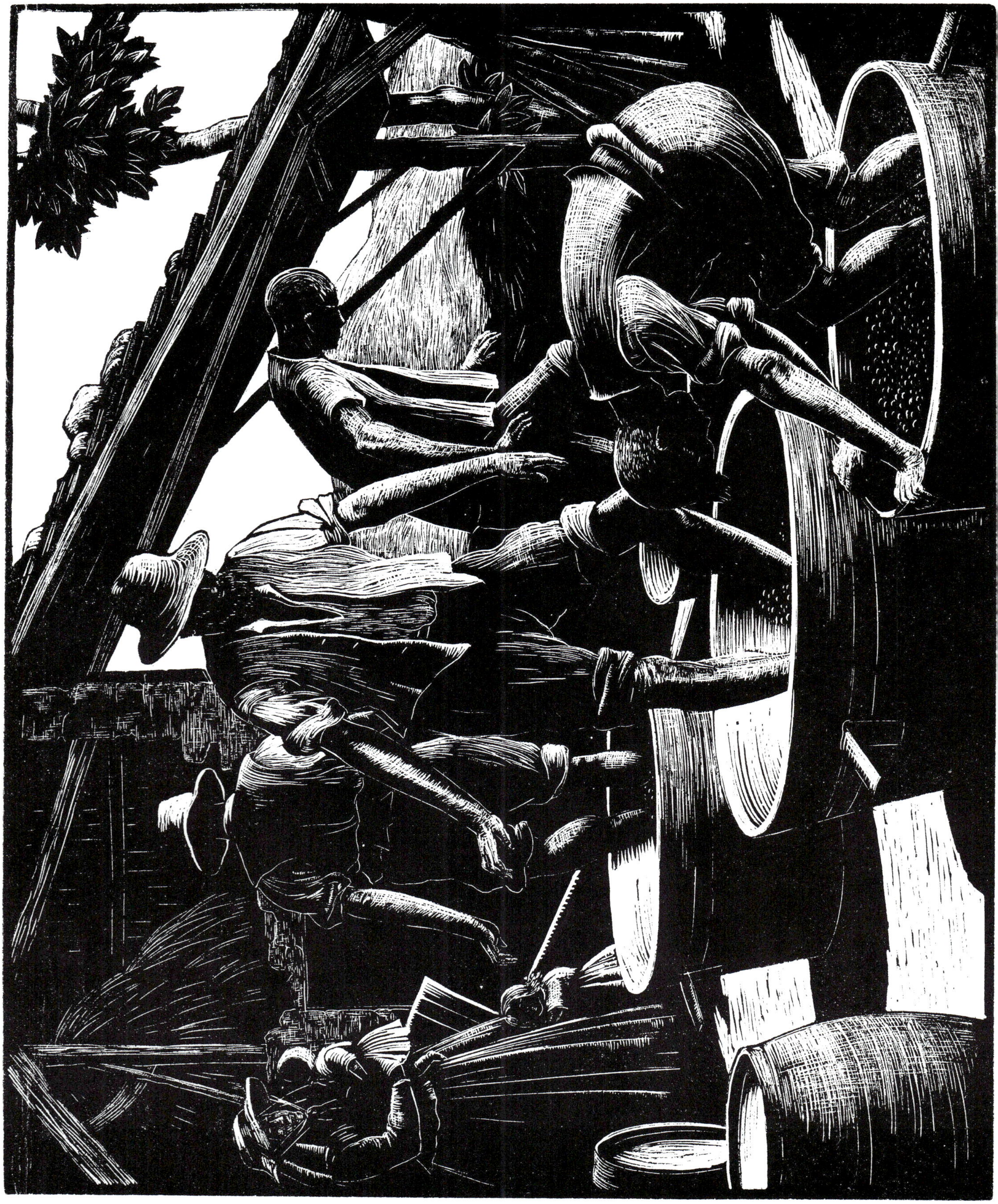

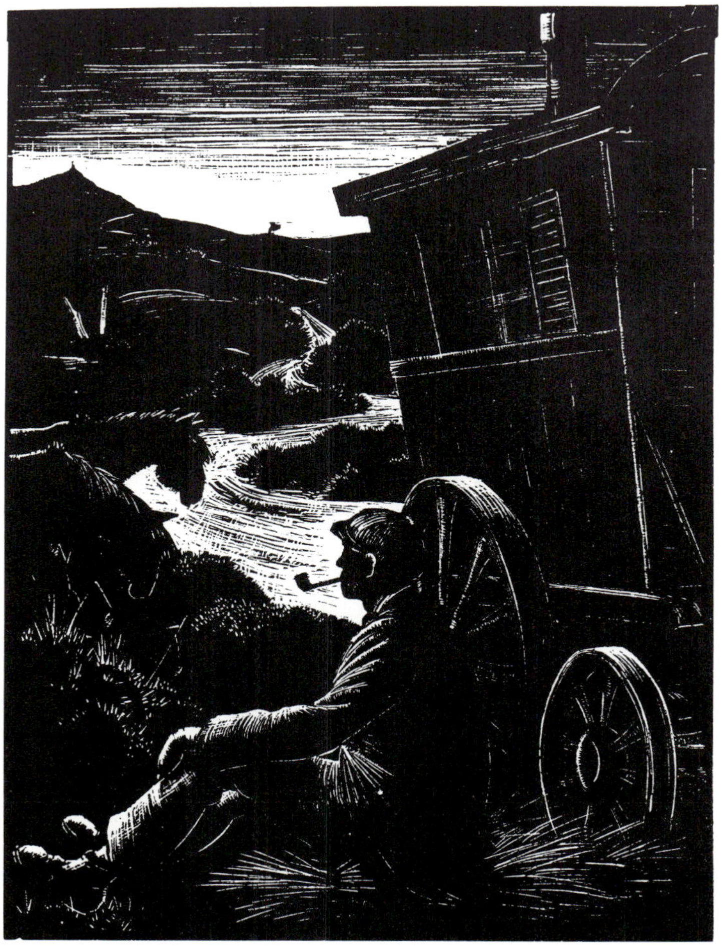

19a. *The Reddleman*, 1928 12.7 × 9.7 cms.: 5 × 3 13/16 ins. frontispiece and dust jacket for Thomas Hardy, *The Return of the Native*, London: Macmillan and Co.; New York: Harper and Brothers, 1929

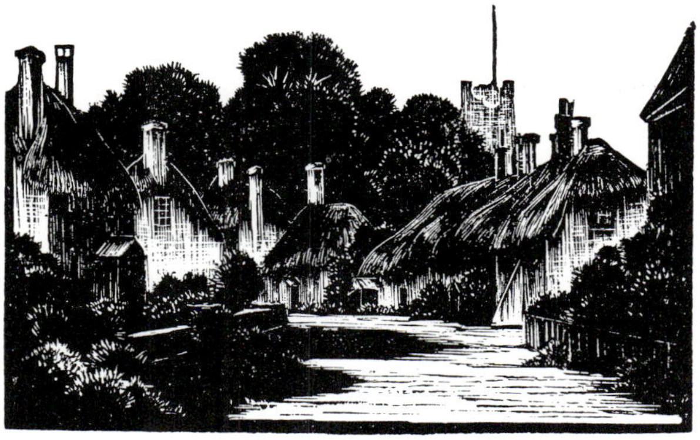

19b. *The Village*, 1928 4.8 × 7.8 cms.: 1 7/8 × 3 1/16 ins., p. 119 and p. 212 in Thomas Hardy, *The Return of the Native*, London: Macmillan and Co.; New York: Harper and Brothers, 1929

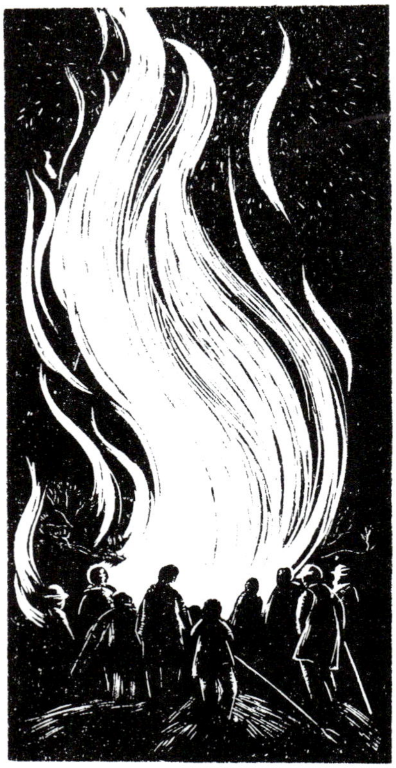

20a. *Bonfire*, 1928 10.2 × 5.3 cms.: 4 × 2¹⁄₁₆ ins. p. 58 and p. 407 in Thomas Hardy, *The Return of the Native*, London: Macmillan and Co.; New York: Harper and Brothers, 1929

20b. *The Heath*, 1928 2.9 × 7.8 cms.: 1⅛ × 3¹⁄₁₆ ins., p. 182 and p. 317 in Thomas Hardy, *The Return of the Native*, London: Macmillan and Co.; New York: Harper and Brothers, 1929

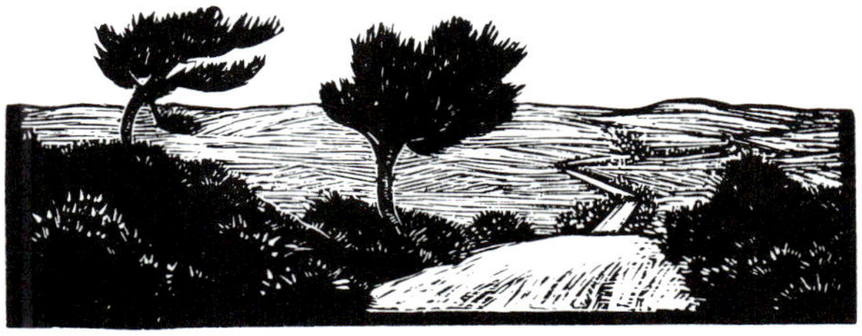

20c. *Wessex Cottage*, 1928 6.2 × 8.6 cms.: 2⁷⁄₁₆ × 3⅜ ins., p. 134 and p. 415 in Thomas Hardy, *The Return of the Native*, London: Macmillan and Co.; New York: Harper and Brothers, 1929

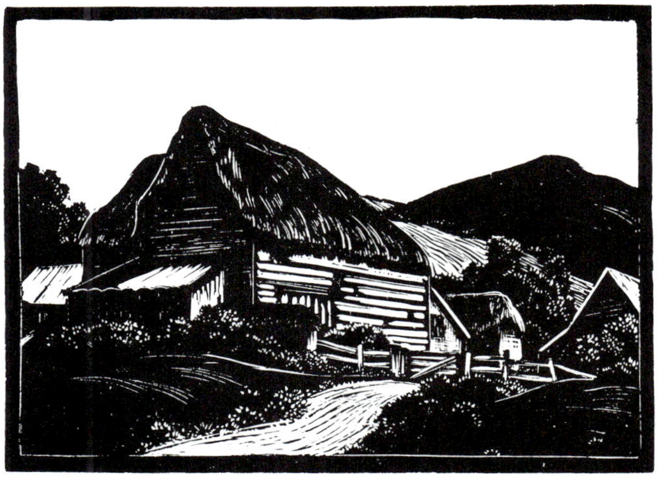

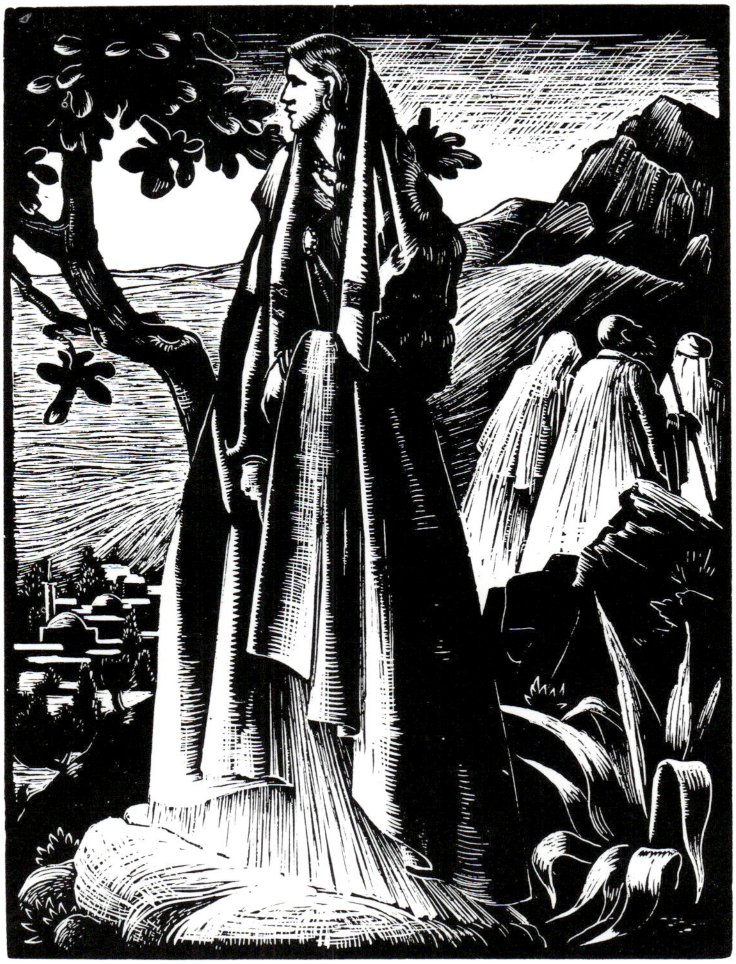

21a. *Lot's Wife*, 1929 12.7 × 9.5 cms.: 5 × 3¾ ins. frontispiece to Joseph Auslander, *Letters to Women*, New York: Harper & Brothers, 1929

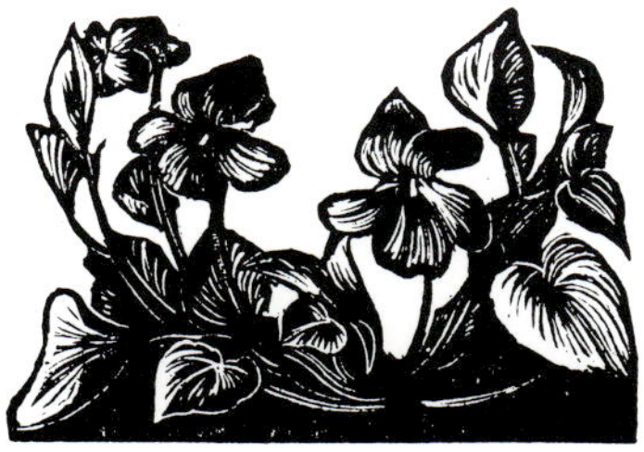

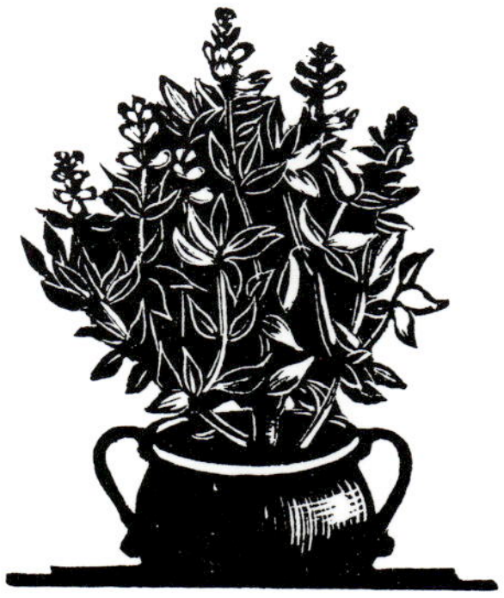

21b. *Violets*, 1929 3.2 × 4.6 cms.: 1¼ × 1¹³⁄₁₆ ins. reverse of title page to Joseph Auslander, *Letters to Women*, New York: Harper & Brothers, 1929

21c. *Skyscraper*, 1929 5.1 × 3.8 cms.: 2 × 1½ ins. p. 9 in Joseph Auslander, *Letters to Women*, New York, Harper & Brothers, 1929

21d. *Thyme*, 1929 4.4 × 3.5 cms.: 1¾ × 1⅜ ins. p. 57 in Joseph Auslander, *Letters to Women*, New York, Harper & Brothers, 1929

22a. *Brother Juniper*, 1929 11.9 × 7.6 cms.: 4$^{11}/_{16}$ × 3 ins. frontispiece to Thornton Wilder, *The Bridge of San Luis Rey*, London: Longmans Green and Co., 1929

22b. *Loading the Boat*, 1929 10.8 × 8.3 cms.: 4¼ × 3¼ ins. facing p. 52 in Thornton Wilder, *The Bridge of San Luis Rey*, London: Longmans Green and Co., 1929

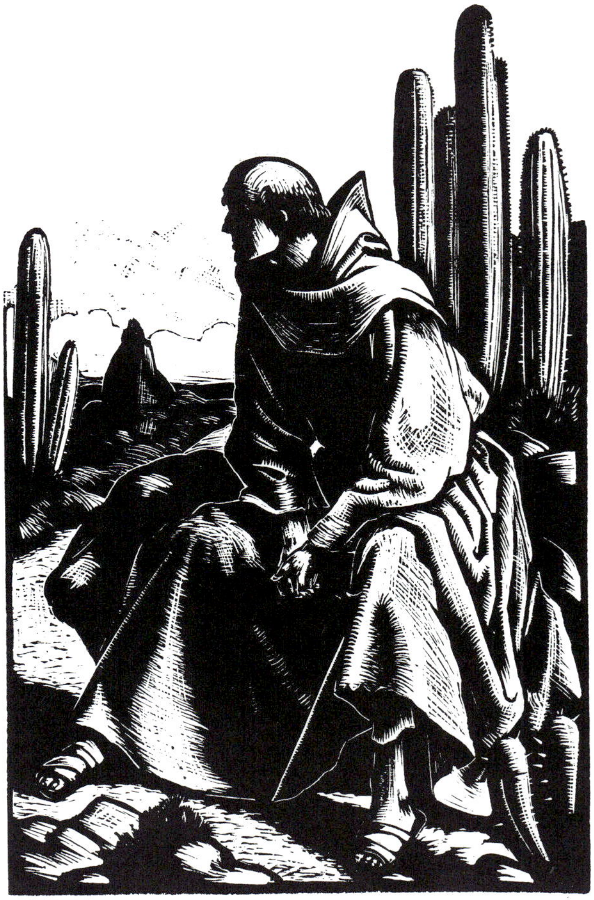

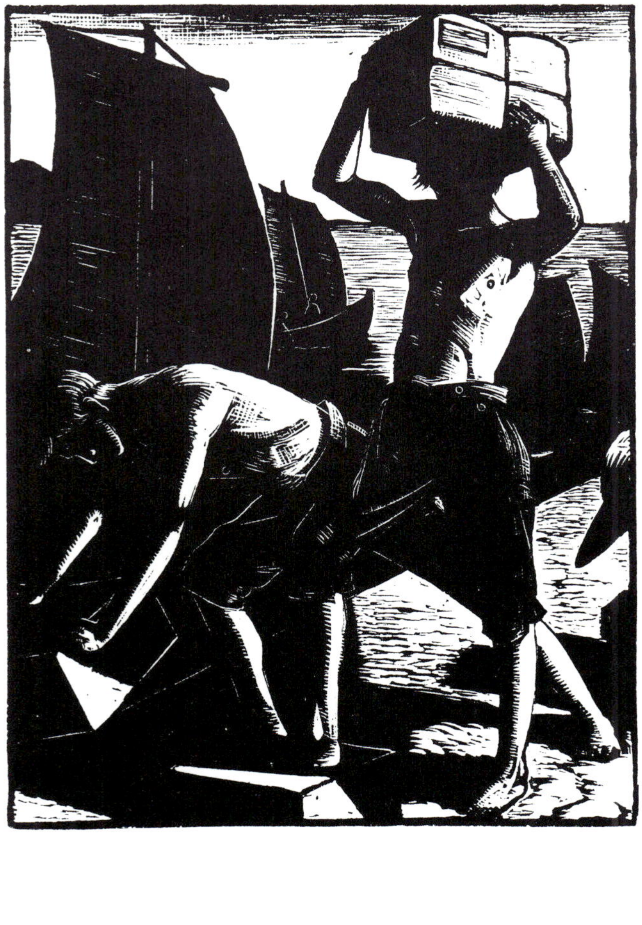

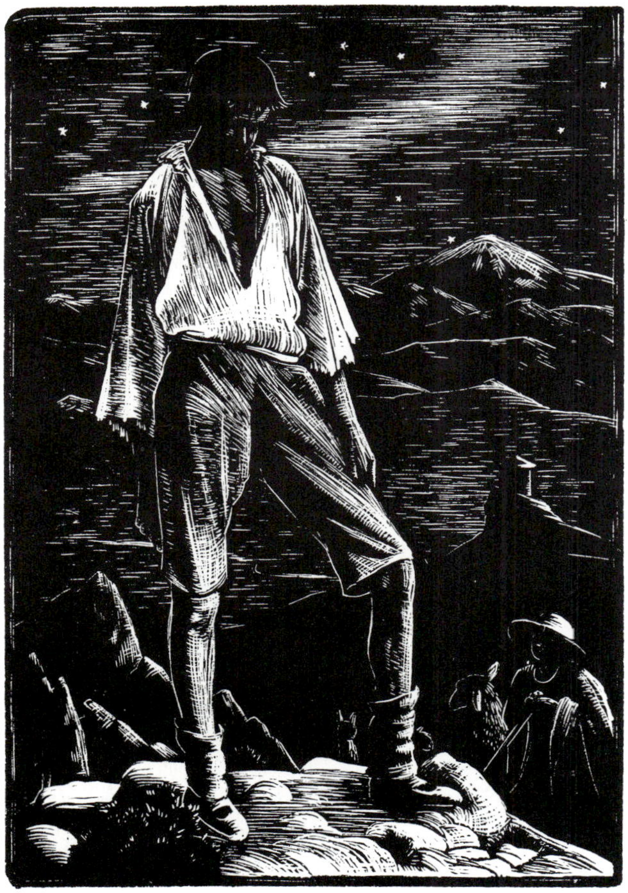

23a. *Esteban*, 1929 11.8 × 8.3 cms.: 4⅝ × 3¼ ins. facing p. 71 in Thornton Wilder, *The Bridge of San Luis Rey*, London: Longmans Green and Co., 1929

23b. *Uncle Pio*, 1929 11.4 × 8.3 cms.: 4½ × 3¼ ins. facing p. 121 in Thornton Wilder, *The Bridge of San Luis Rey*, London: Longmans Green and Co., 1929

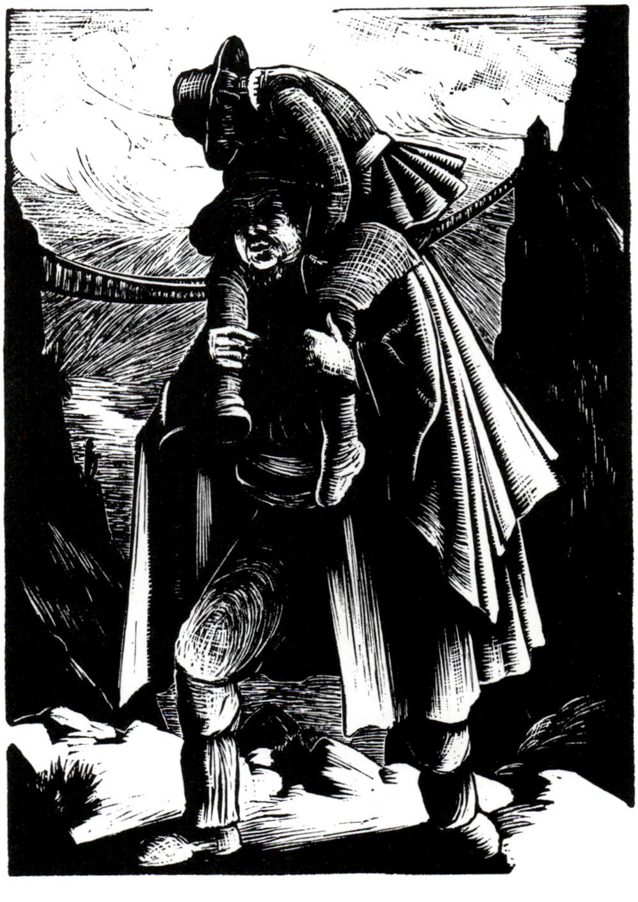

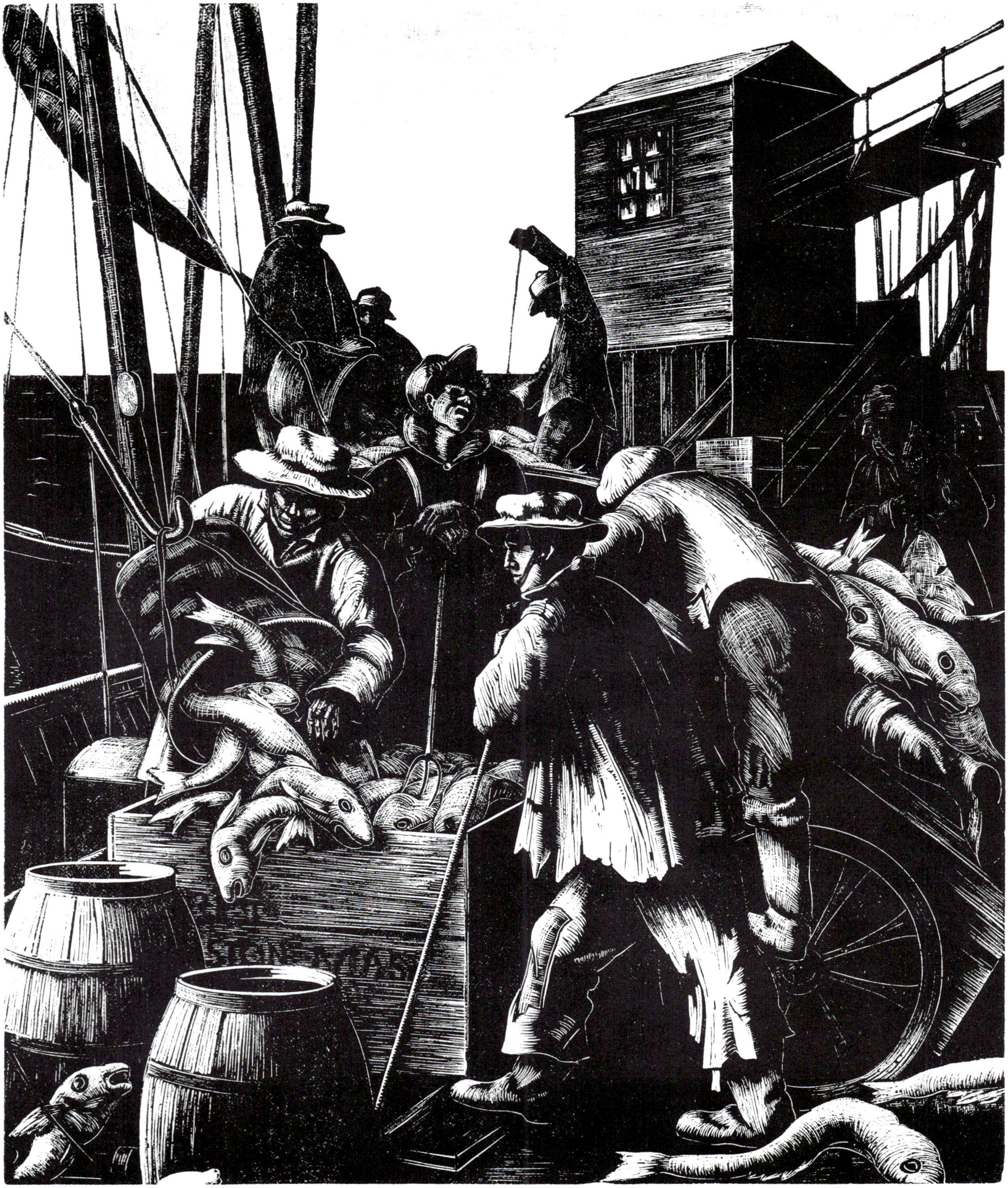

24. *Boston Cod*, 1929 24 × 20.5 cms.: $9\frac{7}{16} \times 8\frac{1}{16}$ ins.

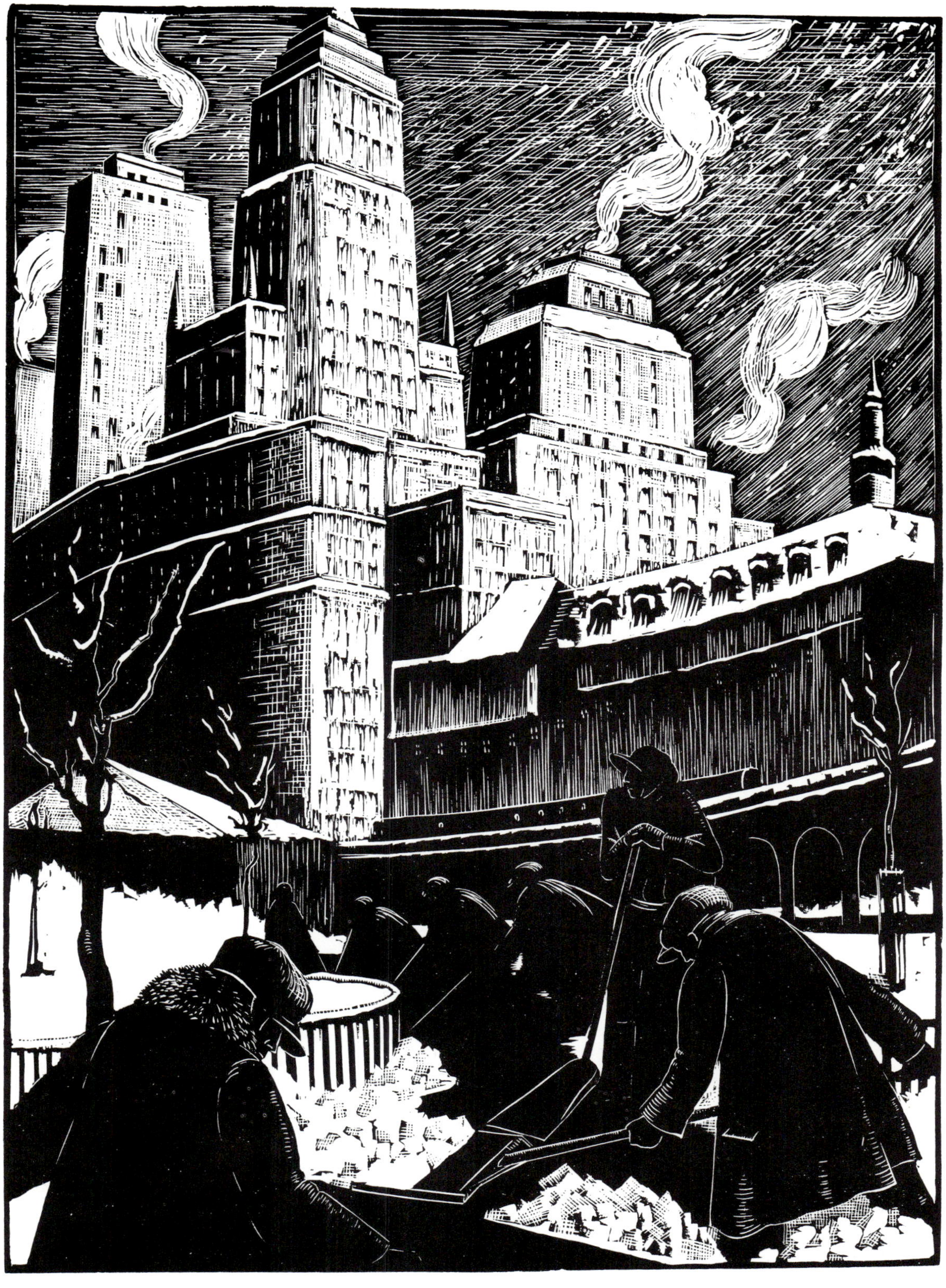

25. *Snow Shovellers: New York*, 1929 20.3 × 15.3 cms.: 8 × 6 ins. commissioned for *The Legion Book*, edited by Captain H. Cotton Minchin, London. Privately published; printed at the Curwen Press, 1929

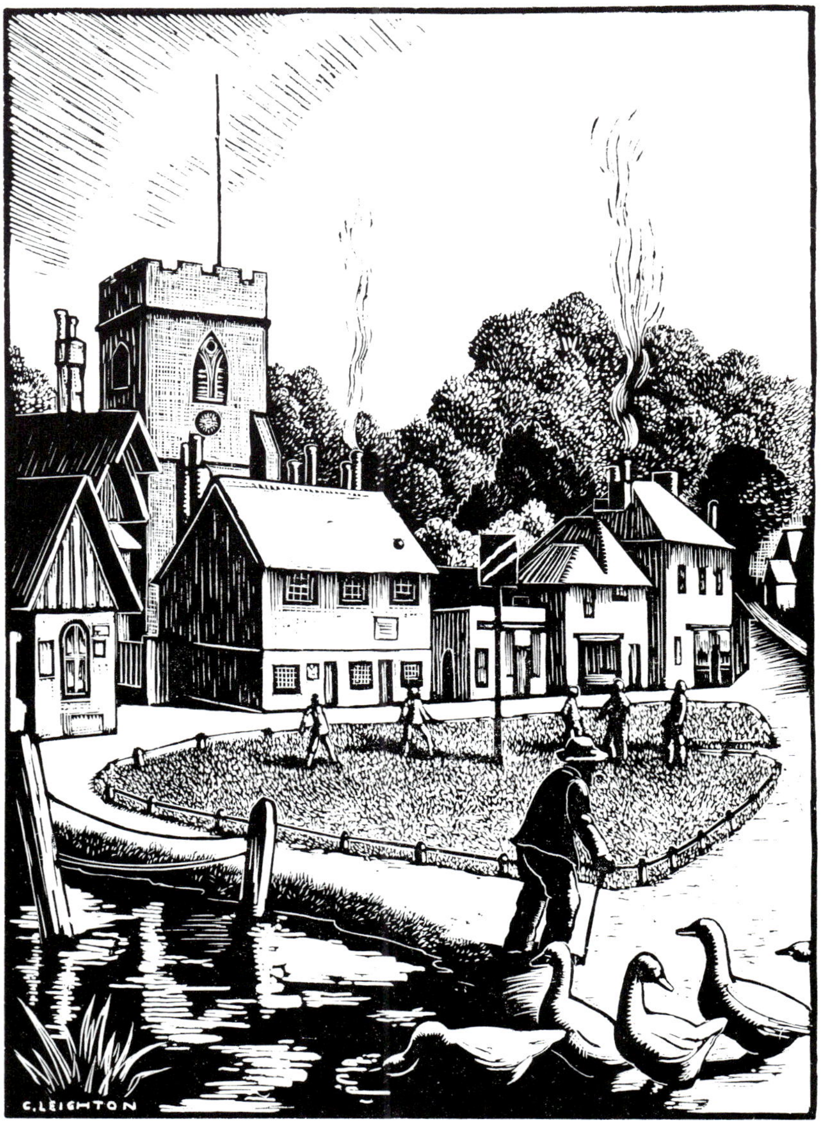

26. *Chalfont St. Giles*, 1929–30 14.8 × 10.8 cms.: 5 13/16 × 4¼ ins. commissioned for the London General Omnibus Company D.L.

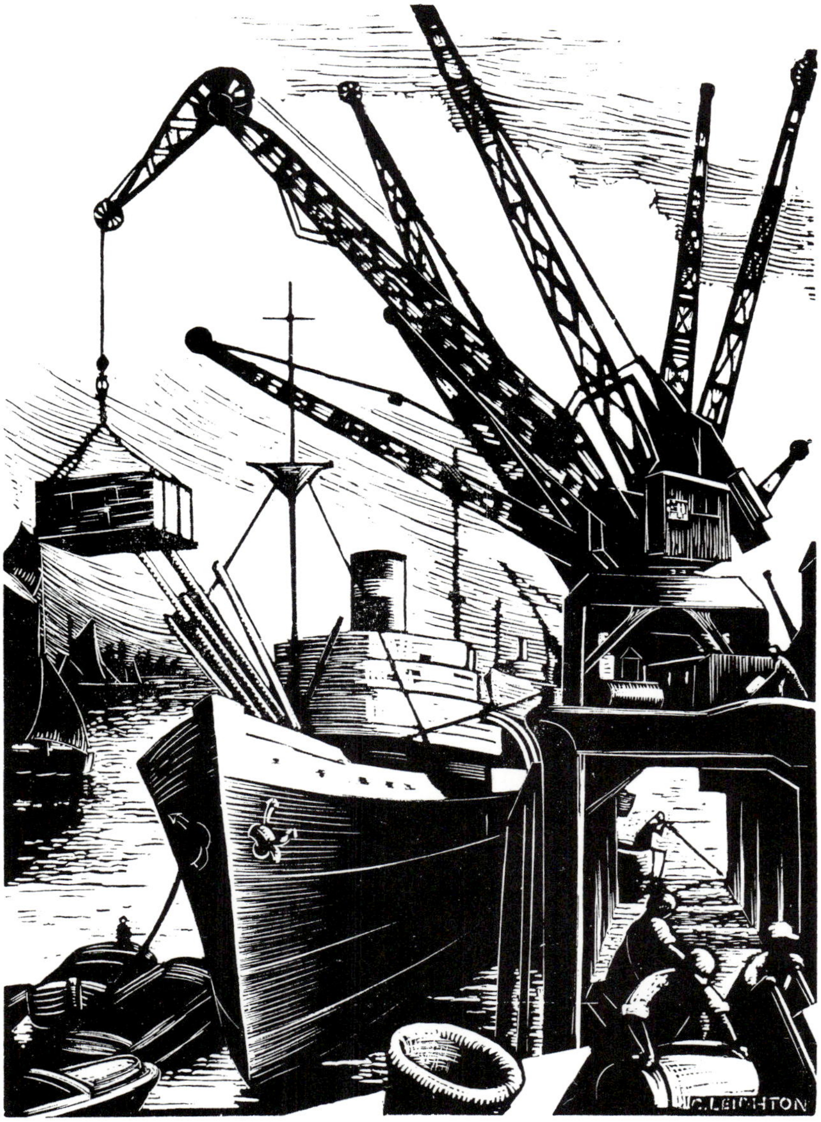

27. *The Docks*, 1929–30 14.8 × 10.8 cms.: 5¹³⁄₁₆ × 4¼ ins.
commissioned for The London General Omnibus Company D.L.

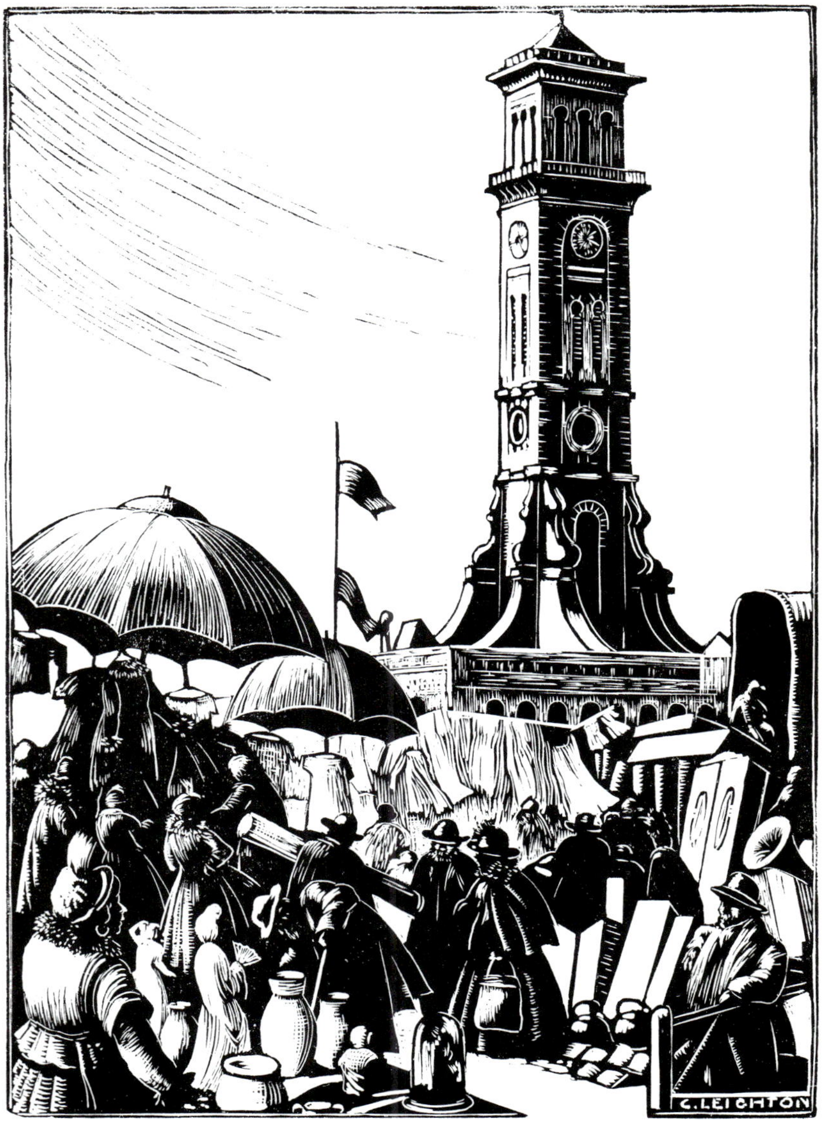

28. *Caledonian Market*, 1929–30 14.8 × 10.6 cms.: 5 13/16 × 4 3/16 ins. commissioned for The London General Omnibus Company D.L.

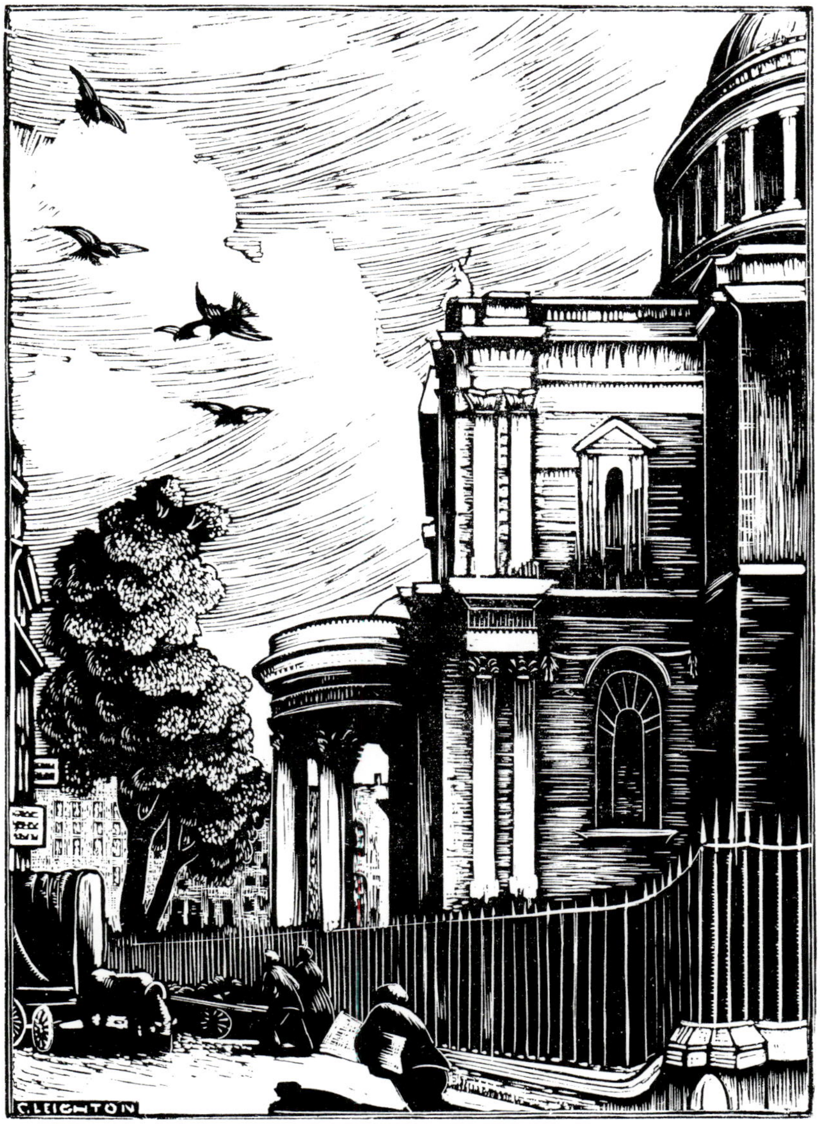

29. *St. Paul's Cathedral*, 1929–30 14.8 × 10.8 cms.: 5 13/16 × 4 1/4 ins. commissioned for The London General Omnibus Company D.L.

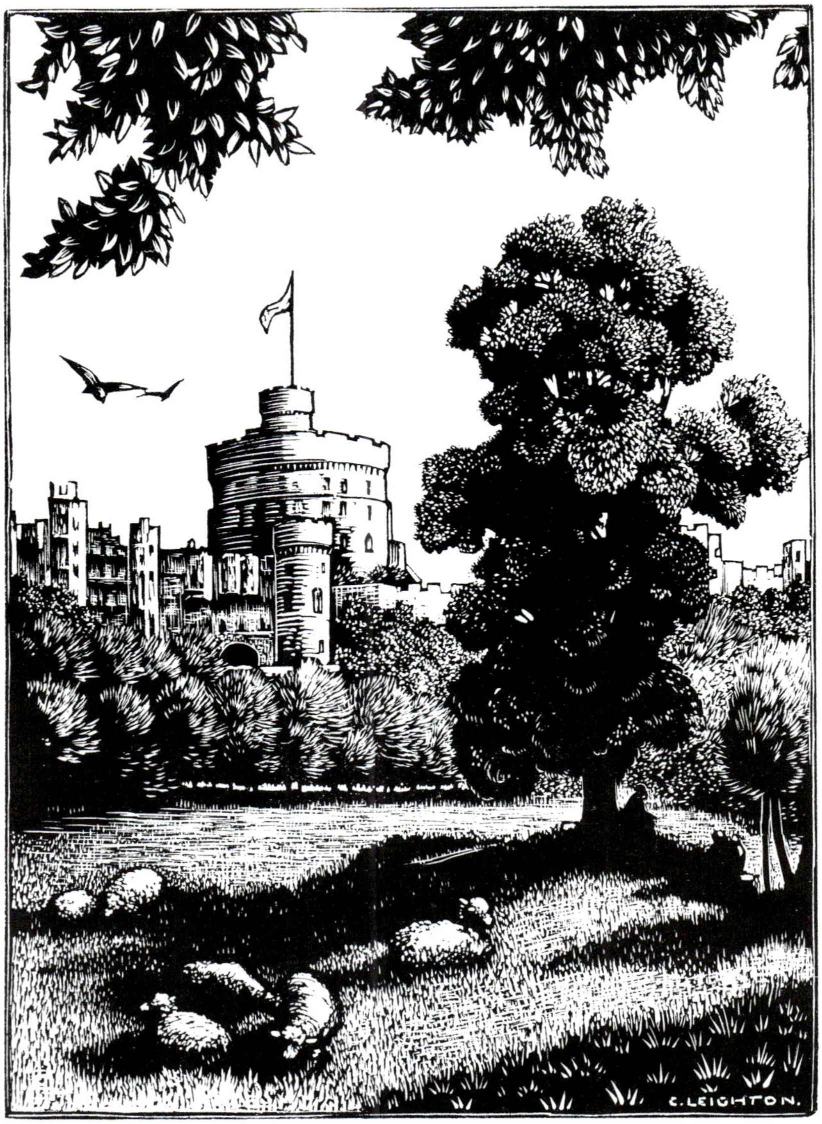

30. *Windsor Castle*, 1929–30 14.8 × 10.6 cms.: $5^{13}/_{16}$ × $4^{3}/_{16}$ ins. commissioned for The London General Omnibus Company D.L.

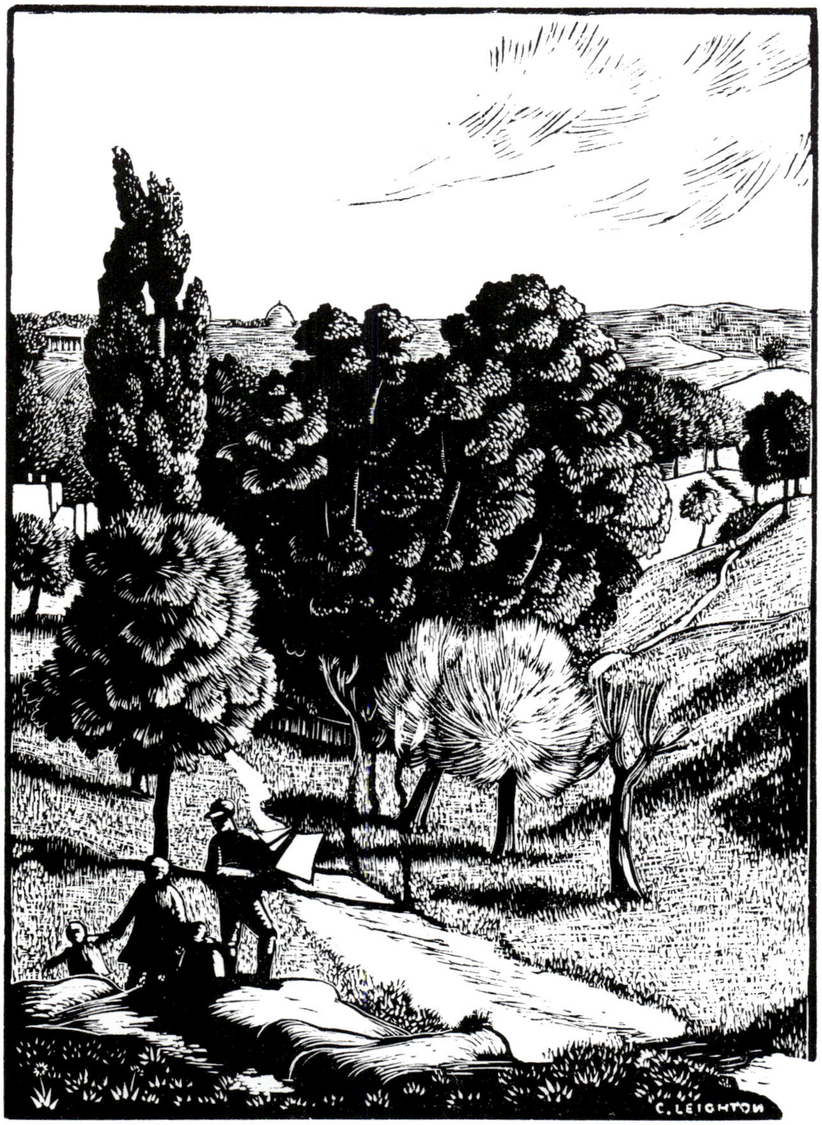

31. *Hampstead Heath*, 1930 14.8 × 10.6 cms.: 5 13/16 × 4 3/16 ins. commissioned for The London General Omnibus Company D.L.

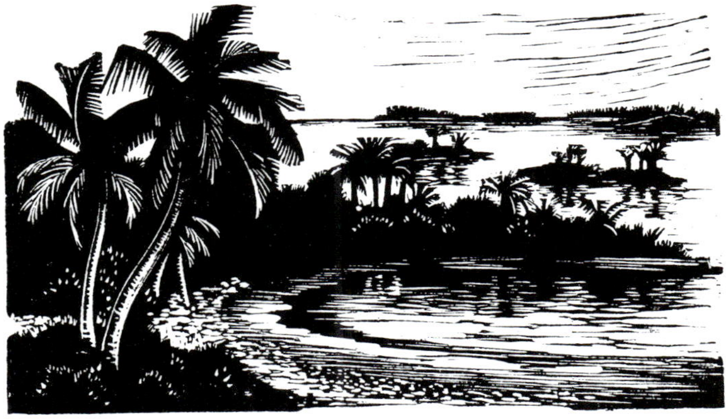

32a. *Tropical Bay*, 1930 5.1 × 8.9 cms.: 2 × 3½ ins. headpiece p. 105 in H.M. Tomlinson, *The Sea and the Jungle*, London: Duckworth; New York: Harper and Brothers, 1930

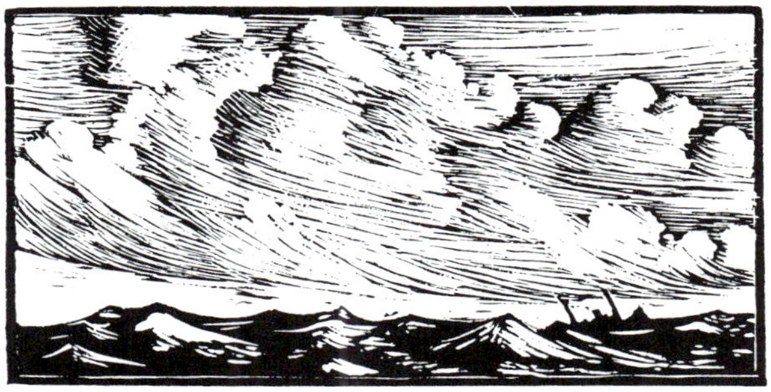

32b. *Stormy Sea*, 1930 3.8 × 7.6 cms.: 1½ × 3 ins. tailpiece p. 104 in H.M. Tomlinson, *The Sea and the Jungle*, London: Duckworth; New York: Harper and Brothers, 1930

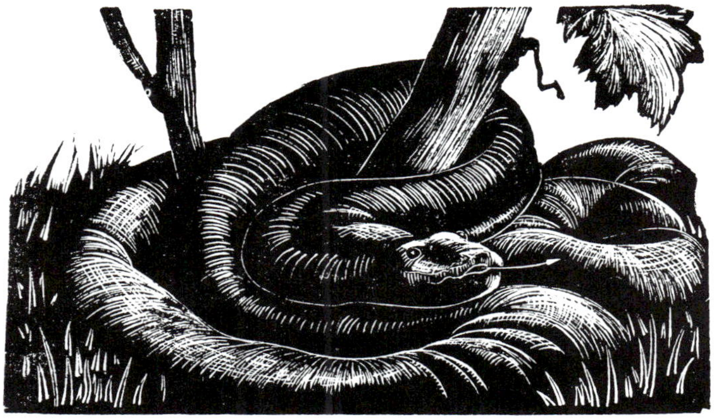

32c. *The Snake*, 1930 5.1 × 8.9 cms.: 2 × 3½ ins. headpiece p. 256 in H.M. Tomlinson, *The Sea and the Jungle*, London: Duckworth; New York: Harper and Brothers, 1930

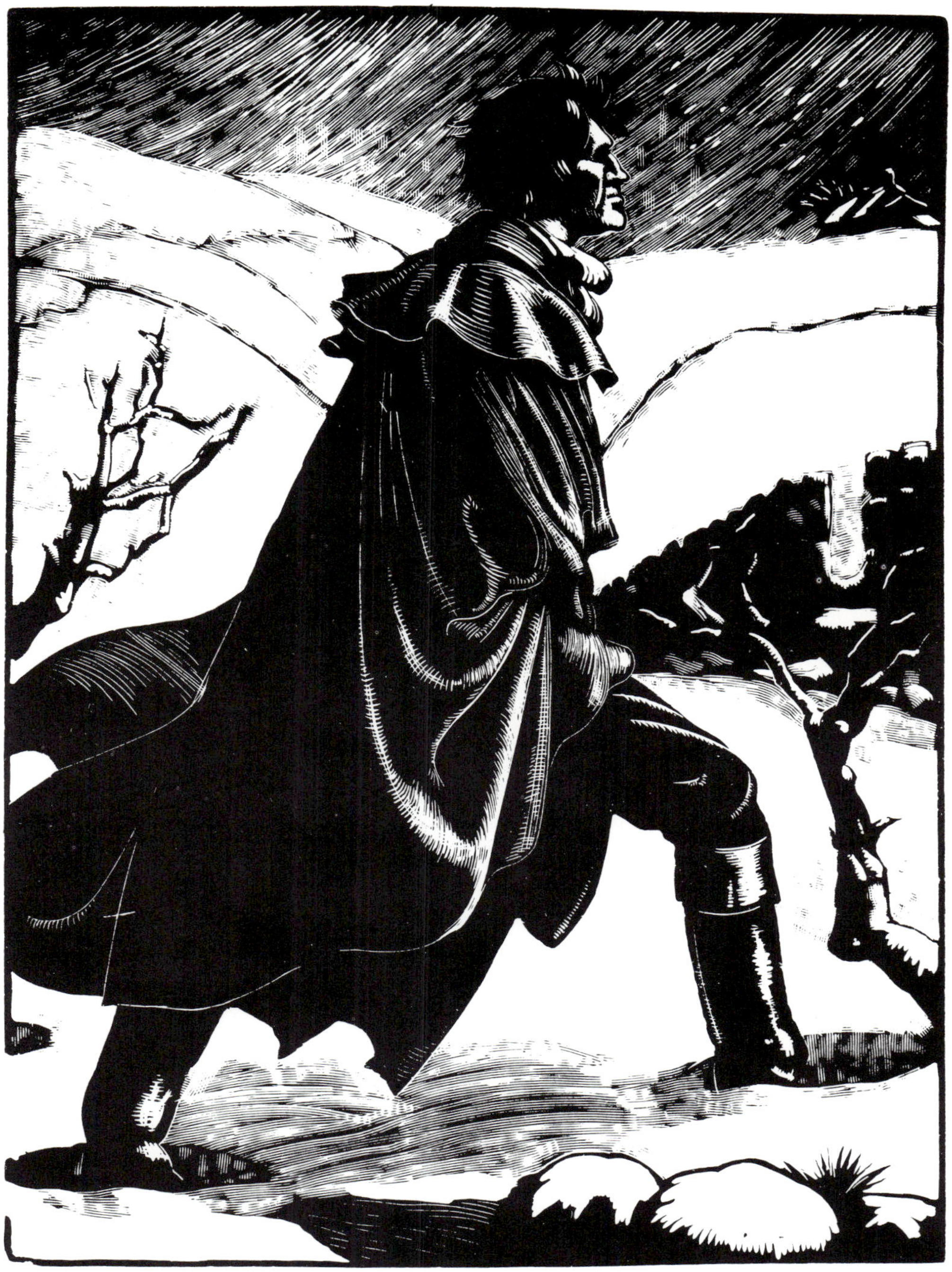

33. *Heathcliff in the Snow*, 1930 17.9 × 13.5 cms.: 7¹⁄₁₆ × 5⁵⁄₁₆ ins., between pp. 30 and 31 in Emily Brontë, *Wuthering Heights*, London: Duckworth; New York: Random House, 1931

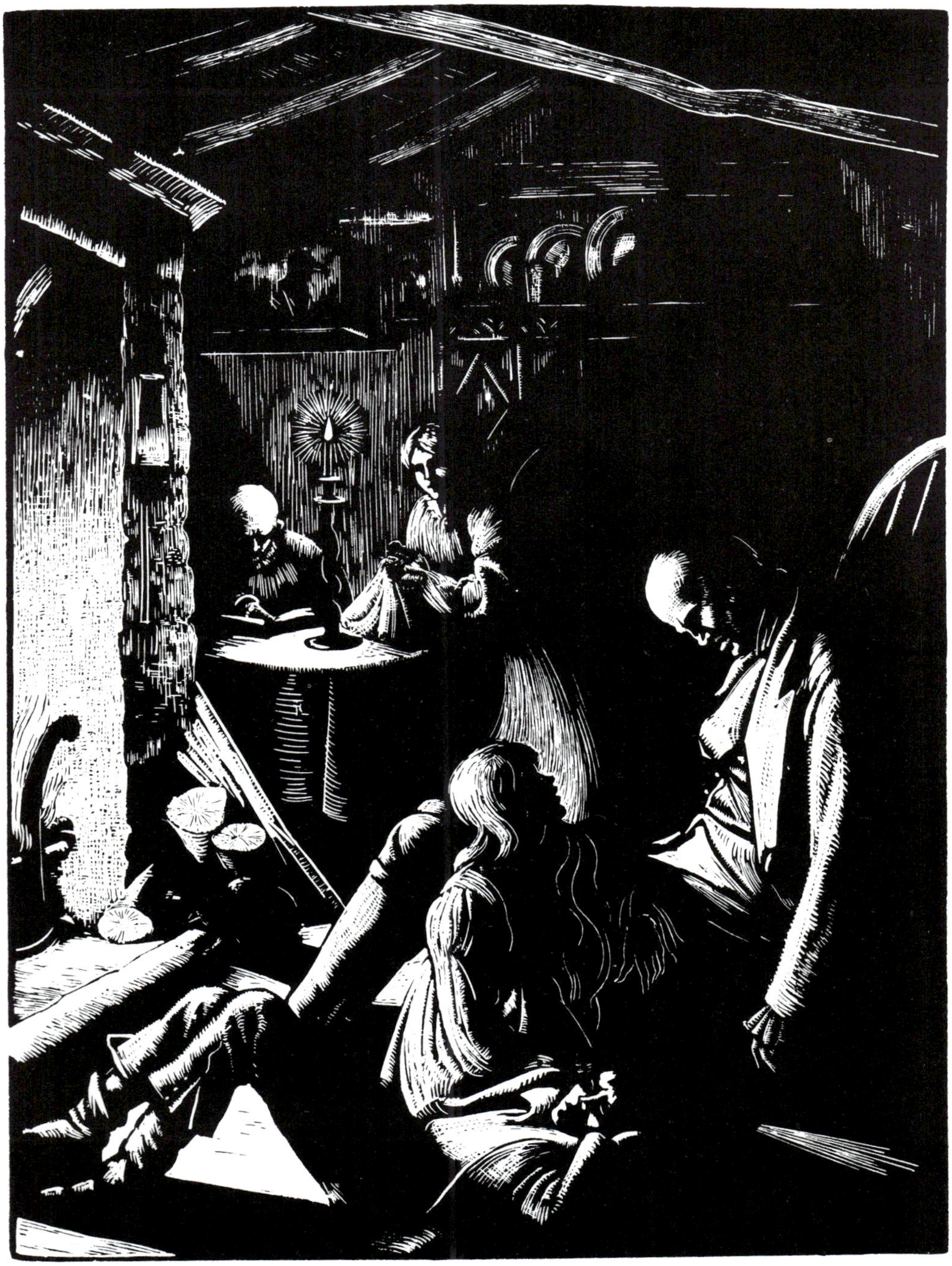

34. *The Death of Earnshaw*, 1930 17.8 × 13.5 cms.: 7 × 5$\frac{5}{16}$ ins., between pp. 42 and 43 in Emily Brontë, *Wuthering Heights*, London: Duckworth; New York: Random House, 1931

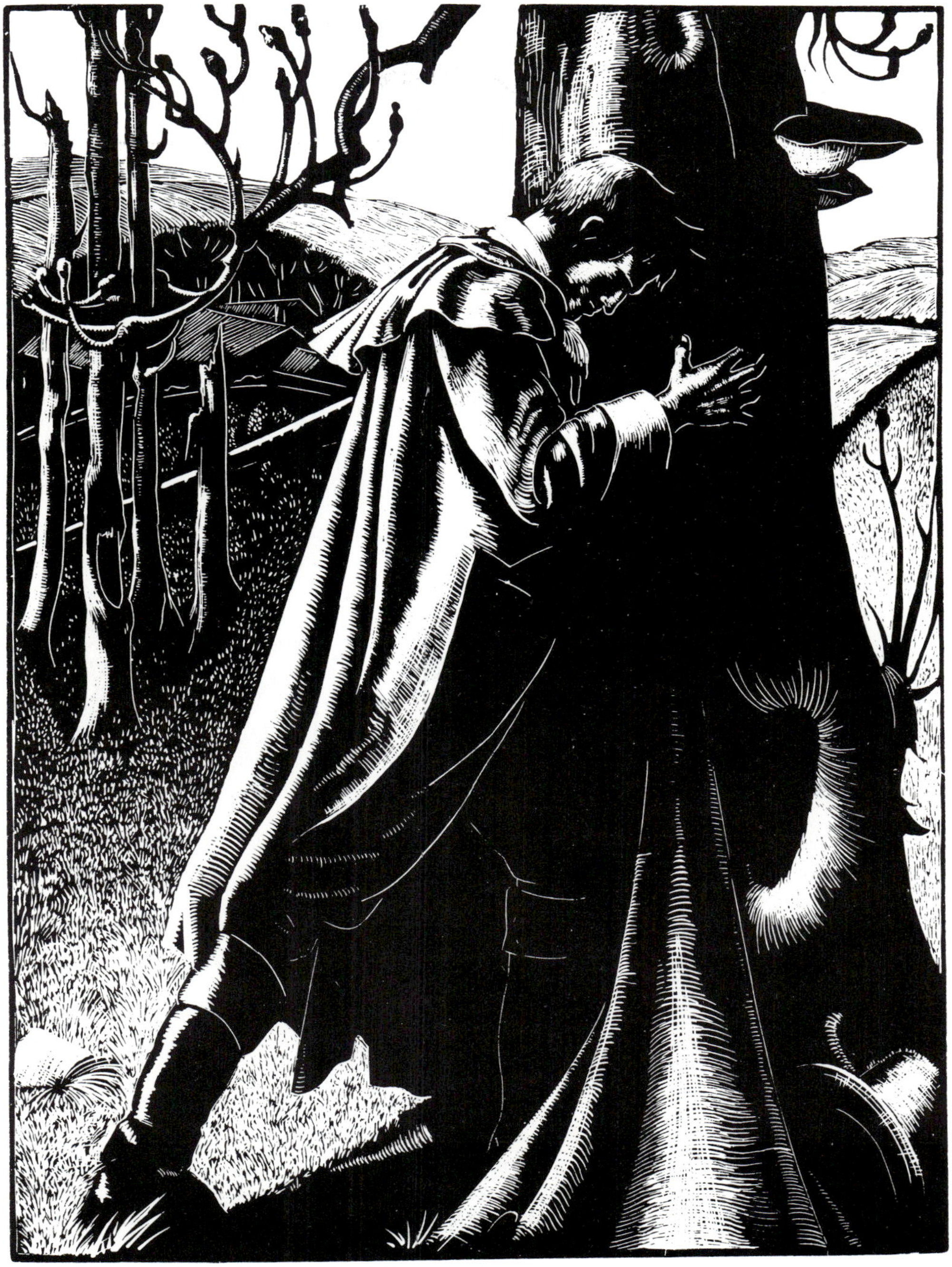

35. *Heathcliff's Grief*, 1930 17.8 × 13.3 cms.: 7 × 5¼ ins., between pp. 162 and 163 in Emily Brontë, *Wuthering Heights*, London: Duckworth; New York: Random House, 1931

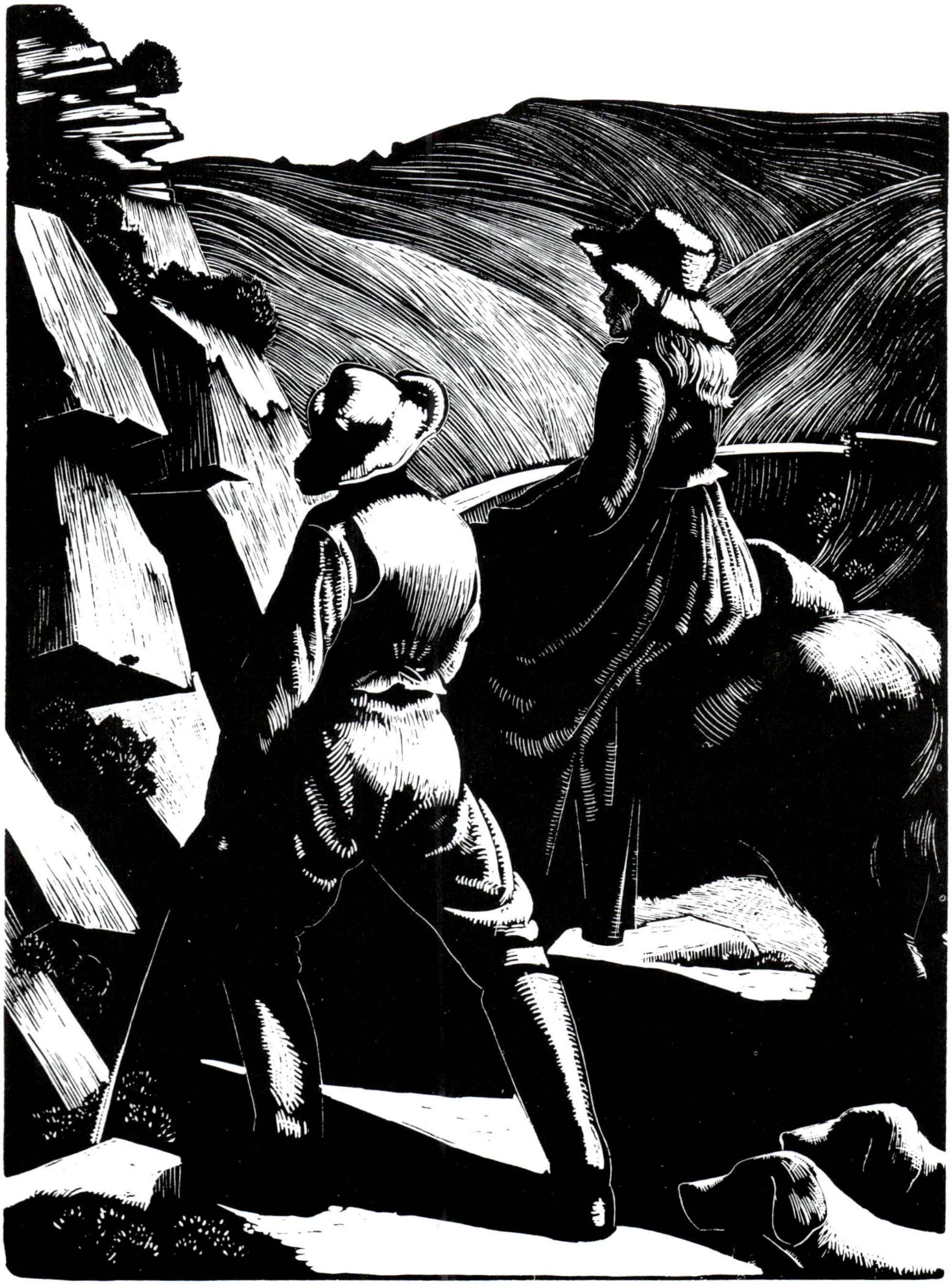

36. *Peniston Crags*, 1930 17.9 × 13.3 cms.: 7⁷⁄₁₆ × 5¼ ins., between pp. 190 and 191 in Emily Brontë, *Wuthering Heights*, London: Duckworth; New York: Random House, 1931

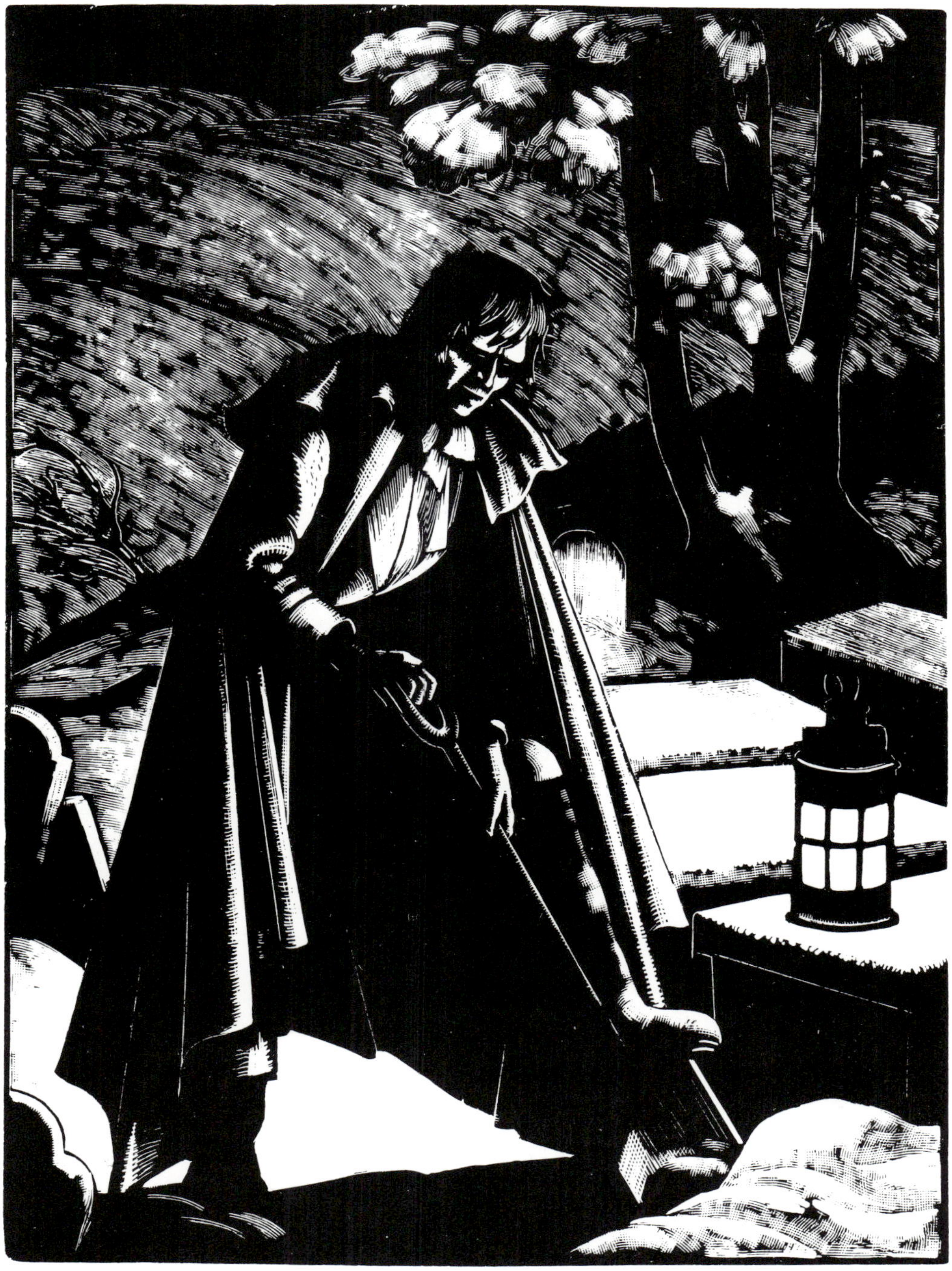

37. *The Graveyard*, 1930 17.9 × 13.3 cms.: 7⅙ × 5¼ ins., between pp. 246 and 247 in Emily Brontë, *Wuthering Heights*, London: Duckworth; New York: Random House, 1931

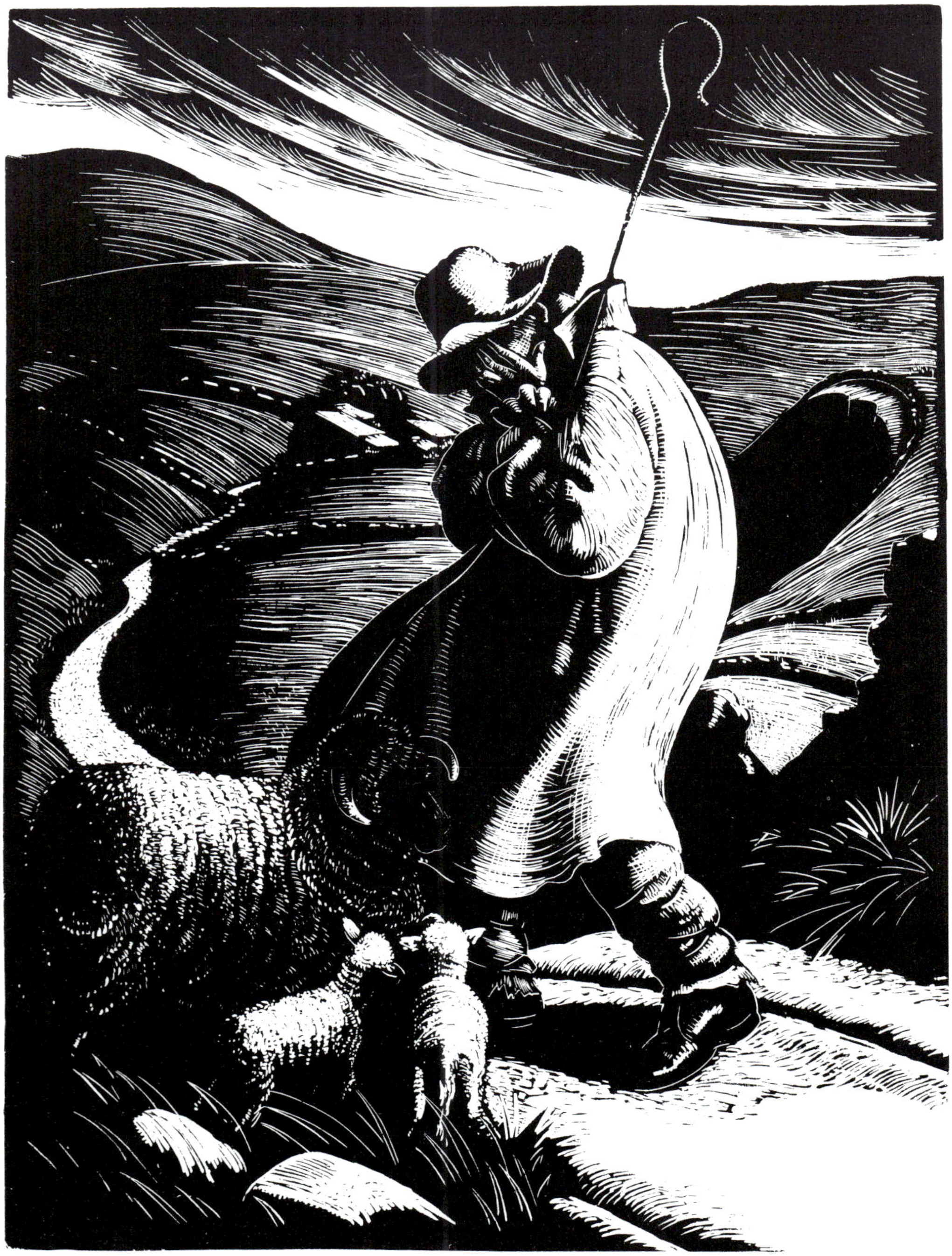

38. *The Frightened Shepherd Boy*, 1930 17.9 × 13.5 cms.: 7¹⁄₁₆ × 5⁵⁄₁₆ ins., between pp. 310 and 311 in Emily Brontë, *Wuthering Heights*, London: Duckworth; New York: Random House, 1931

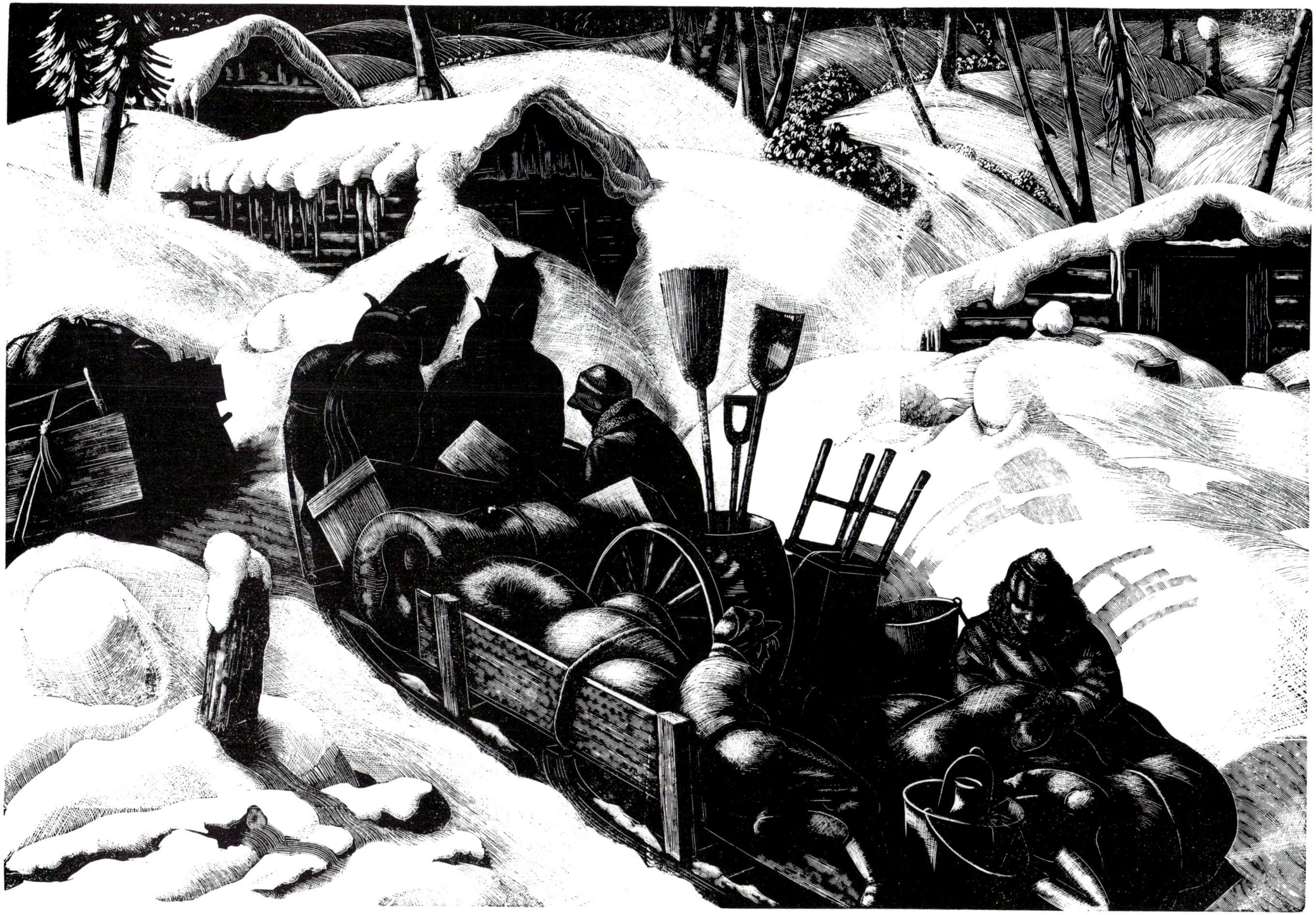

39. *Breaking Camp: Lumber Camp Series*, 1931 22.7 × 33 cms.: $8\frac{15}{16}$ × 13 ins. (here reduced to 70%) D.L.

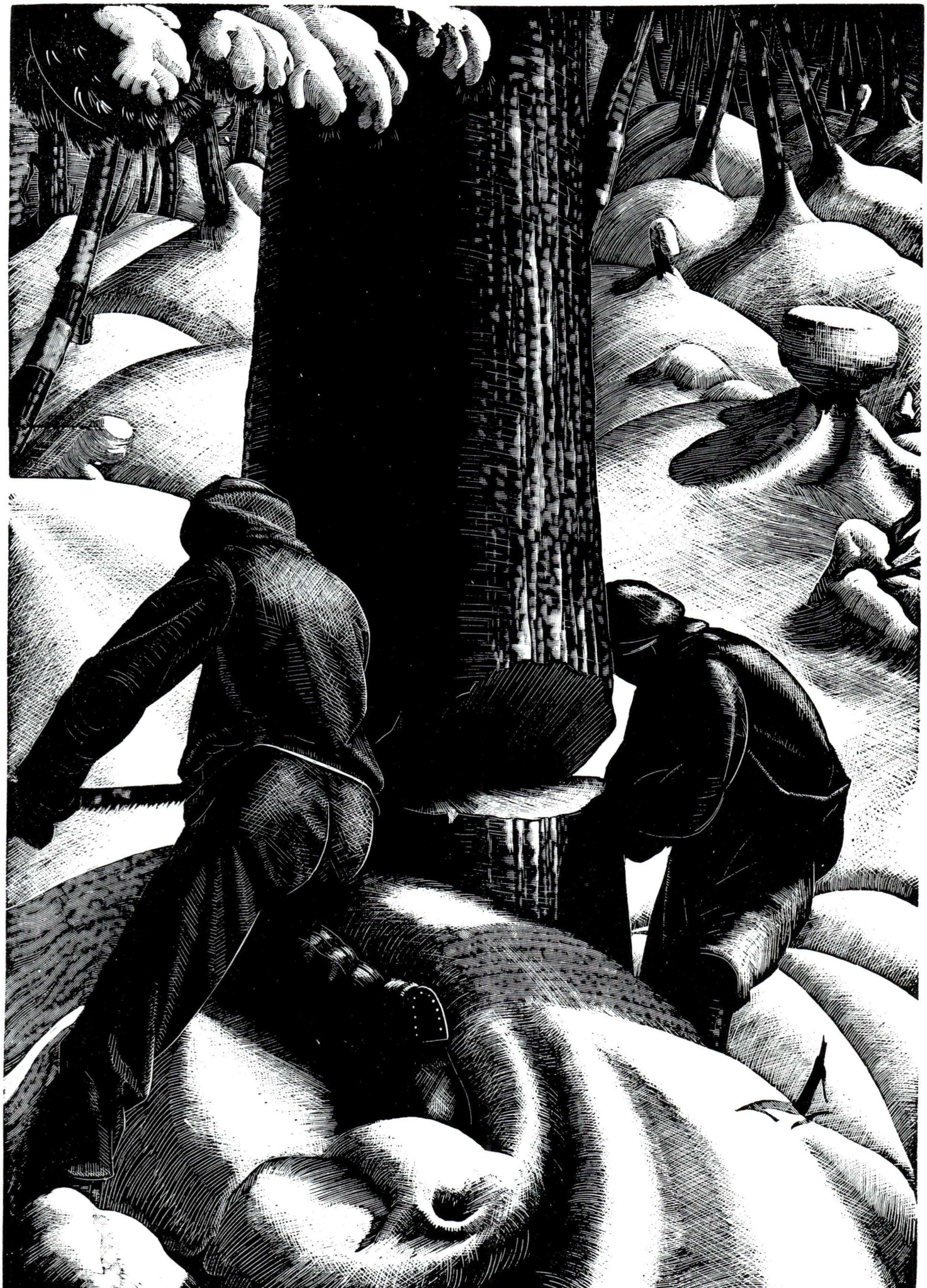

40. *Cutting: Lumber Camp Series*, 1931 28.9 × 20.3 cms.: 11⅜ × 8 ins. (here reduced to 81%) D.L.

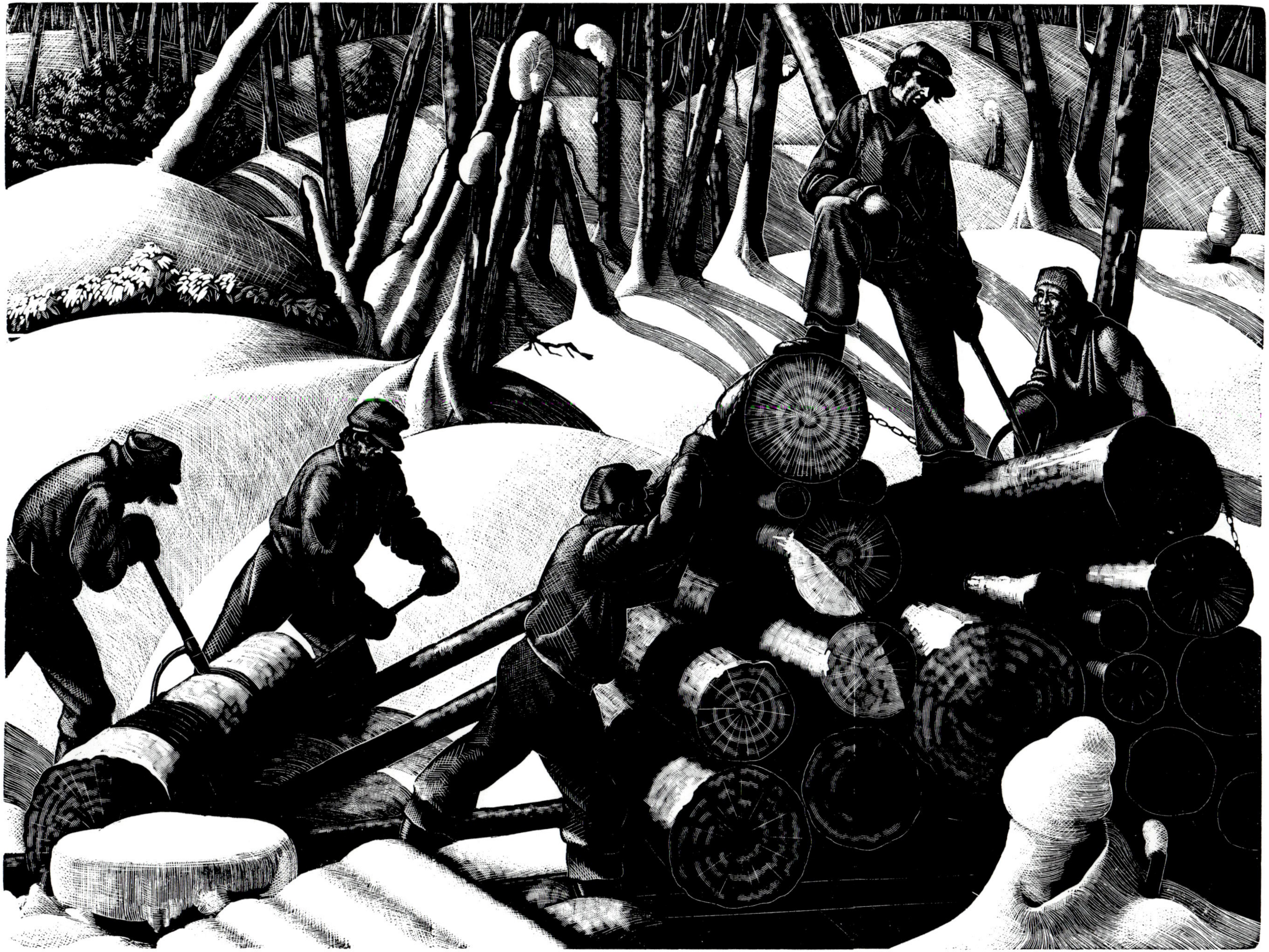

41. *Loading: Lumber Camp Series*, 1931 22.7 × 30.2 cms.: 8 15/16 × 11⅞ ins. (here reduced to 77%) D.L.

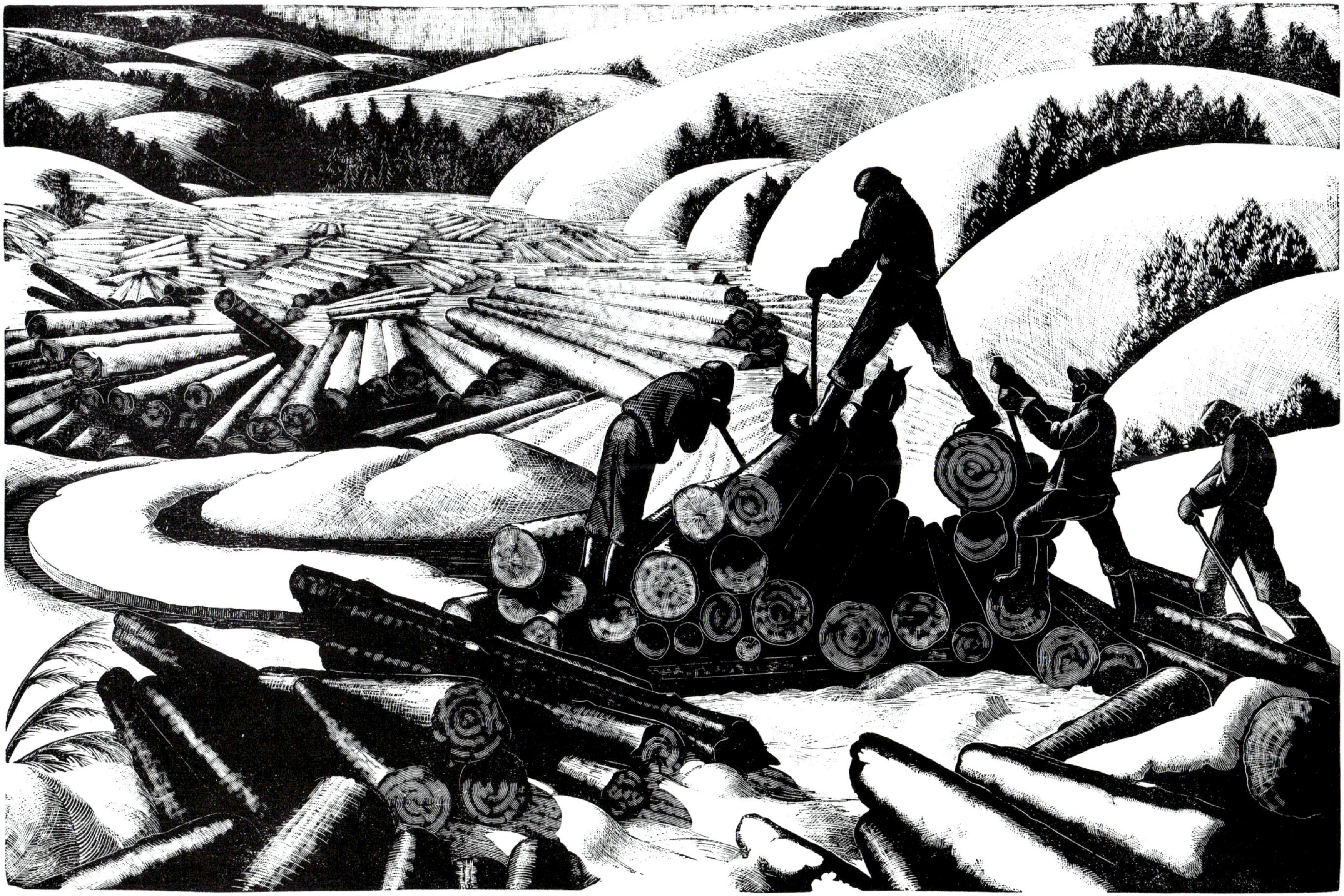

42. *Landing: Lumber Camp Series*, 1931 21 × 31.8 cms.: 8¼ × 12½ ins. (here reduced to 73%) D.L.

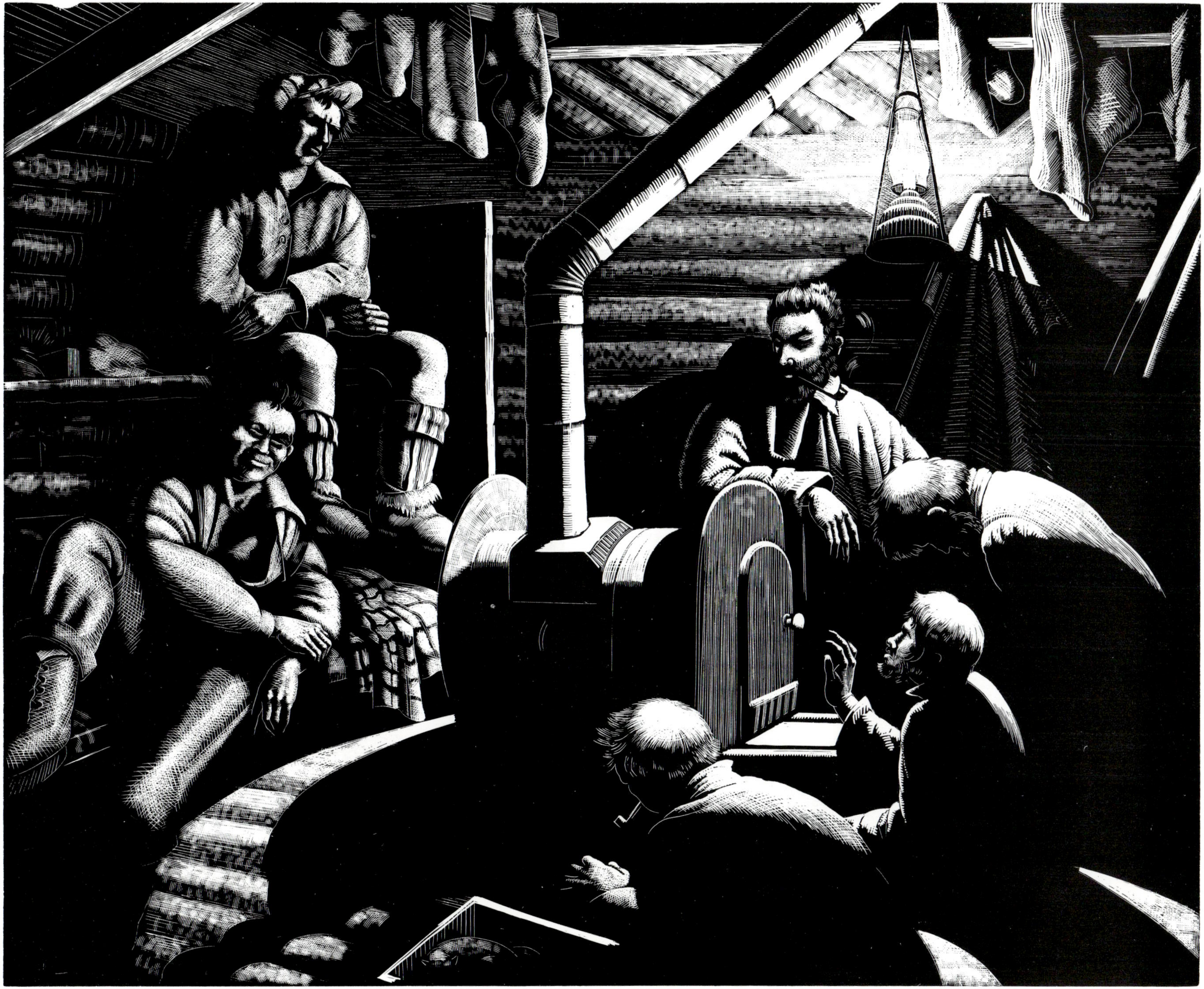

43. *Resting: Lumber Camp Series*, 1931 23 × 28.1 cms.: 9⁹⁄₁₆ × 11¹⁄₁₆ ins. (here reduced to 82%) D.L.

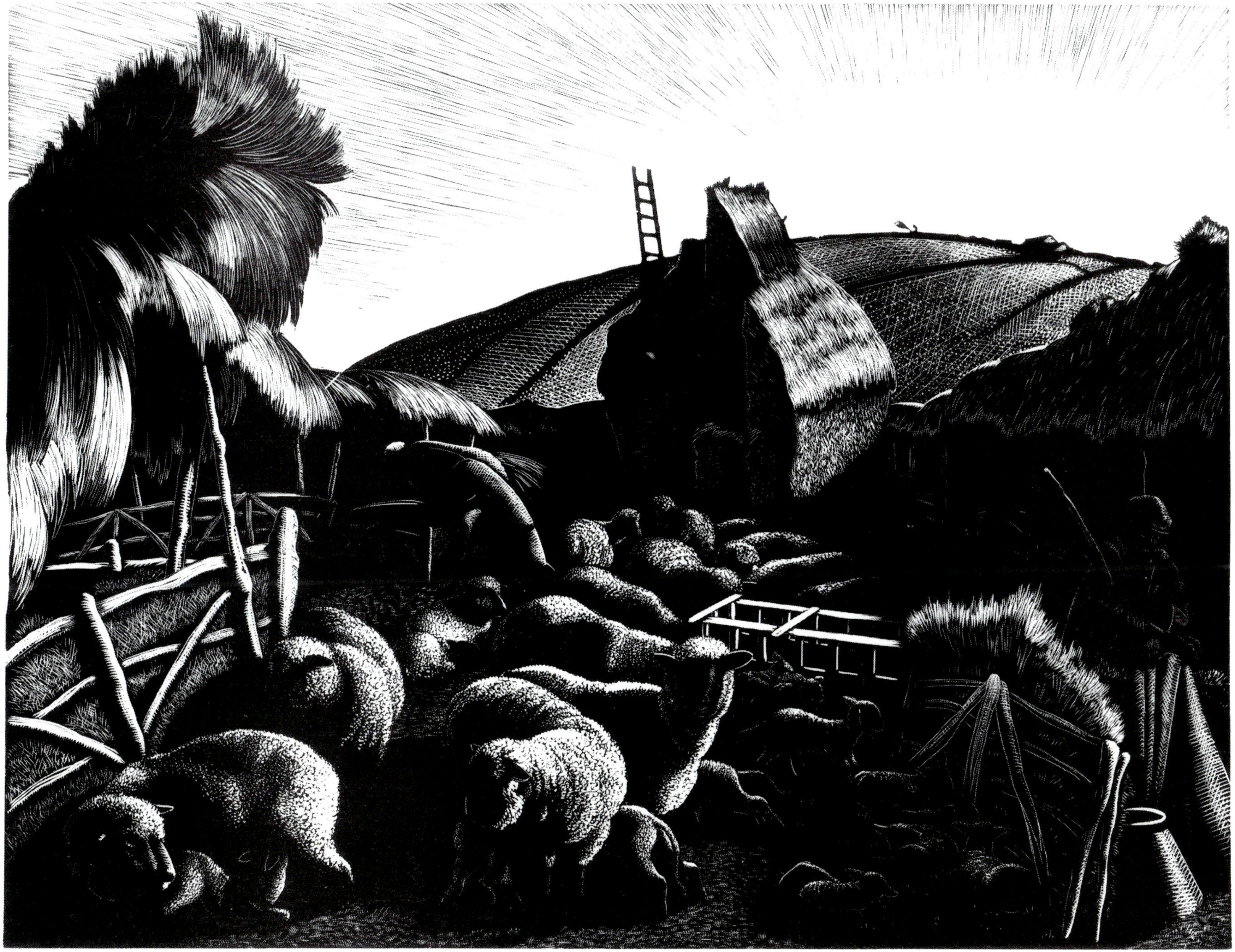

44. *January: Lambing*, 1931–2 20.3 × 26.7 cms.: 8 × 10½ ins. (here reduced to 86%), p. 2 in Clare Leighton, *The Farmer's Year*, London: Collins & Co., 1933 (repr. from an impression in the Department of Western Art, Ashmolean Museum, Oxford, numbered 11/30, signed and inscribed 'To Martin Hardie, because he liked it'). Hardie has noted'? since destroyed. Rare 1st. state. Ladder against sky later taken out.'

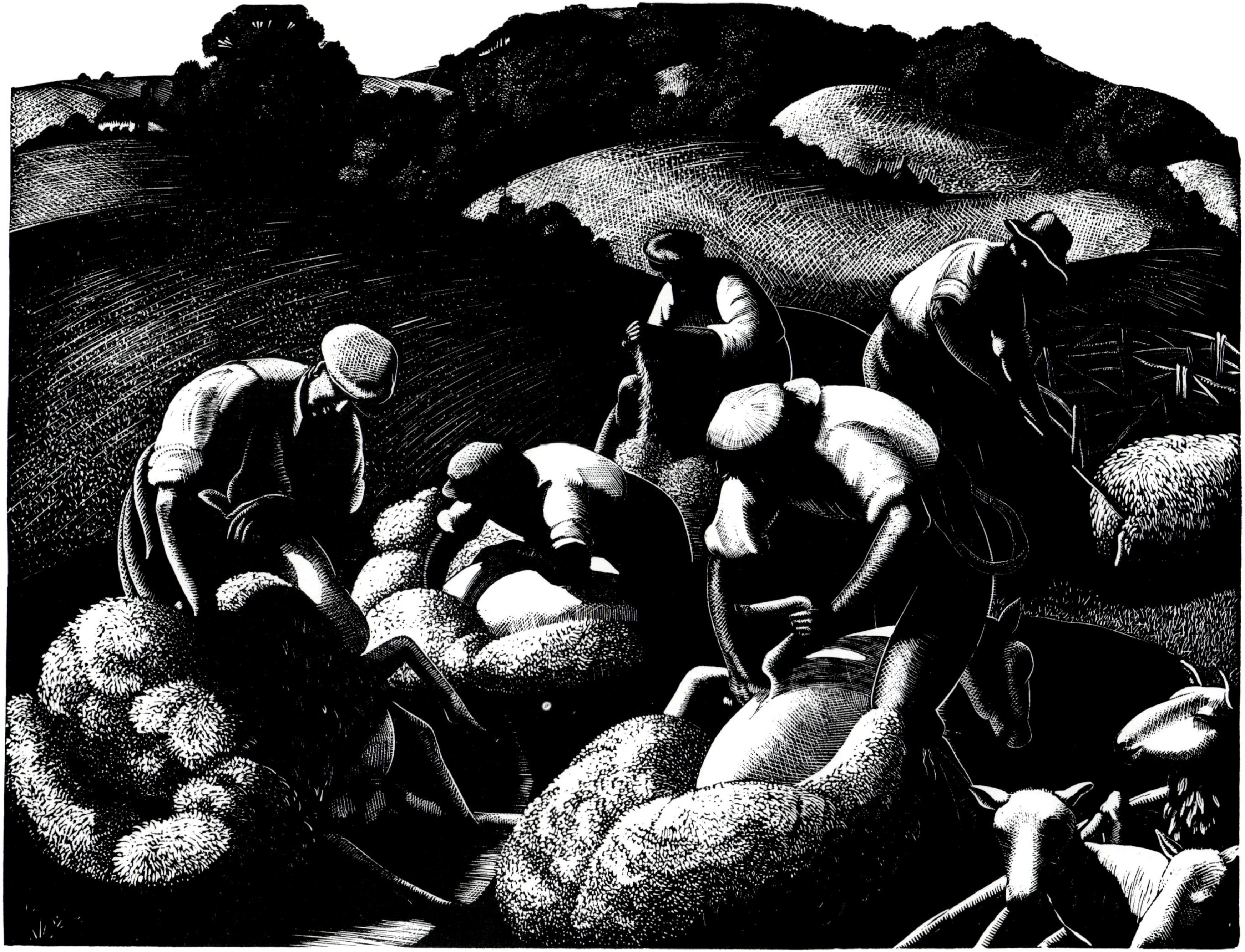

45. *May: Sheep Shearing*, 1931–2 20.3 × 26.7 cms.: 8 × 10½ ins. (here reduced to 86%), p. 20 in Clare Leighton, *The Farmer's Year*, London: Collins & Co., 1933

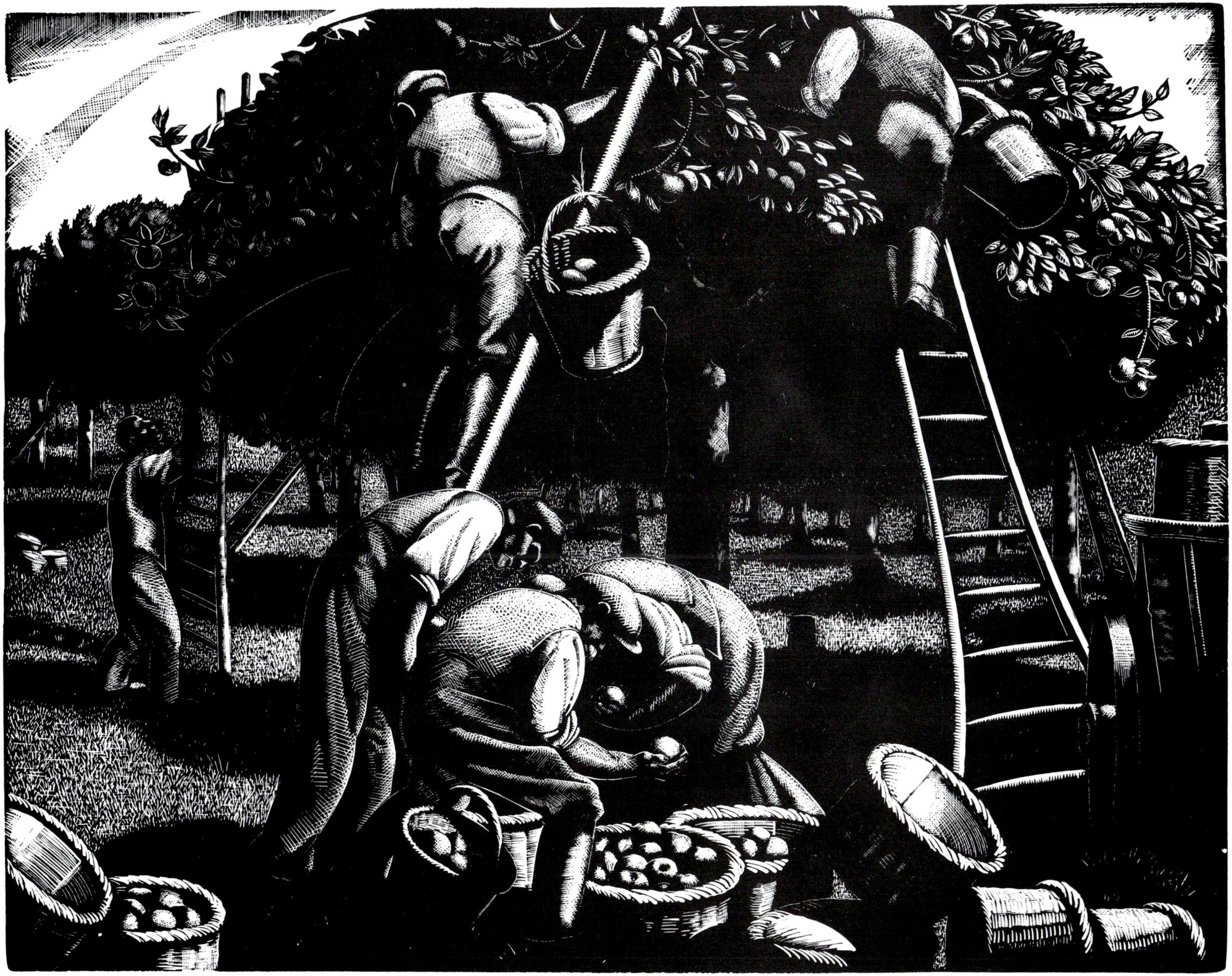

46. *September: Apple-Picking*, 1931–2 22.1 × 28 cms.: 8¹¹⁄₁₆ × 11 ins. (here reduced to 82%), p. 40 in Clare Leighton, *The Farmer's Year*, London: Collins & Co., 1933 (repr. from an impression in the Department of Western Art, Ashmolean Museum, Oxford, numbered 7/30, signed and inscribed 'to Martin Hardie, in friendliness from Clare Leighton')

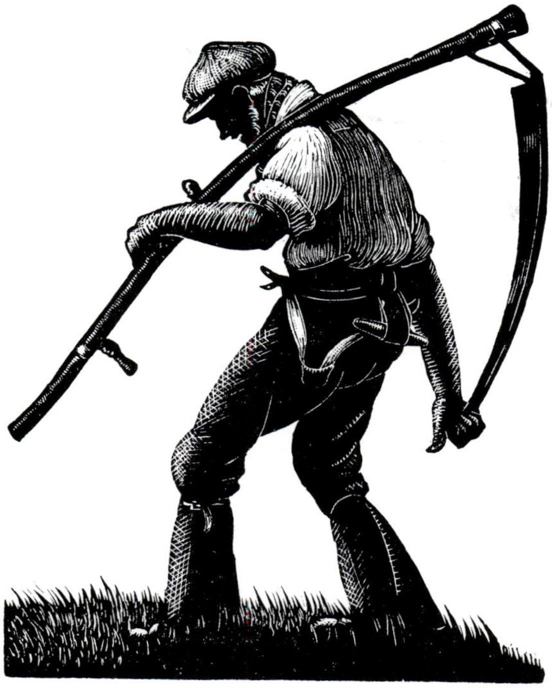

47a. *The Reaper*, 1931–2 9.1 × 7.2 cms.: 3⁹⁄₁₆ × 2¹³⁄₁₆ ins., title page in Clare Leighton, *The Farmer's Year*, London: Collins & Co., 1933

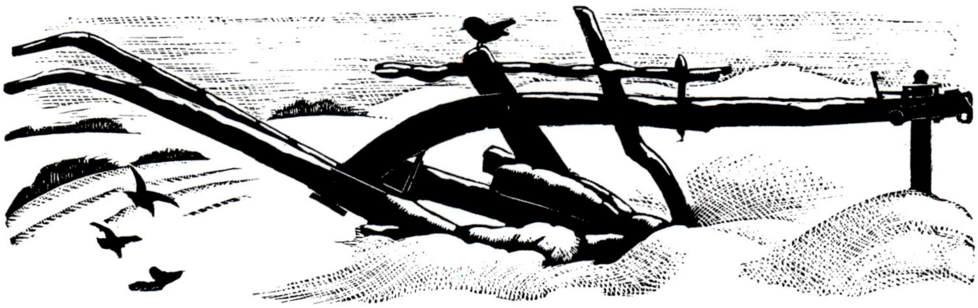

47b. *Plough in the Snow*, 1931–2 3.8 × 12.7 cms.: 1½ × 5 ins., p. 10 in Clare Leighton, *The Farmer's Year*, Collins & Co., 1933

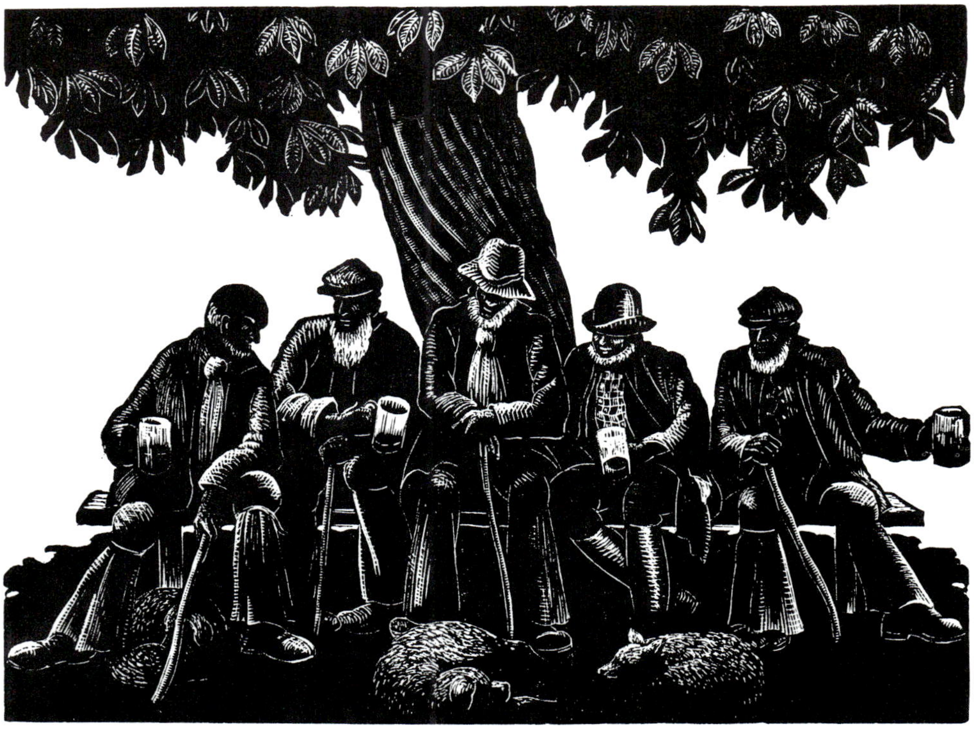

48a. *The Sages*, 1931–2 9.5 × 12.7 cms.: 3¾ × 5 ins. p. 29 in Clare Leighton, *The Farmer's Year*, London: Collins & Co., 1933

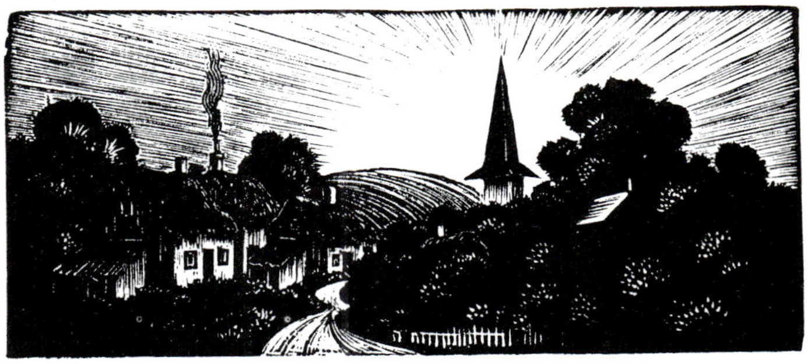

48b. *The Village*, 1931–2 3.8 × 8.9 cms.: 1½ × 3½ ins. p. 46 in Clare Leighton, *The Farmer's Year*, London: Collins & Co., 1933

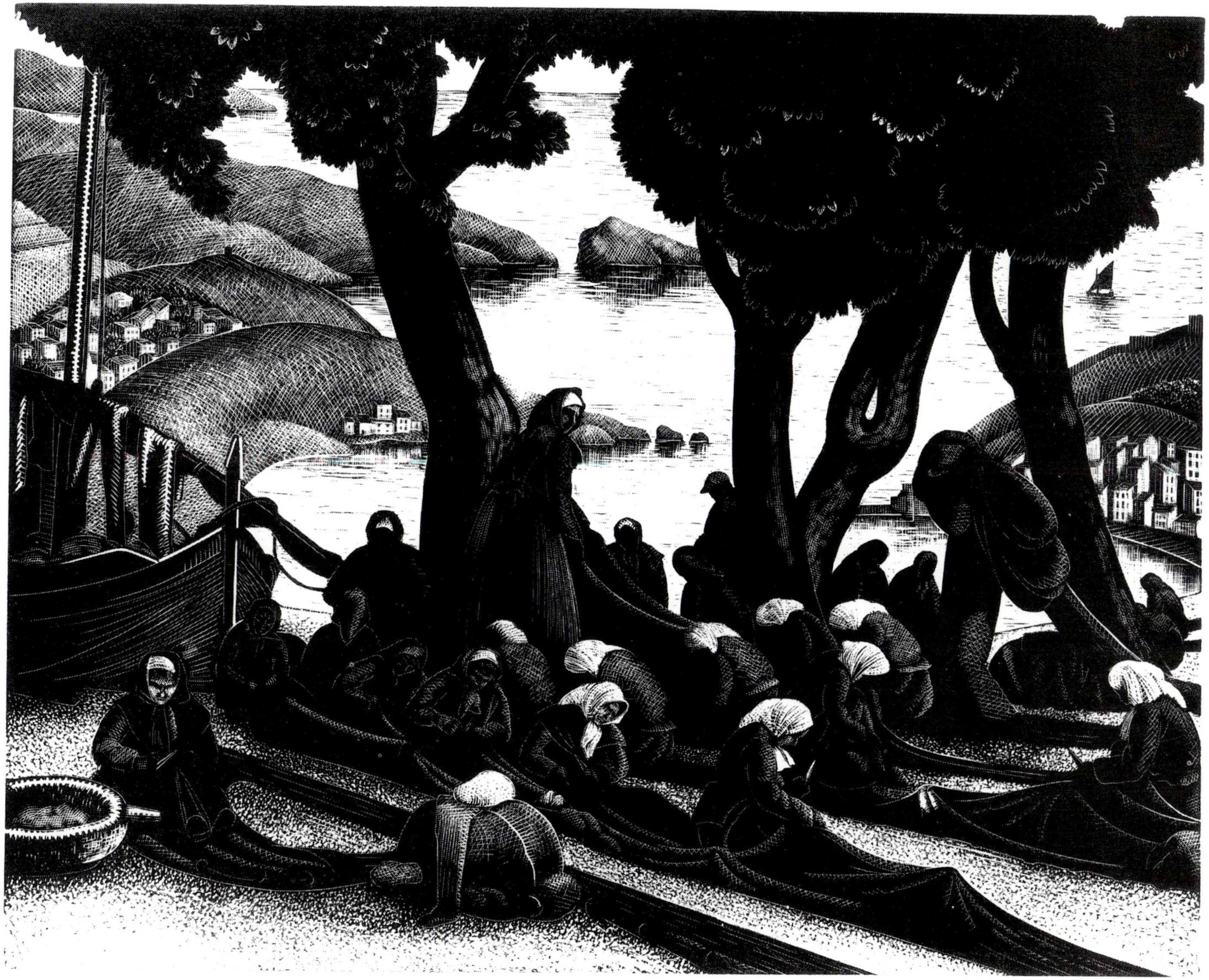

49. *The Net Menders*, 1933 15.4 × 19.1 cms.: $6\frac{1}{16} \times 7\frac{1}{2}$ ins. commission for The Woodcut Society, Kansas City, 1933 (here reproduced from an impression in the Department of Western Art, Ashmolean Museum, Oxford, signed, numbered 181/200, dated 1933 and inscribed 'To Martin Hardie who caused its existence')

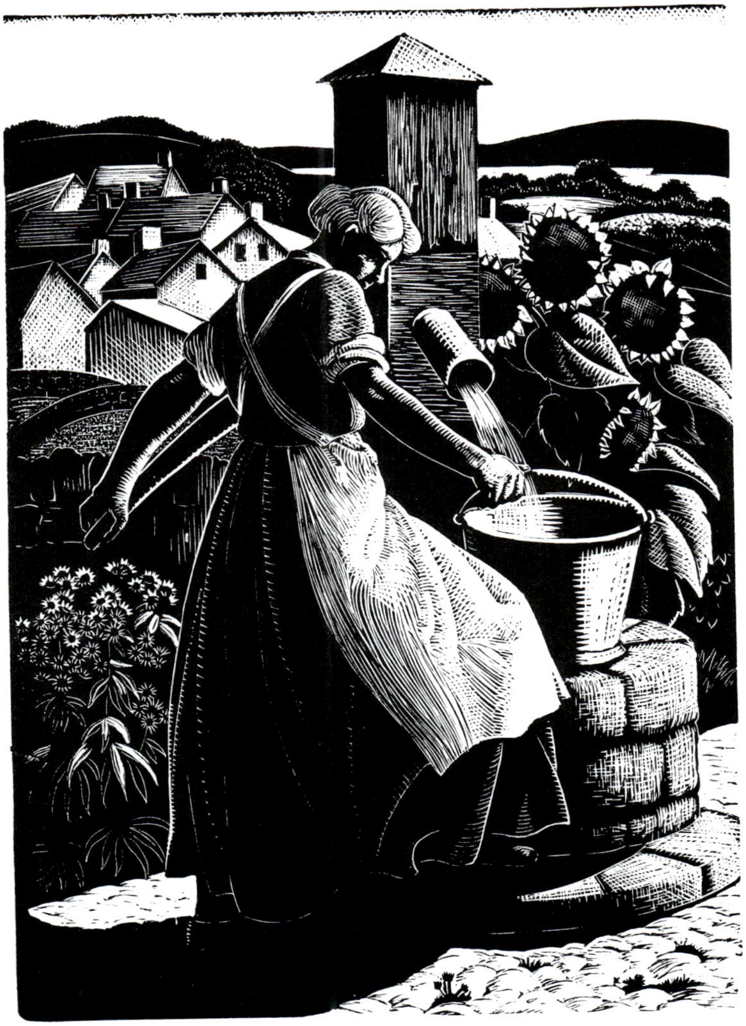

50. *At the Pump*, 1934 13.4 × 12.1 cms.: 5¼ × 4¾ ins., between pp. 16 and 17 in Constance Holme, *The Trumpet in the Dust*, London: Ivor Nicholson and Watson, 1934

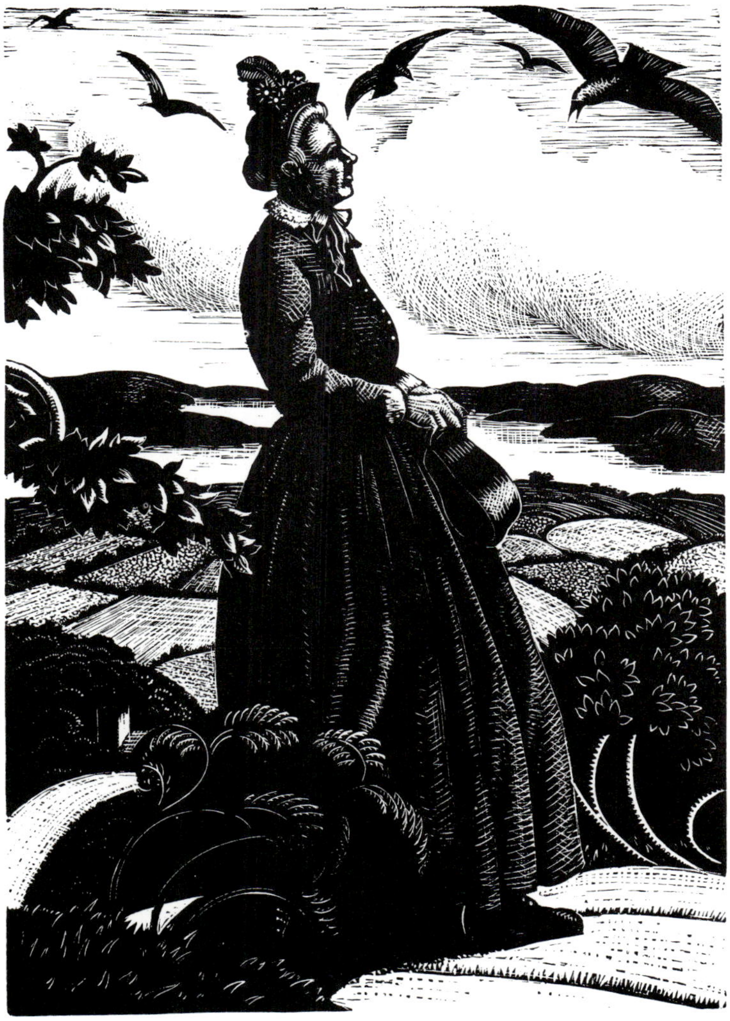

51. *Mrs. Clapham*, 1934 13.4 × 12.1 cms.: 5¼ × 4¾ ins., between pp. 138 and 139 in Constance Holme, *The Trumpet in the Dust*, London: Ivor Nicholson and Watson, 1934

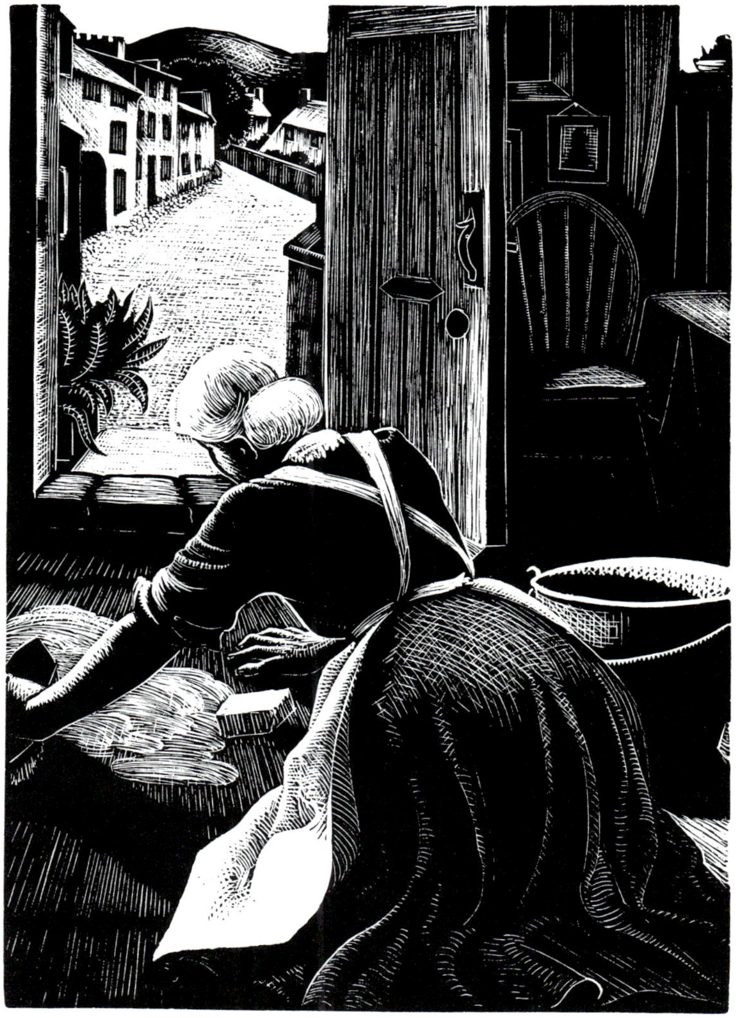

52. *Finale*, 1934 13.4 × 12.1 cms.: 5¼ × 4¾ ins., between pp. 254 and 255 in Constance Holme, *The Trumpet in the Dust*, London: Ivor Nicholson and Watson, 1934

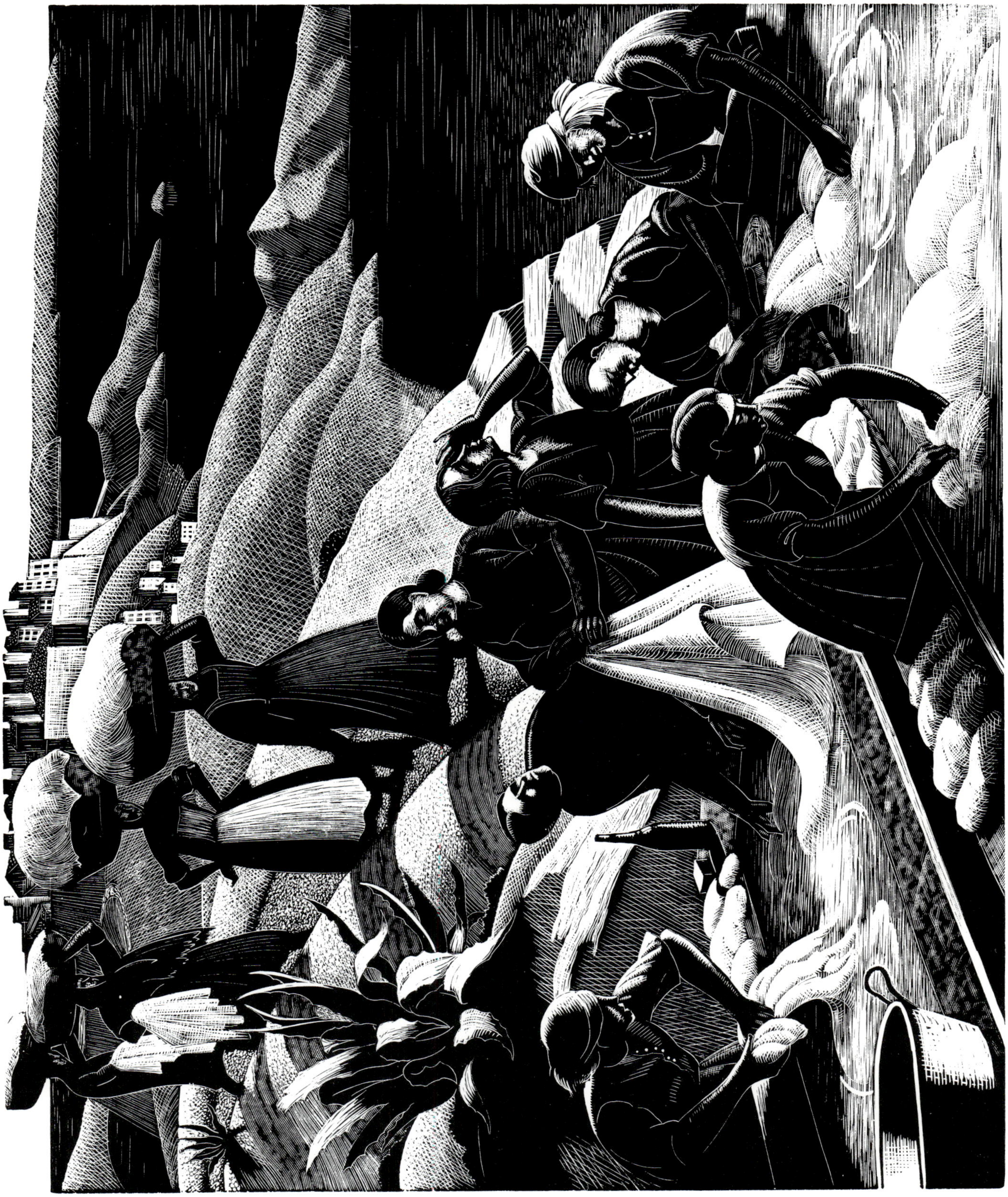

53. *Washing Clothes*, *Corsica*, 1934 21.6 × 26.7 cms.: 8½ × 10½ ins., commission for the Cleveland Print Club, 1934 (here reduced to 83%) D.L.

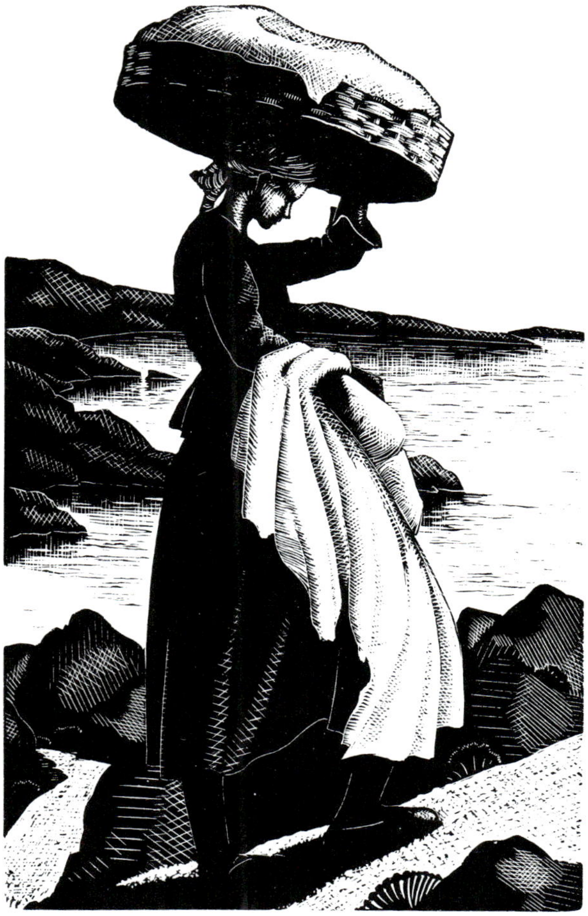

54. *Corsican Laundress*, 1934 12.1 × 7.6 cms.: 4¾ × 3 ins., commission for The Albany Print Club, 1934 D.L.

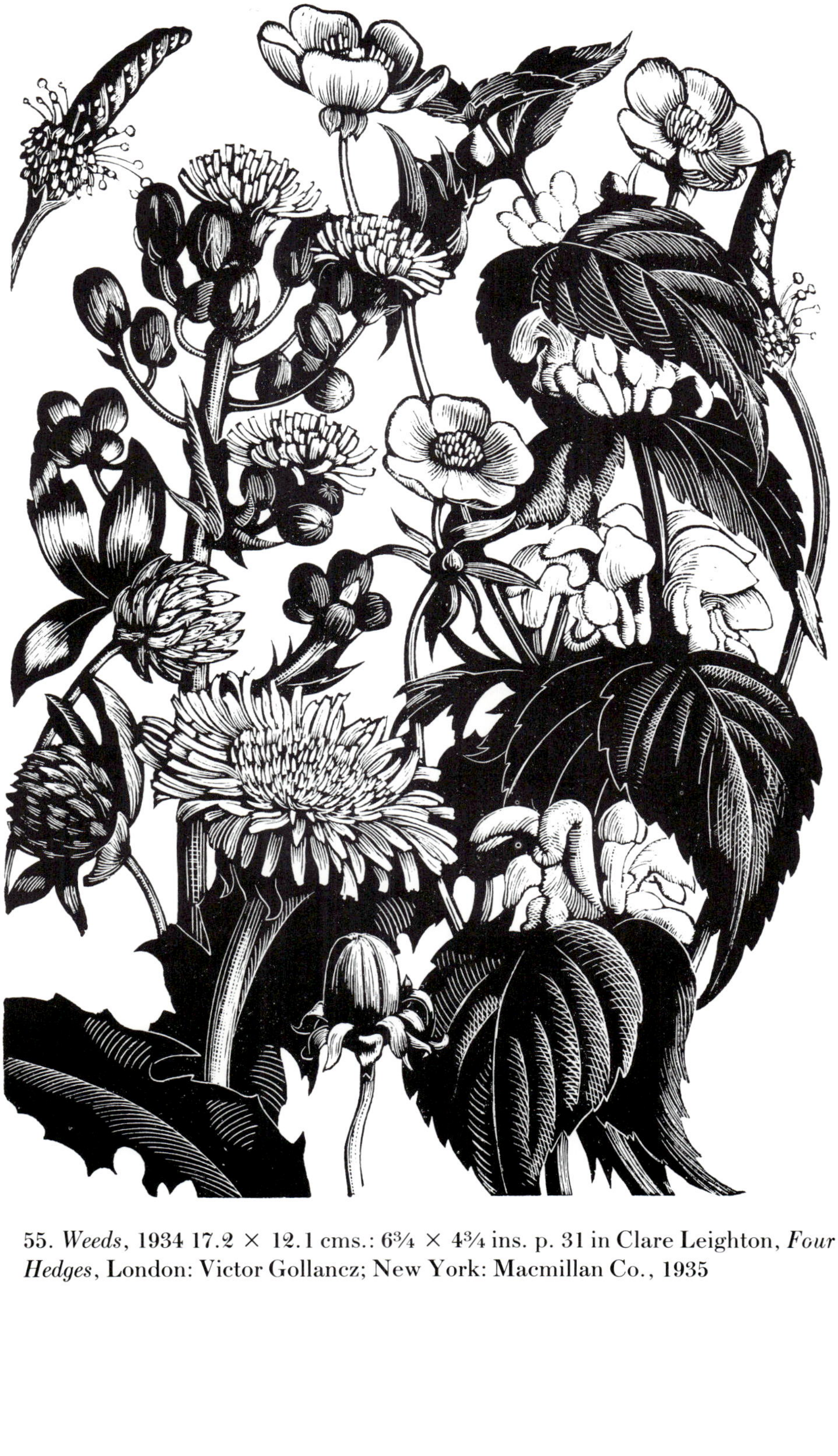

55. *Weeds*, 1934 17.2 × 12.1 cms.: 6¾ × 4¾ ins. p. 31 in Clare Leighton, *Four Hedges*, London: Victor Gollancz; New York: Macmillan Co., 1935

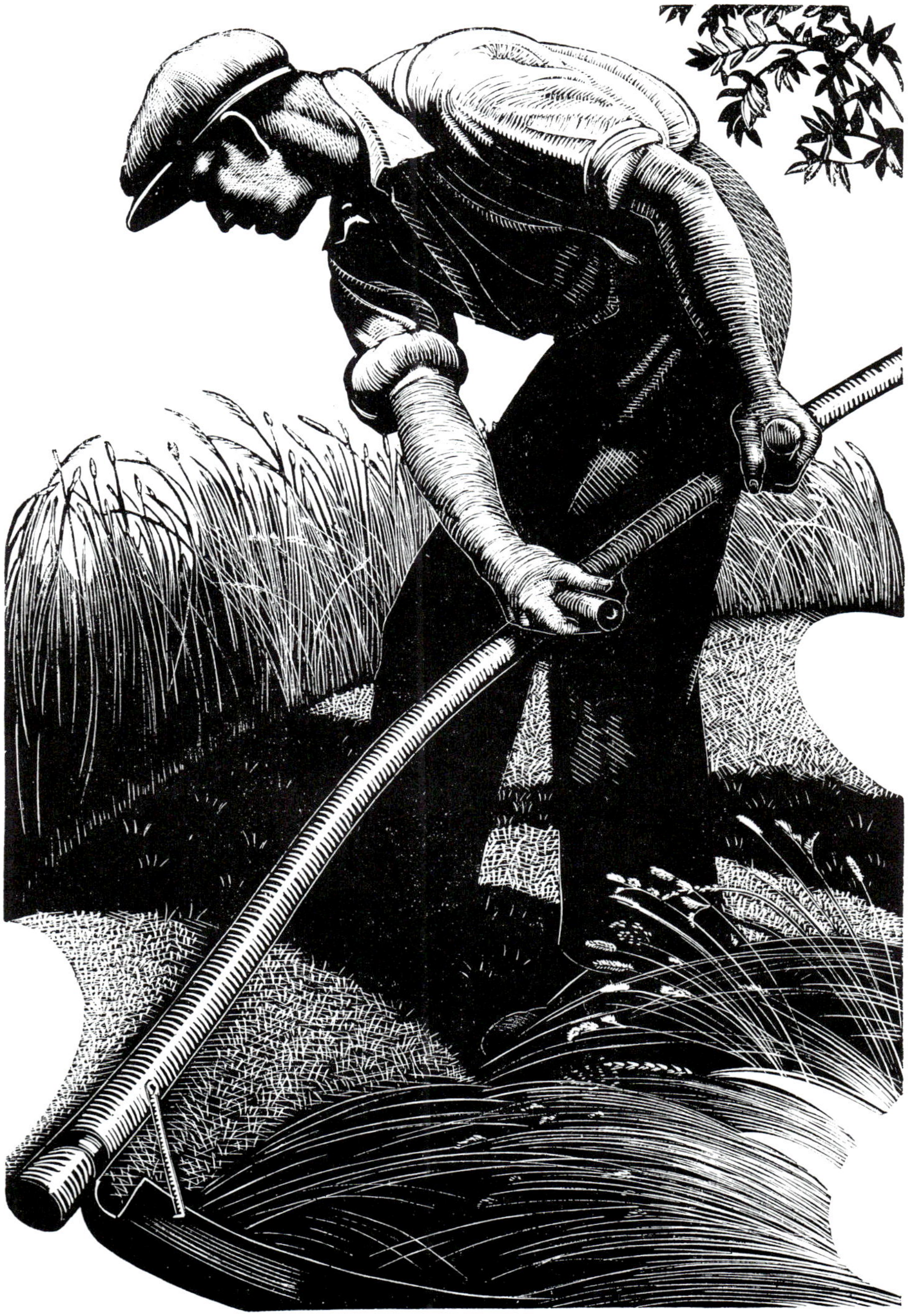

56. *Scything*, 1934 17.8 × 12.4 cms.: 7 × 4⅞ ins. p. 59 in Clare Leighton, *Four Hedges*, London: Victor Gollancz; New York: Macmillan Co., 1935

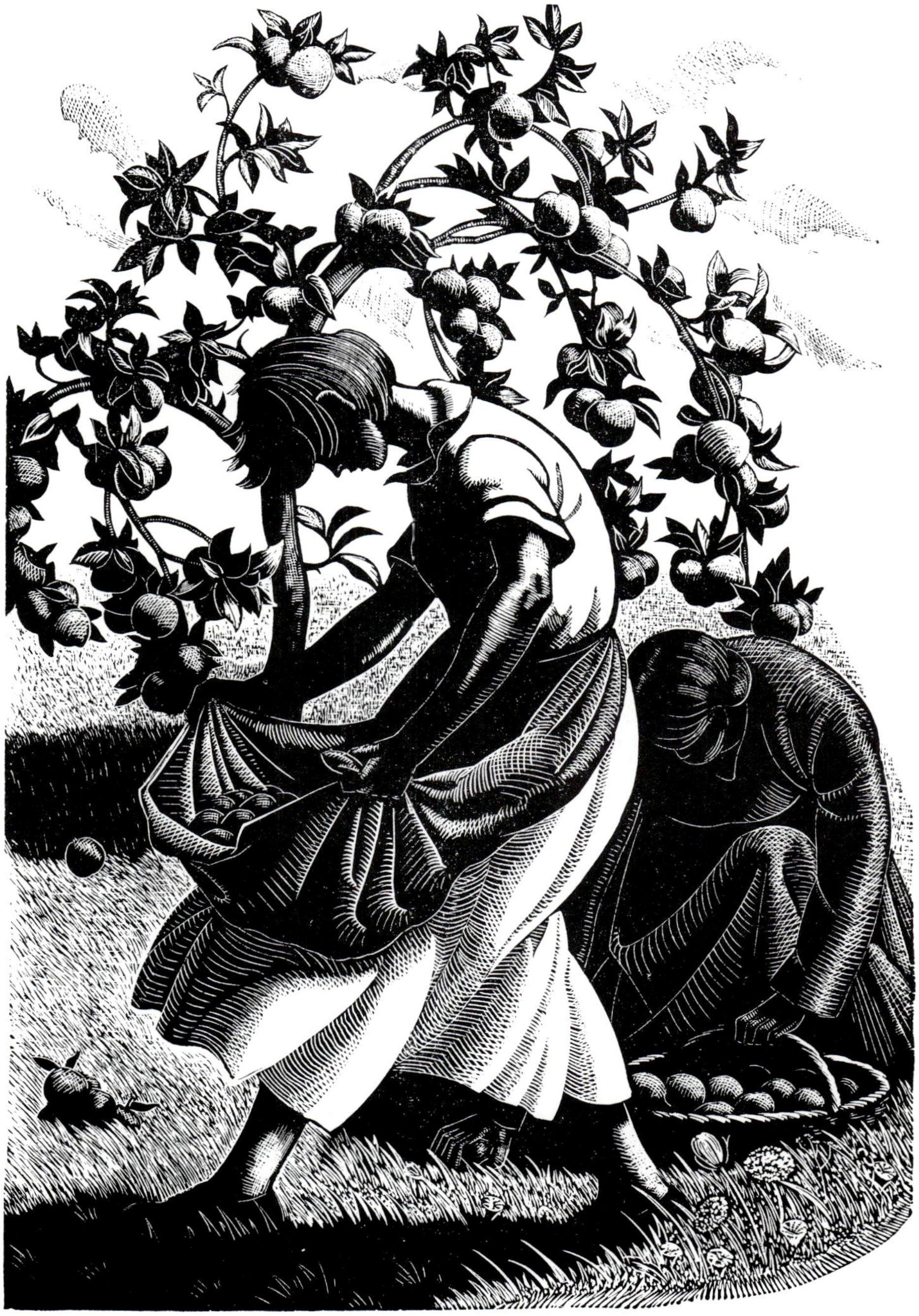

57. *A Lapful of Windfalls*, 1934 20 × 12.1 cms.: 7⅞ × 4¾ ins. p. 85 in Clare Leighton, *Four Hedges*, London: Victor Gollancz; New York: Macmillan Co., 1935

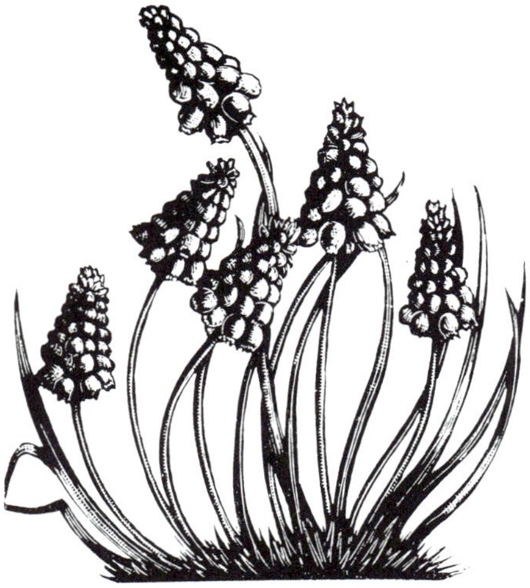

58a. *Grape Hyacinths*, 1934 6.4 × 5.7 cms.: 2½ × 2¼ ins. p. 13 in Clare Leighton, *Four Hedges*, London: Victor Gollancz; New York: Macmillan Co., 1935

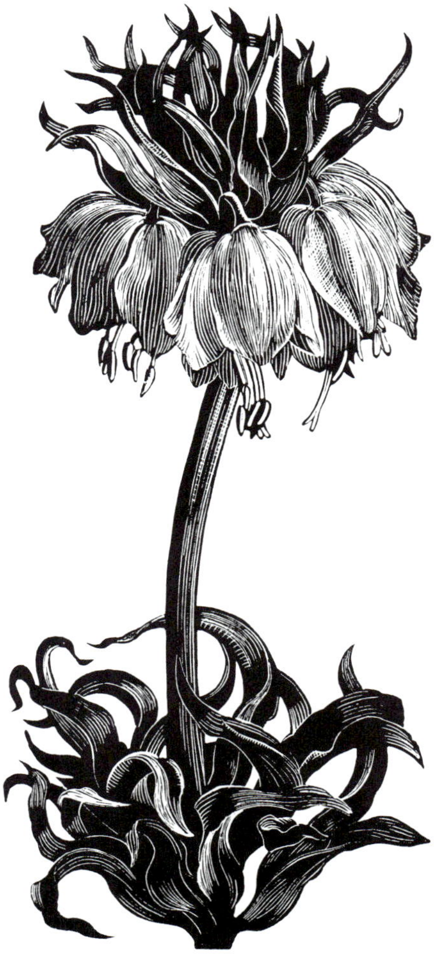

58b. *Crown Imperial*, 1934 12.6 × 5.7 cms.: 4¹⁵⁄₁₆ × 2¼ ins. p. 27 in Clare Leighton, *Four Hedges*, London: Victor Gollancz; New York: Macmillan Co., 1935

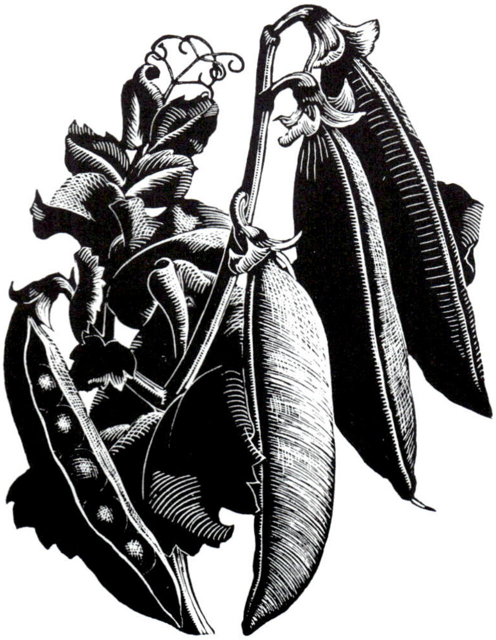

58c. *Peas*, 1934 8.3 × 6.4 cms.: 3¼ × 2½ ins. p. 50 in Clare Leighton, *Four Hedges*, London: Victor Gollancz; New York: Macmillan Co., 1935

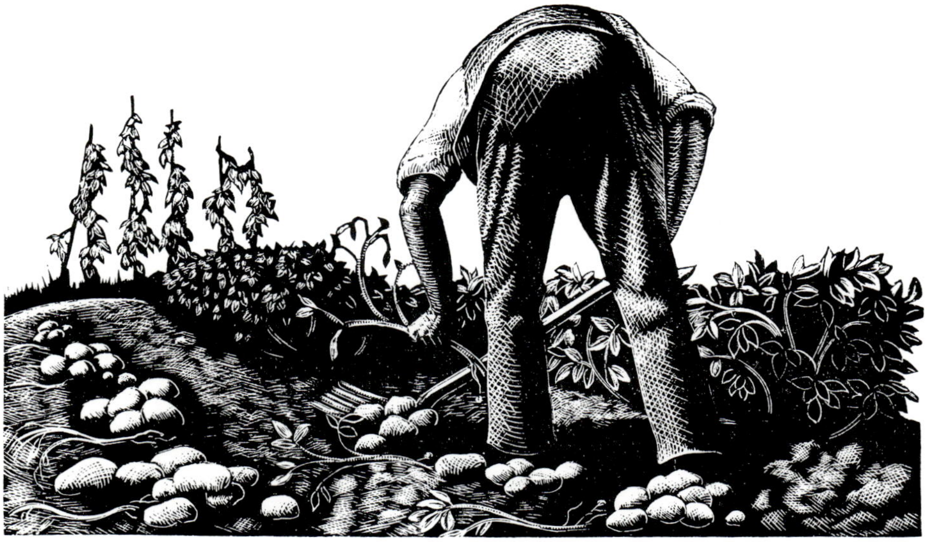

59a. *Digging Potatoes*, 1934 7.2 × 12.1 cms.: $2^{13}/_{16}$ × $4^{3}/_{4}$ ins. p. 94 in Clare Leighton, *Four Hedges*, London: Victor Gollancz; New York: Macmillan Co., 1935

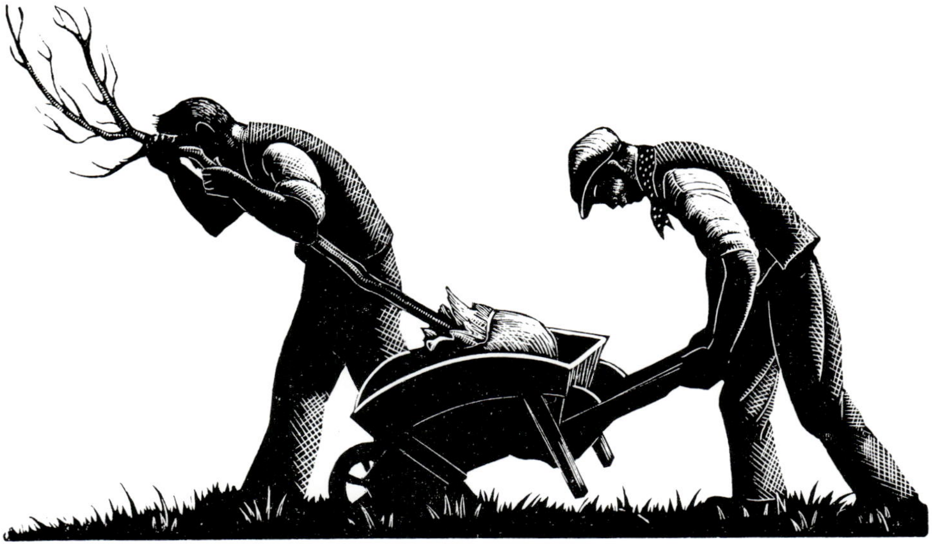

59b. *Transplanting Walnut Tree*, 1934 7 × 12.3 cms.: $2^{3}/_{4}$ × $4^{13}/_{16}$ ins. p. 108 in Clare Leighton, *Four Hedges*, London: Victor Gollancz; New York: Macmillan Co., 1935

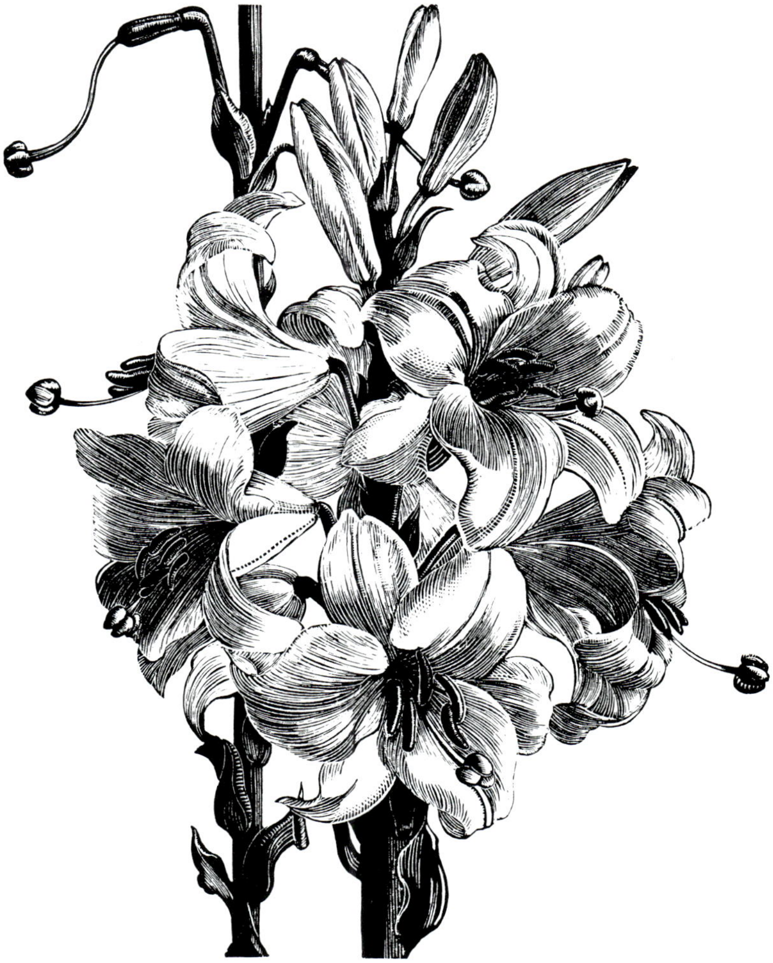

60a. *Lily*, 1934 12.7 × 9.8 cms.: 5 × 3⅞ ins. p. 64 in Clare Leighton, *Four Hedges*, London: Victor Gollancz; New York: Macmillan Co., 1935

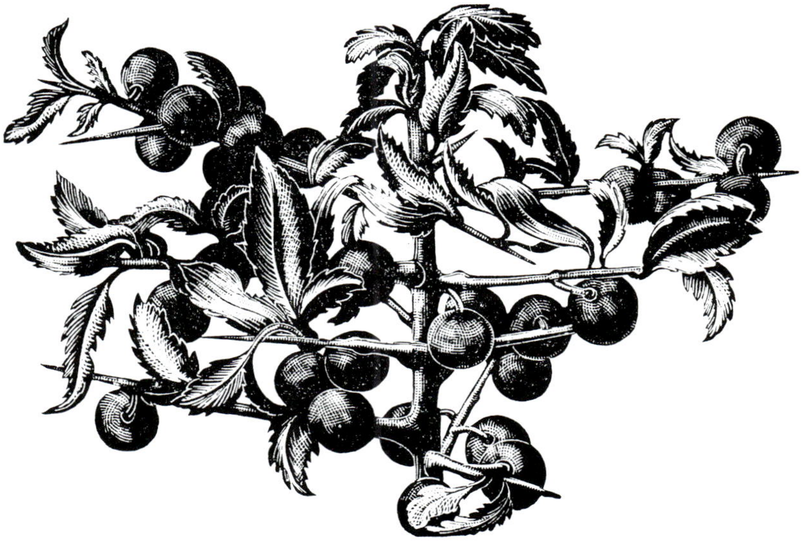

60b. *Sloe*, 1934 7 × 10.3 cms.: 2¾ × 4¹⁄₁₆ ins. p. 97 in Clare Leighton, *Four Hedges*, London: Victor Gollancz; New York: Macmillan Co., 1935

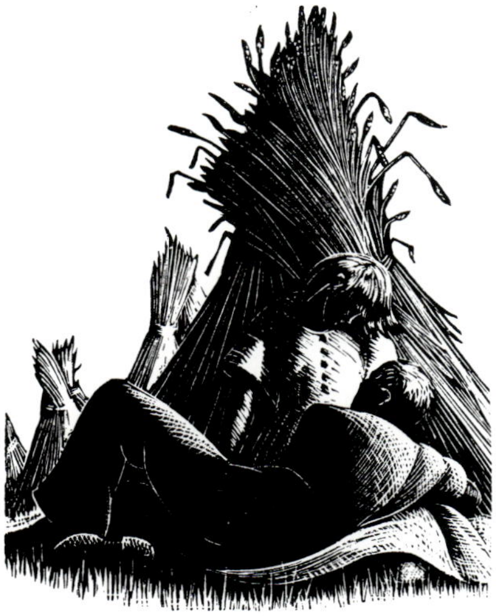

61a. *Title Page Design*, 1936 6.5 × 5.2 cms.: 2⁹⁄₁₆ × 2¹⁄₁₆ ins. in Clare Leighton, *Country Matters*, London: Victor Gollancz; New York: Macmillan Co., 1937

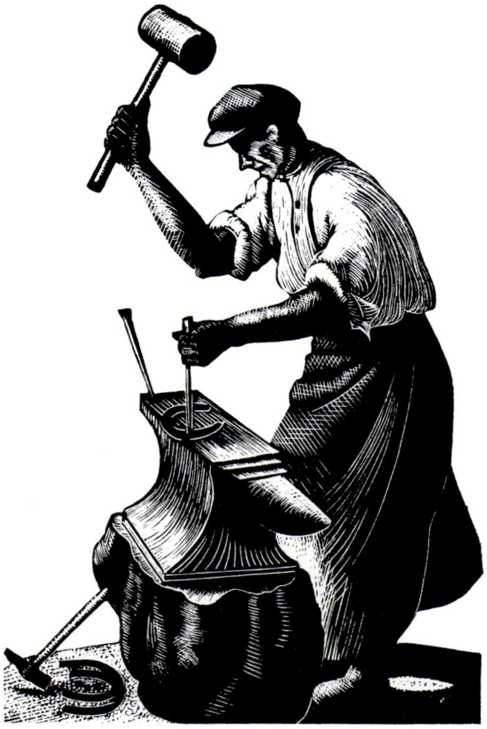

61b. *The Blacksmith*, 1936 9.5 × 6.3 cms.: 3¾ × 2½ ins. p. 21 in Clare Leighton, *Country Matters*, London: Victor Gollancz; New York: Macmillan Co., 1937

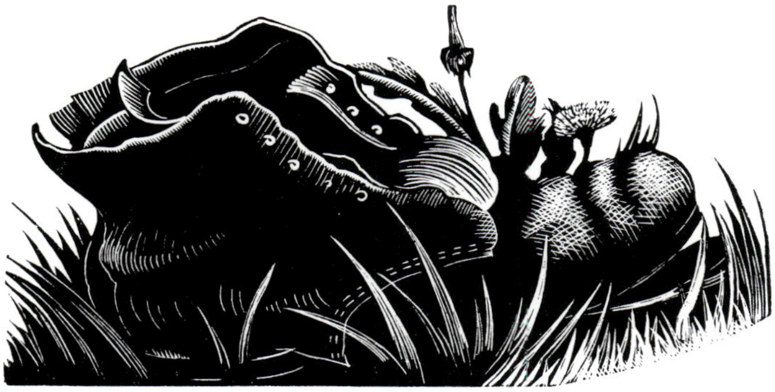

61c. *Old Boot*, 1936 4.3 × 8.9 cms.: 1¹¹⁄₁₆ × 3½ ins. p. 16 in Clare Leighton, *Country Matters*, London: Victor Gollancz; New York: Macmillan Co., 1937

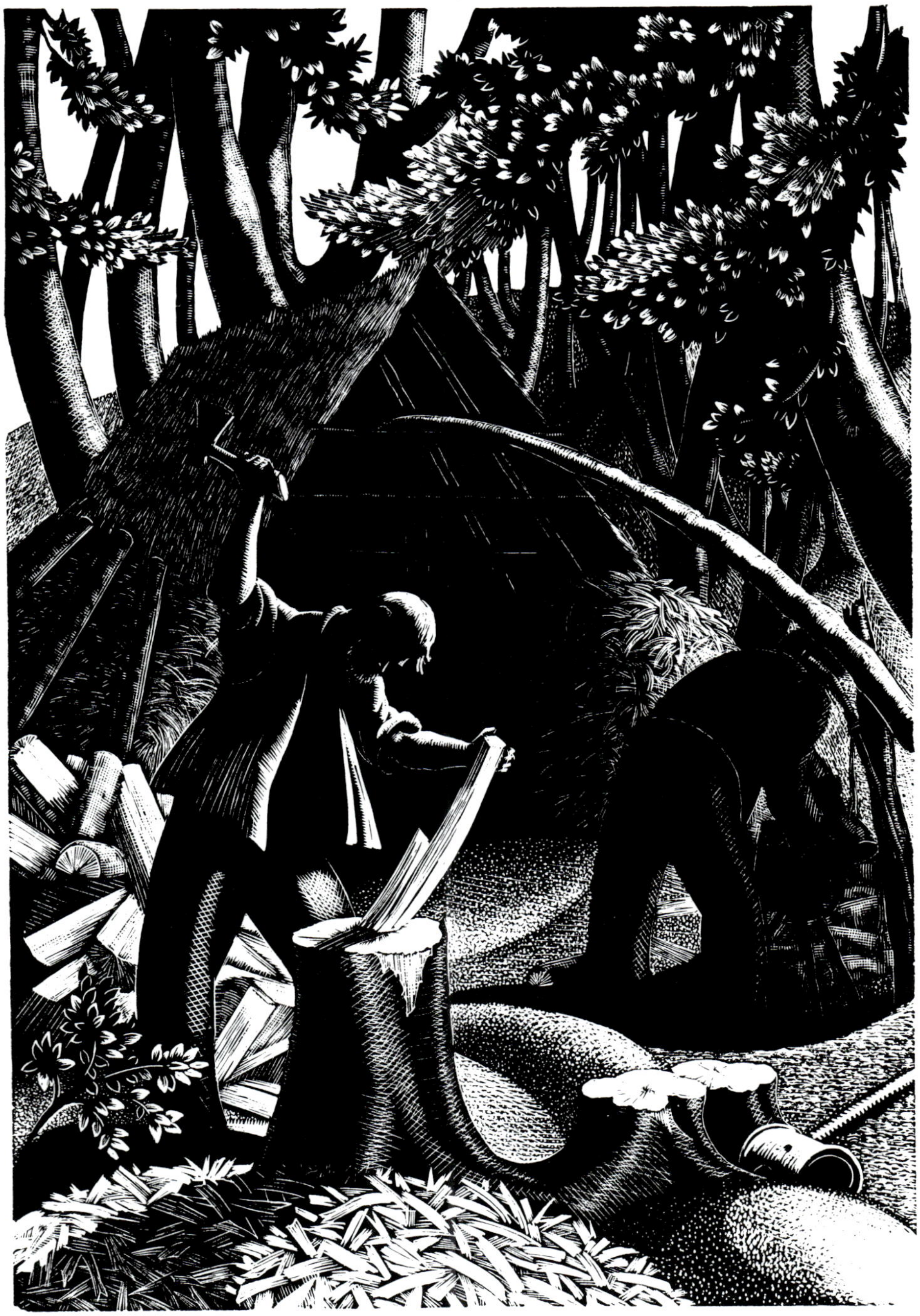

62. *Chair Bodgers*, 1936 17.5 × 10.2 cms.: 6⅞ × 4 ins. p. 67 in Clare Leighton, *Country Matters*, London: Victor Gollancz; New York: Macmillan Co., 1937

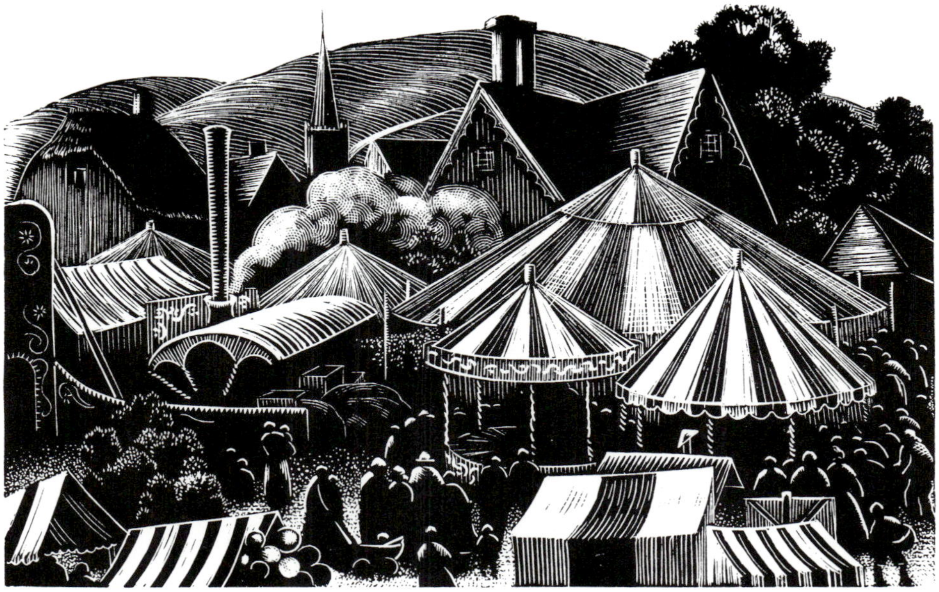

63a. *The Village Fair*, 1936 7.6 × 12.1 cms.: 3 × 4¾ ins. p. 41 in Clare Leighton, *Country Matters*, London: Victor Gollancz; New York: Macmillan Co., 1937

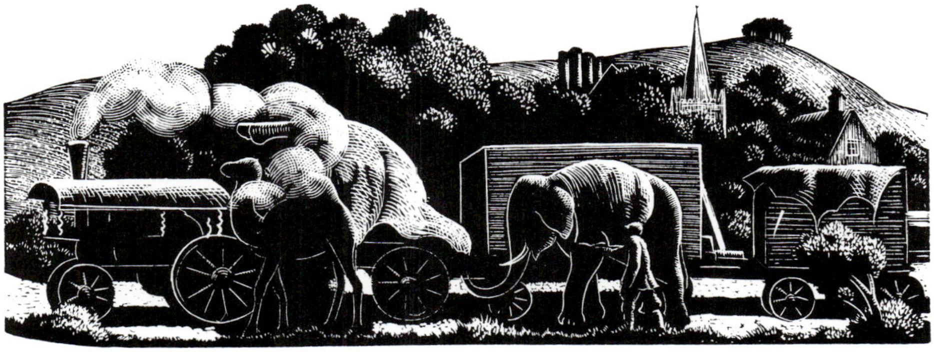

63b. *The Fair Goes Down the Street*, 1936 4.4 × 12.1 cms.: 1¾ × 4¾ ins. p. 43 in Clare Leighton, *Country Matters*, London: Victor Gollancz; New York, Macmillan Co., 1937

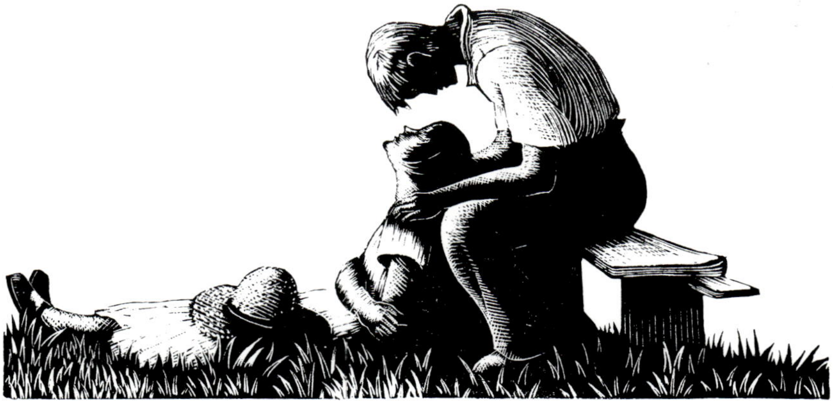

63c. *Henry and Amy*, 1936 5.1 × 10.8 cms.: 2 × 4¼ ins. p. 51 in Clare Leighton, *Country Matters*, London: Victor Gollancz; New York: Macmillan Co., 1937

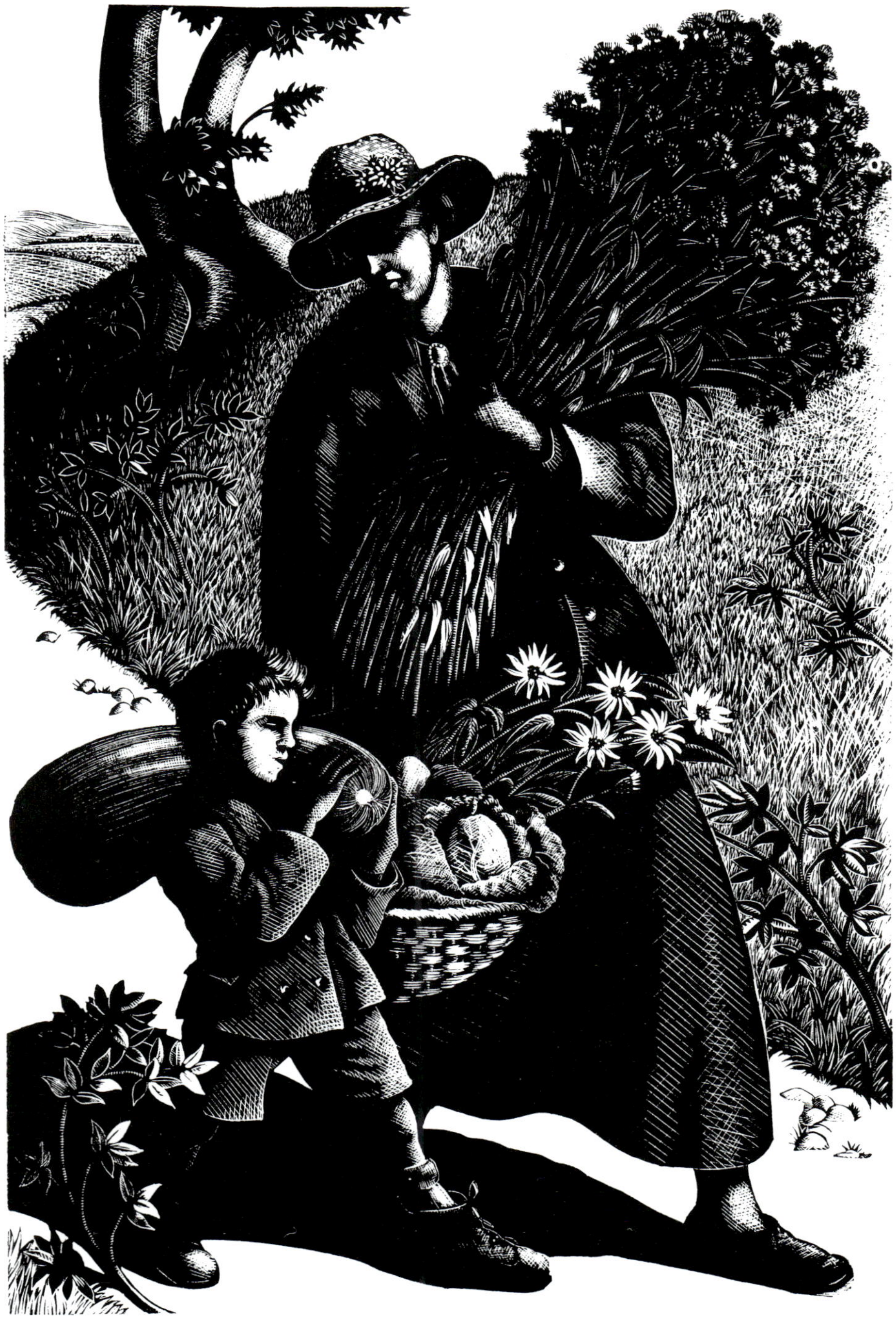

64. *Going to the Festival*, 1936 17.8 × 12.1 cms.: 7 × 4¾ ins. p. 101 in Clare Leighton, *Country Matters*, London: Victor Gollancz; New York: Macmillan Co., 1937

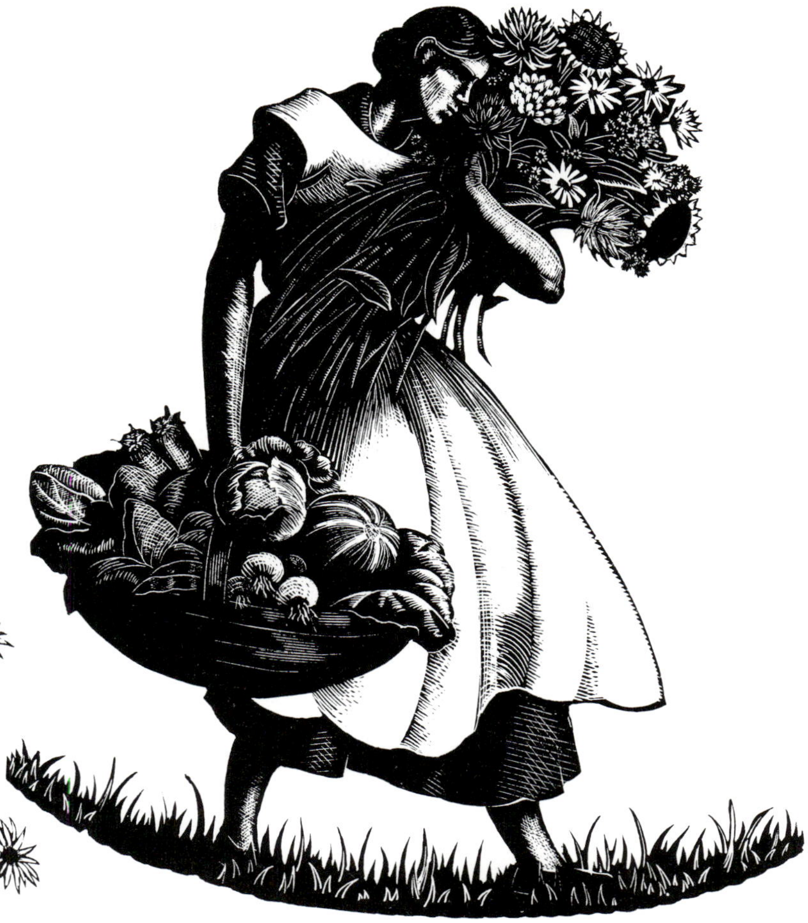

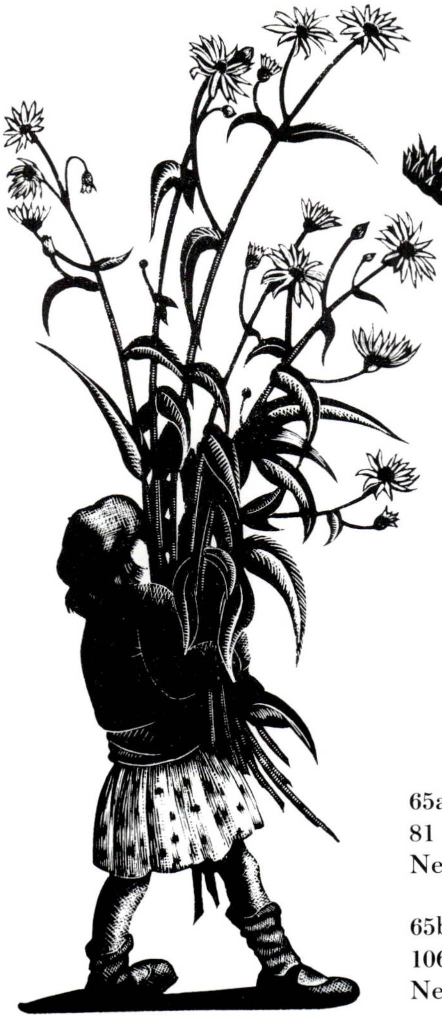

65a. *Woman with Flowers*, 1936 12.1 × 10.5 cms.: 4¾ × 4⅛ ins. p. 81 in Clare Leighton, *Country Matters*, London: Victor Gollancz; New York: Macmillan Co., 1937

65b. *Child with Flowers*, 1936 13.3 × 5.7 cms.: 5¼ × 2¼ ins. p. 106 in Clare Leighton, *Country Matters*, London: Victor Gollancz; New York: Macmillan Co., 1937

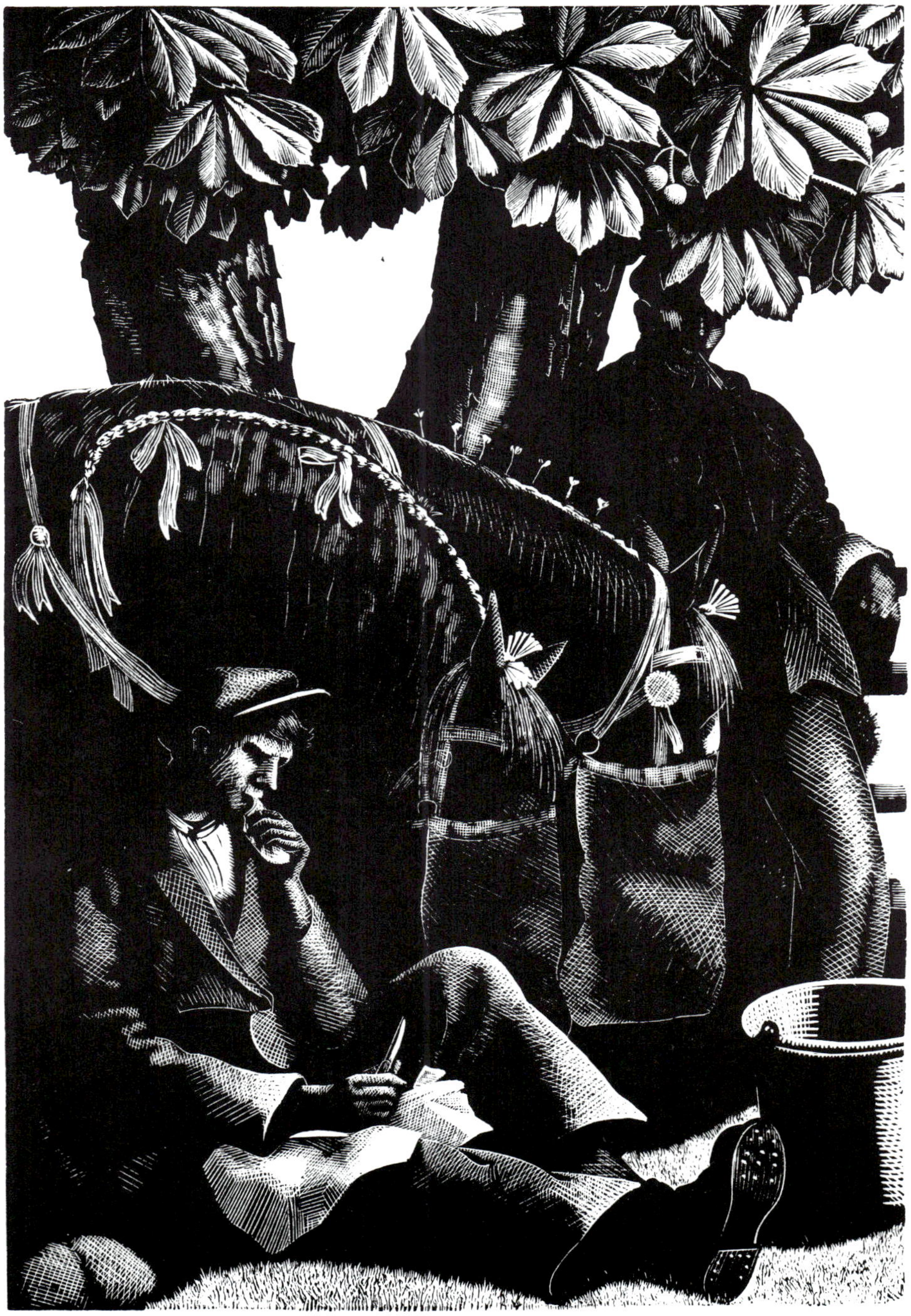

66. *Dinner Time at the Show*, 1936 17.8 × 12.1 cms.: 7 × 4¾ ins. p. 119 in Clare Leighton, *Country Matters*, London: Victor Gollancz; New York: Macmillan Co., 1937

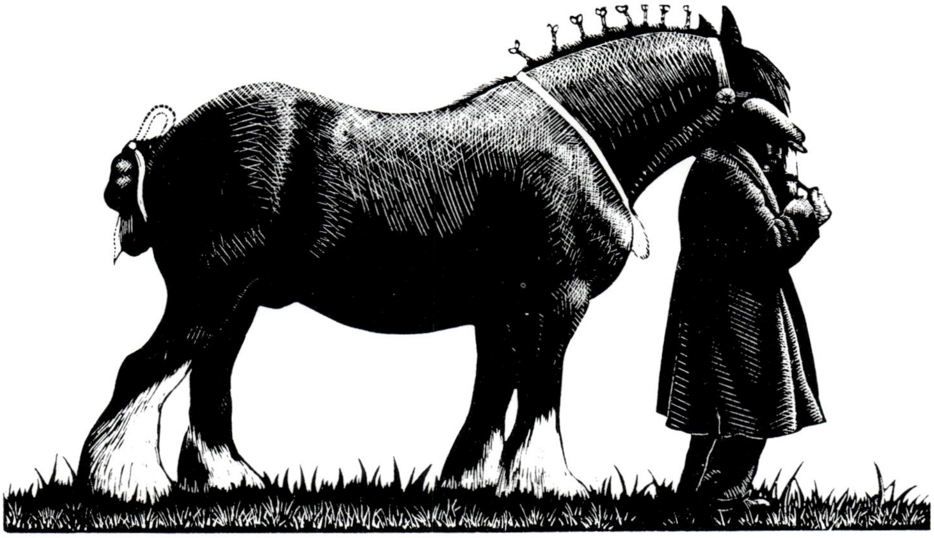

67a. *Shire Horse*, 1936 7.2 × 12.4 cms.: $2^{13}/_{16}$ × $4^{7}/_{8}$ ins. p. 113 in Clare Leighton, *Country Matters*, London: Victor Gollancz; New York: Macmillan Co., 1937

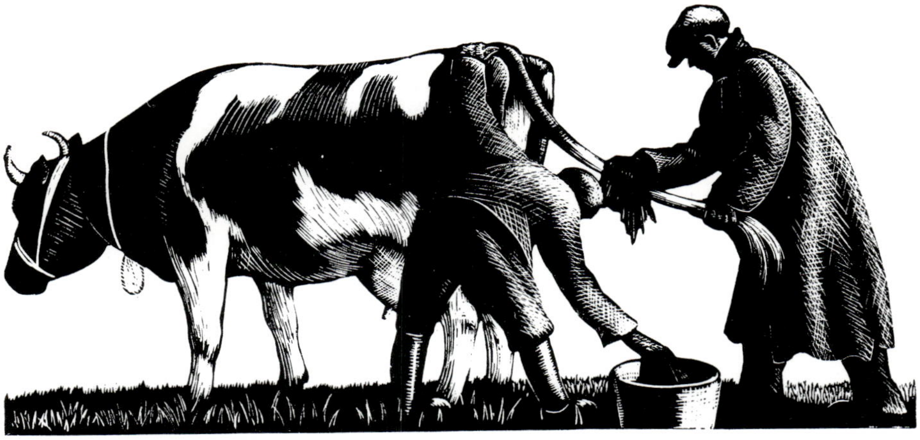

67b. *Washing the Cow's Tail*, 1936 5.7 × 12.1 cms.: $2^{1}/_{4}$ × $4^{3}/_{4}$ ins. p. 115 in Clare Leighton, *Country Matters*, London: Victor Gollancz; New York: Macmillan Co., 1937

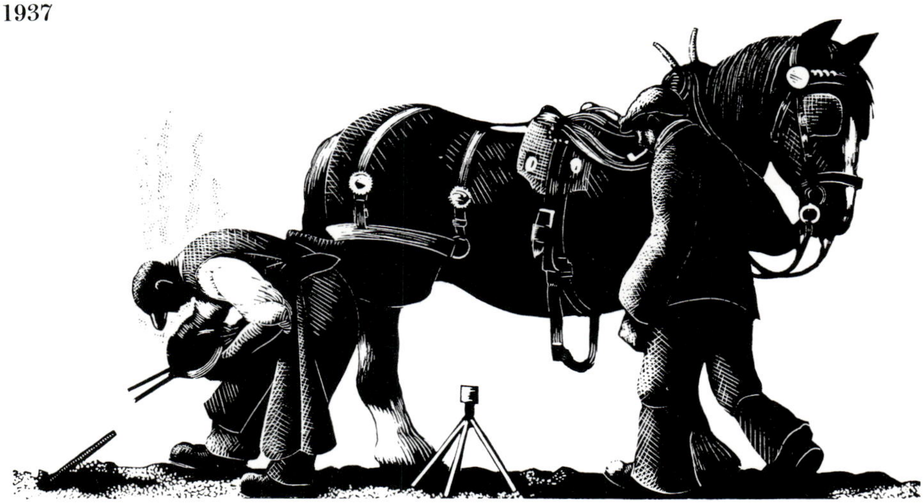

67c. *Shoeing the Horse*, 1936 6.3 × 12.1 cms.: $2^{1}/_{2}$ × $4^{3}/_{4}$ ins. p. 17 in Clare Leighton, *Country Matters*, London: Victor Gollancz; New York: Macmillan Co., 1937

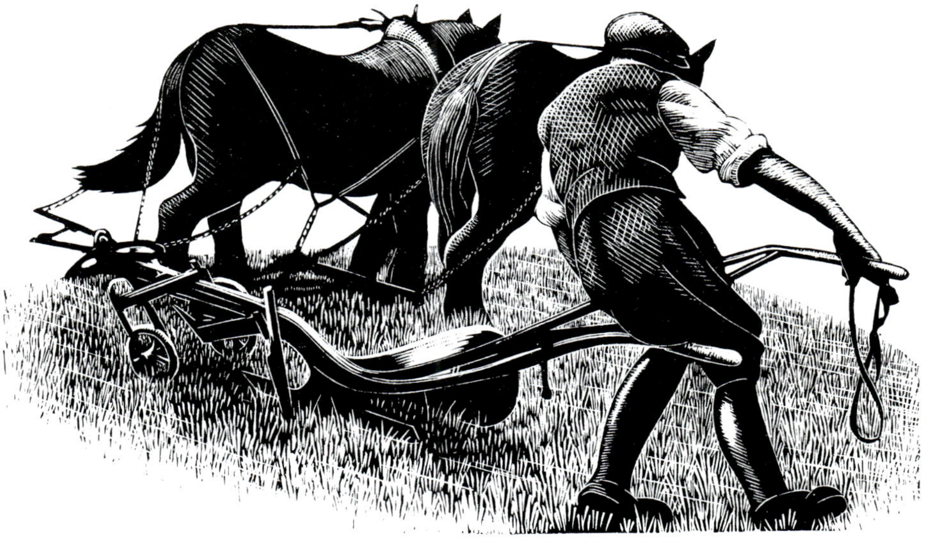

68a. *Turning the Plough*, 1936 7 × 12.1 cms.: 2¾ × 4¾ ins. p. 131 in Clare Leighton, *Country Matters*, London: Victor Gollancz; New York: Macmillan Co., 1937

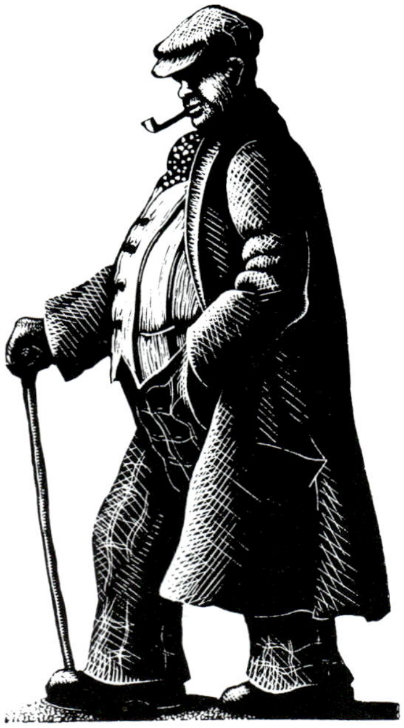

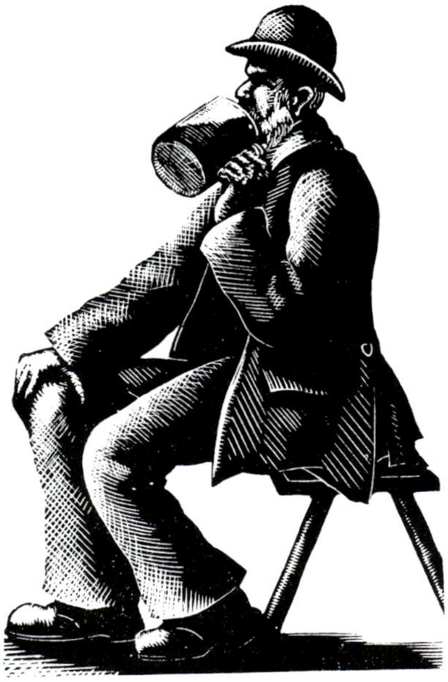

68b. *Going to the Pub*, 1936 8.3 × 4.6 cms.: 3¼ × 1$\frac{13}{16}$ ins. p. 136 in Clare Leighton, *Country Matters*, London: Victor Gollancz; New York: Macmillan Co., 1937

68c. *Man Drinking*, 1936 7.6 × 5.1 cms.: 3 × 2 ins. p. 139 in Clare Leighton, *Country Matters*, London: Victor Gollancz; New York: Macmillan Co., 1937

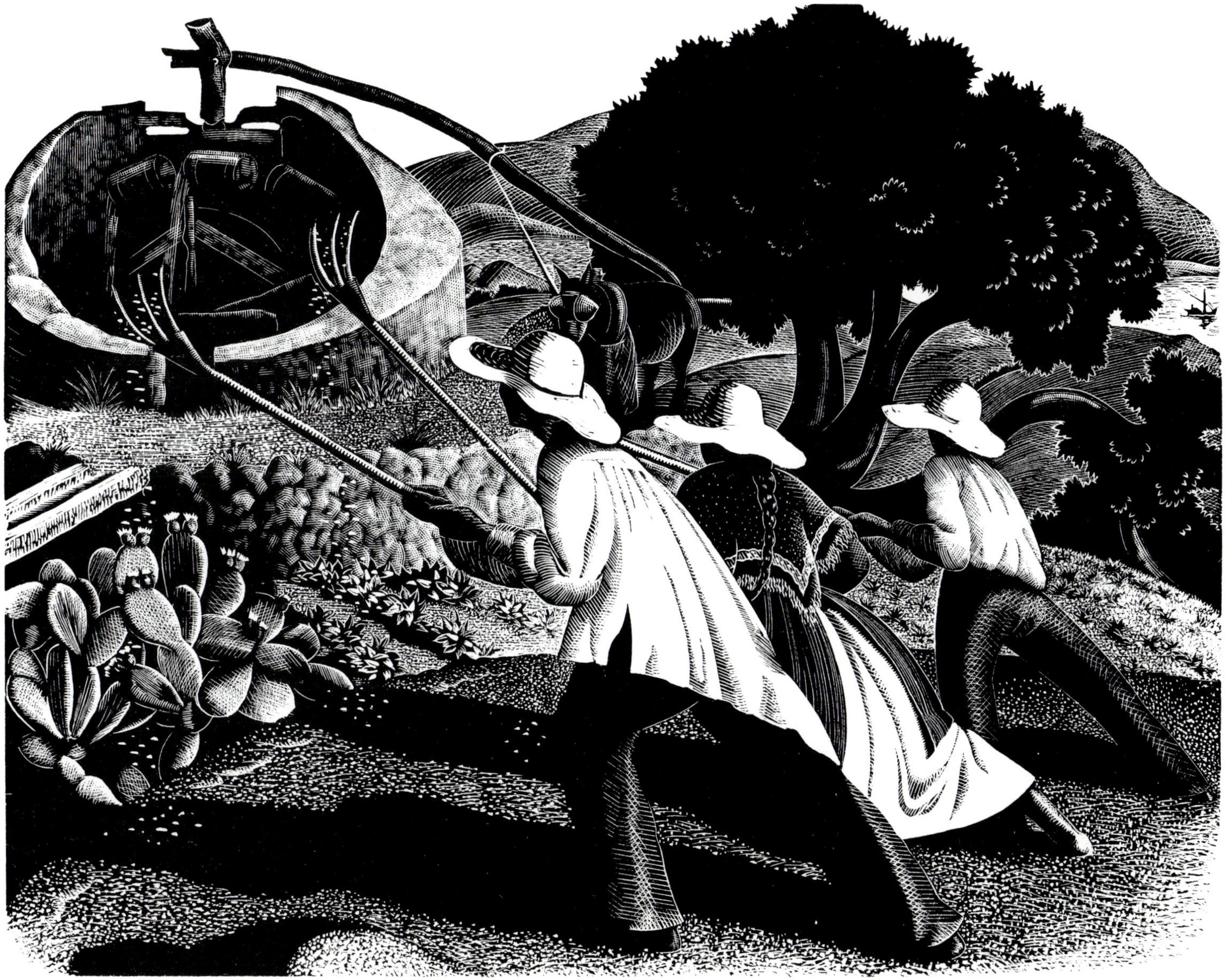

69. *Winnowers*, *Majorca*, 1937 15.6 × 19.4 cms.: 6⅛ × 7⅝ ins., commission for The Woodcut Society, Kansas City, 1937 D.L.

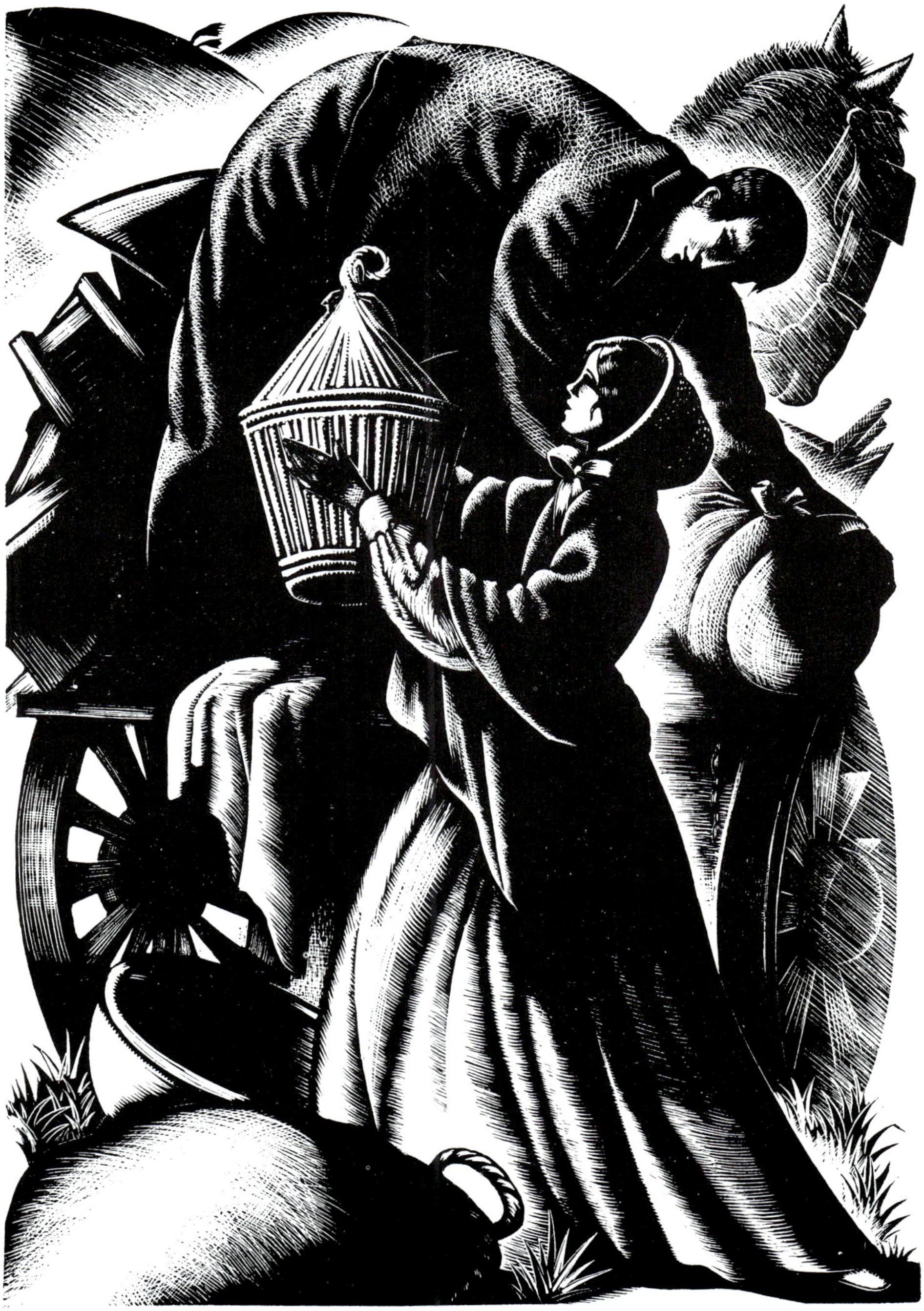

70. *The Birdcage*, 1938–9, 17.8 × 12.5 cms.: 7 × 4 15/16 ins. p. 117 in Thomas Hardy, *Under the Greenwood Tree*, London and New York: Macmillan Co., 1940

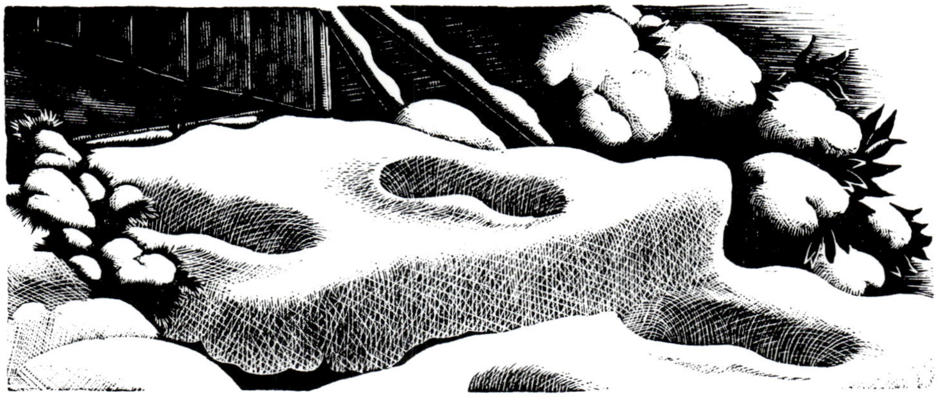

71a. *Snow on the Doorstep*, 1938–9 5.2 × 12.4 cms.: 2¹⁄₁₆ × 4⅞ ins. p. 46 in Thomas Hardy, *Under the Greenwood Tree*, London and New York: Macmillan Co., 1940

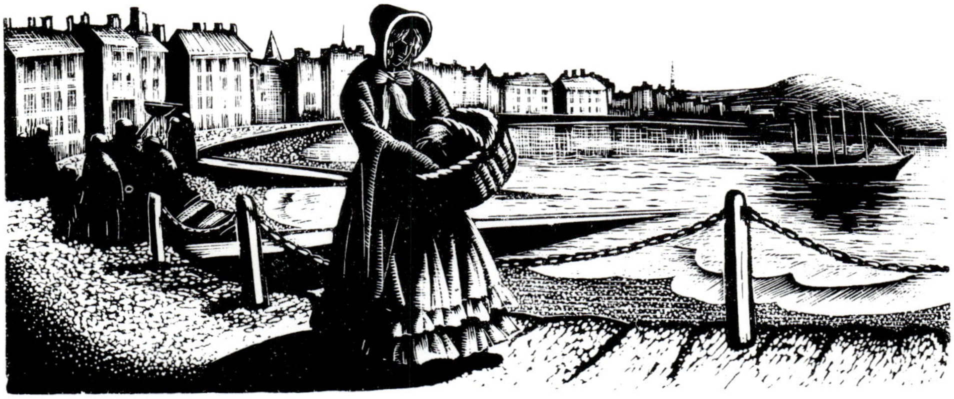

71b. *Bridmouth*, 1938–9 5.2 × 12.4 cms.: 2¹⁄₁₆ × 4⅞ ins. p. 133 in Thomas Hardy, *Under the Greenwood Tree*, London and New York: Macmillan Co., 1940

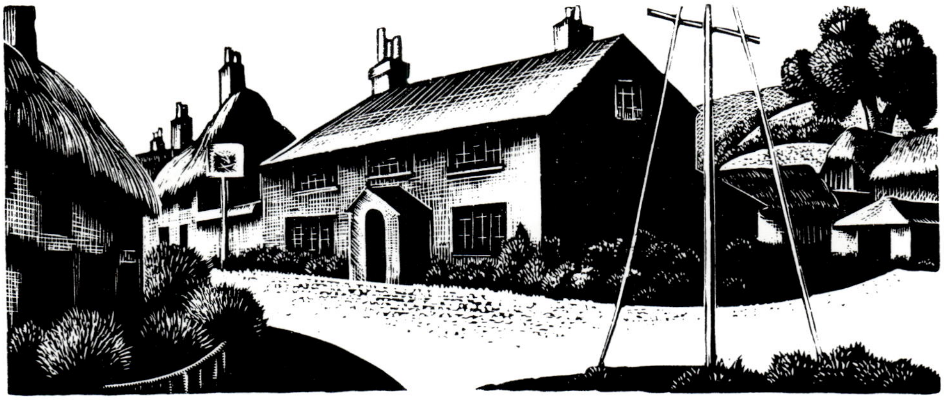

71c. *The Ship Inn*, 1938–9 5.2 × 12.4 cms.: 2¹⁄₁₆ × 4⅞ ins. p. 139 in Thomas Hardy, *Under the Greenwood Tree*, London and New York: Macmillan Co., 1940

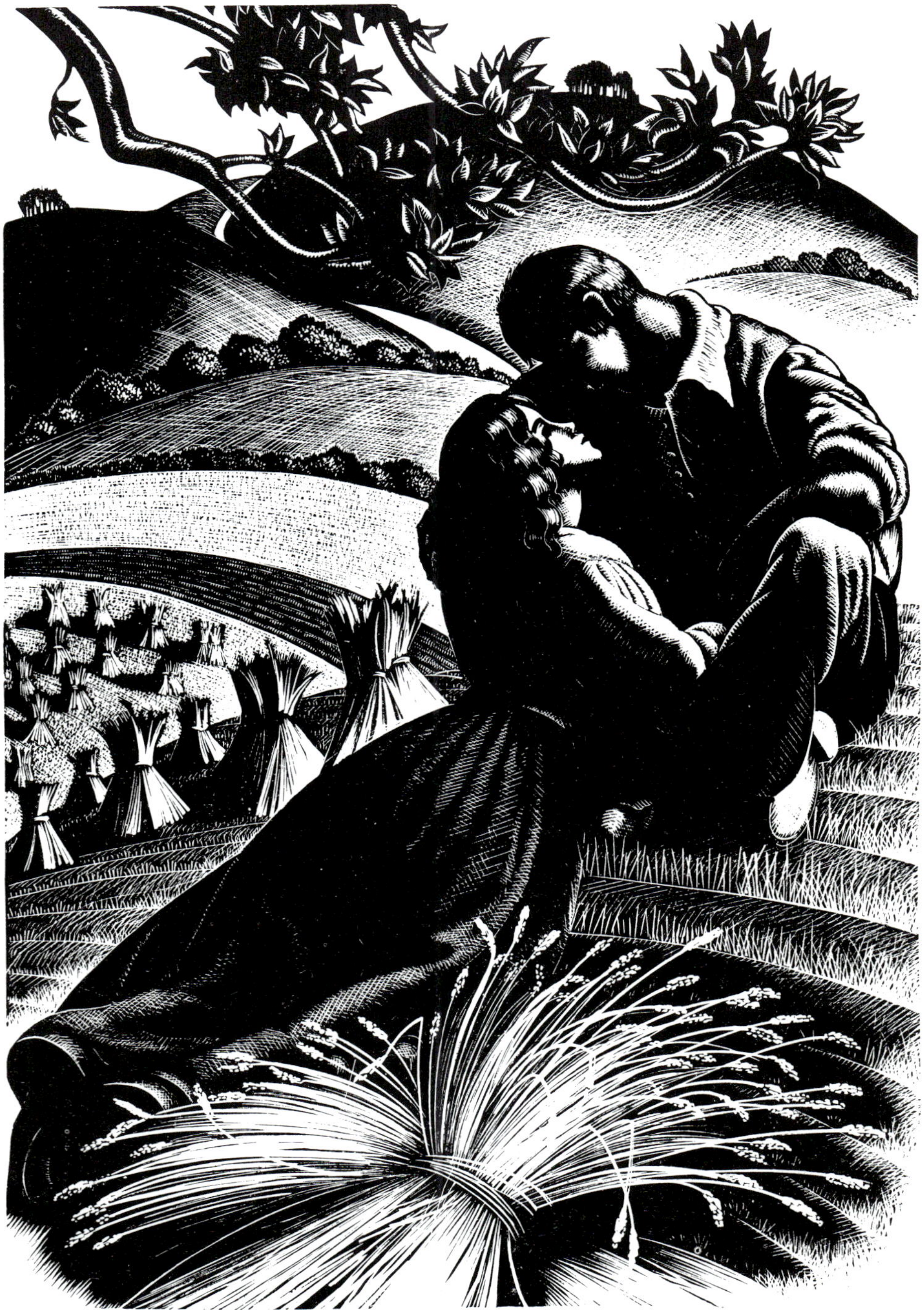

72. *The Lovers*, 1938–9 18 × 12.5 cms.: 7¹⁄₁₆ × 4¹⁵⁄₁₆ ins. p. 193 in Thomas Hardy, *Under the Greenwood Tree*, London and New York: Macmillan Co., 1940

73a. *Grey's Bridge*, 1938–9 5.2 × 7.8 cms.: 2⅟₁₆ × 3⅟₁₆ ins. p. 211 in Thomas Hardy, *Under the Greenwood Tree*, London and New York: Macmillan Co., 1940

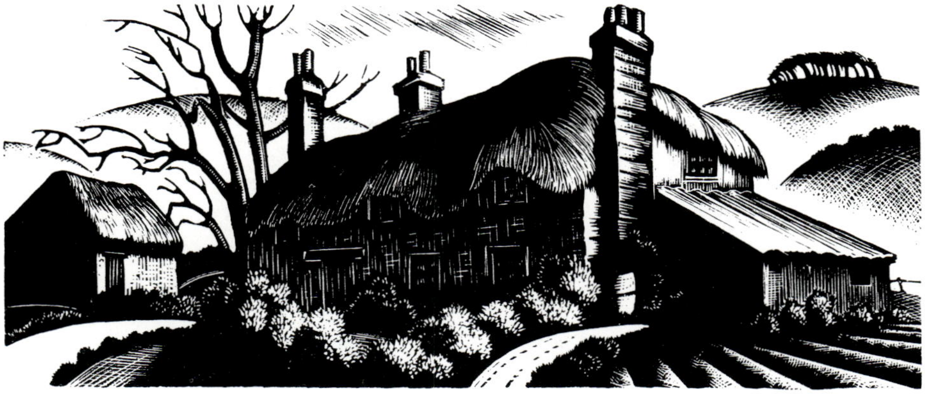

73b. *Tranter's Cottage*, 1938–9 5.2 × 12.5 cms.: 2⅟₁₆ × 4¹⁵⁄₁₆ ins. p. 8 in Thomas Hardy, *Under the Greenwood Tree*, London and New York: Macmillan Co., 1940

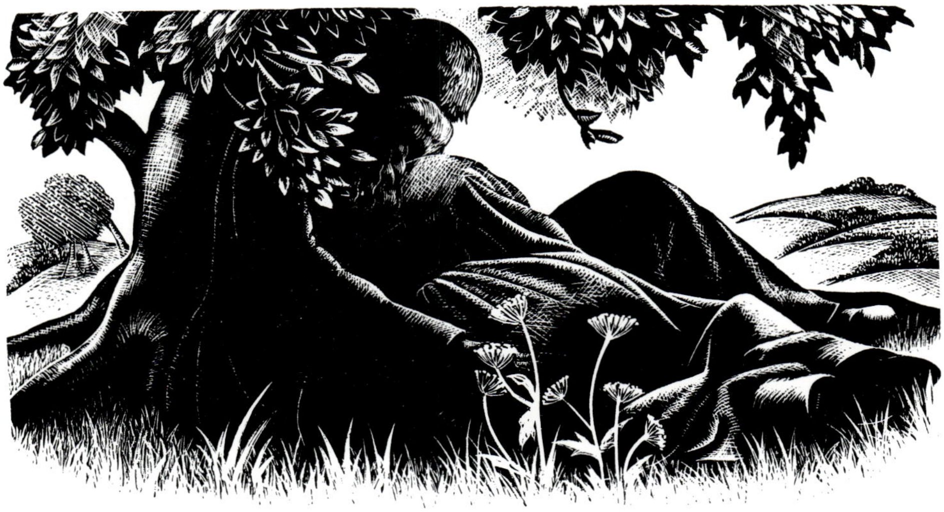

73c. *Under the Greenwood Tree*, 1938–9 6.5 × 12.4 cms.: 2⁹⁄₁₆ × 4⅞ ins. p. 231 in Thomas Hardy, *Under the Greenwood Tree*, London and New York: Macmillan Co., 1940

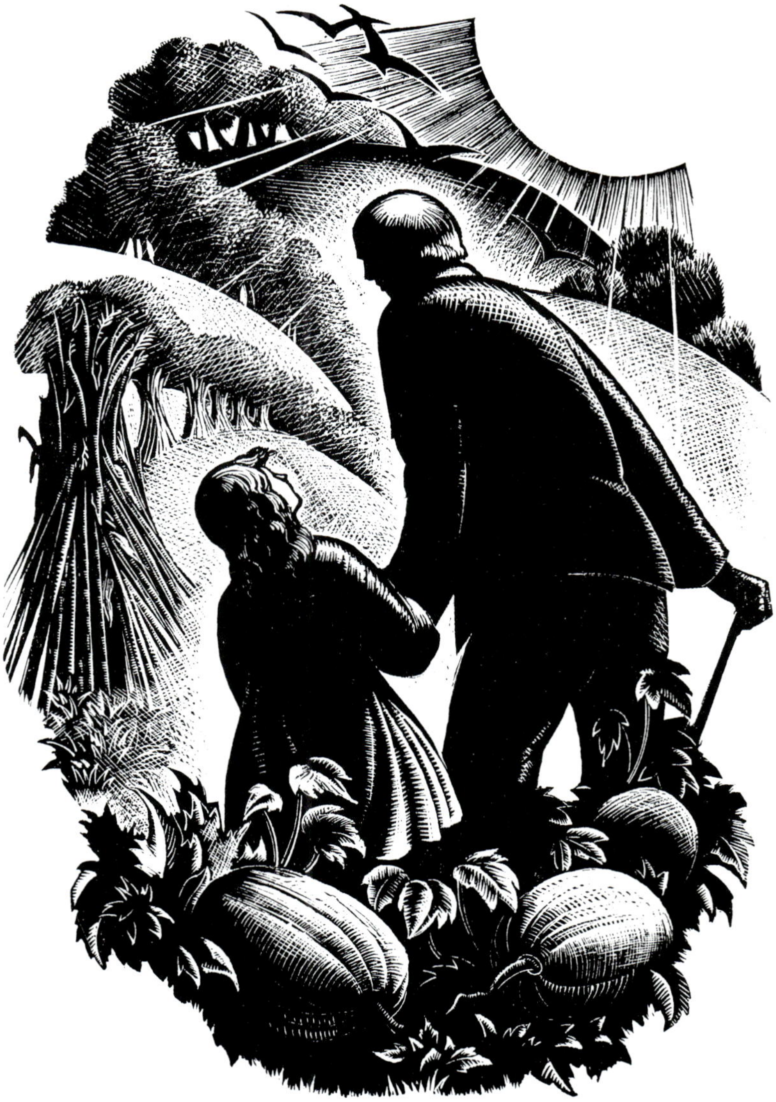

74. *What Power is the Sun's, Daughter*, 1941. 14.6 × 10.3 cms.: 5¾ × 4¹⁄₁₆ ins. p. 12 in Elsie Symington, *By Light of Sun*, New York: G.P. Putnam's Sons, 1941

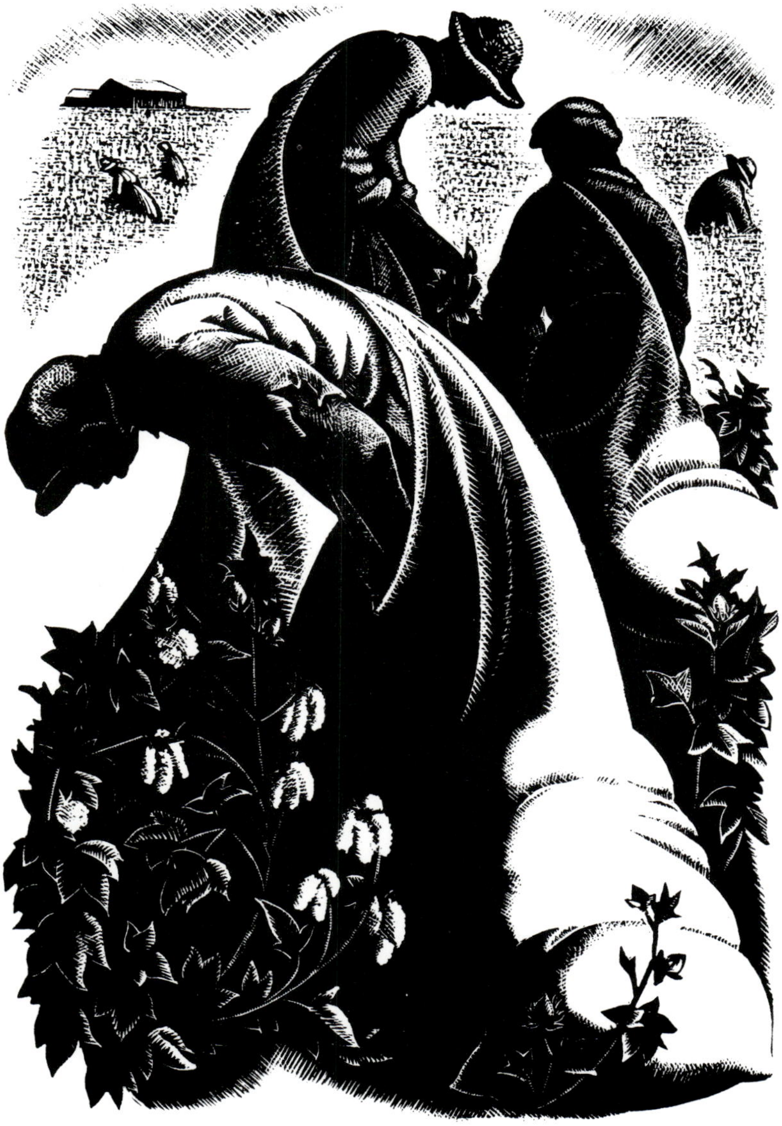

75. *Cotton Pickers*, 1941 14.8 × 10.3 cms.: 5$^{13}/_{16}$ × 4$^{1}/_{16}$ ins. commission for The Print Club of Rochester, 1941

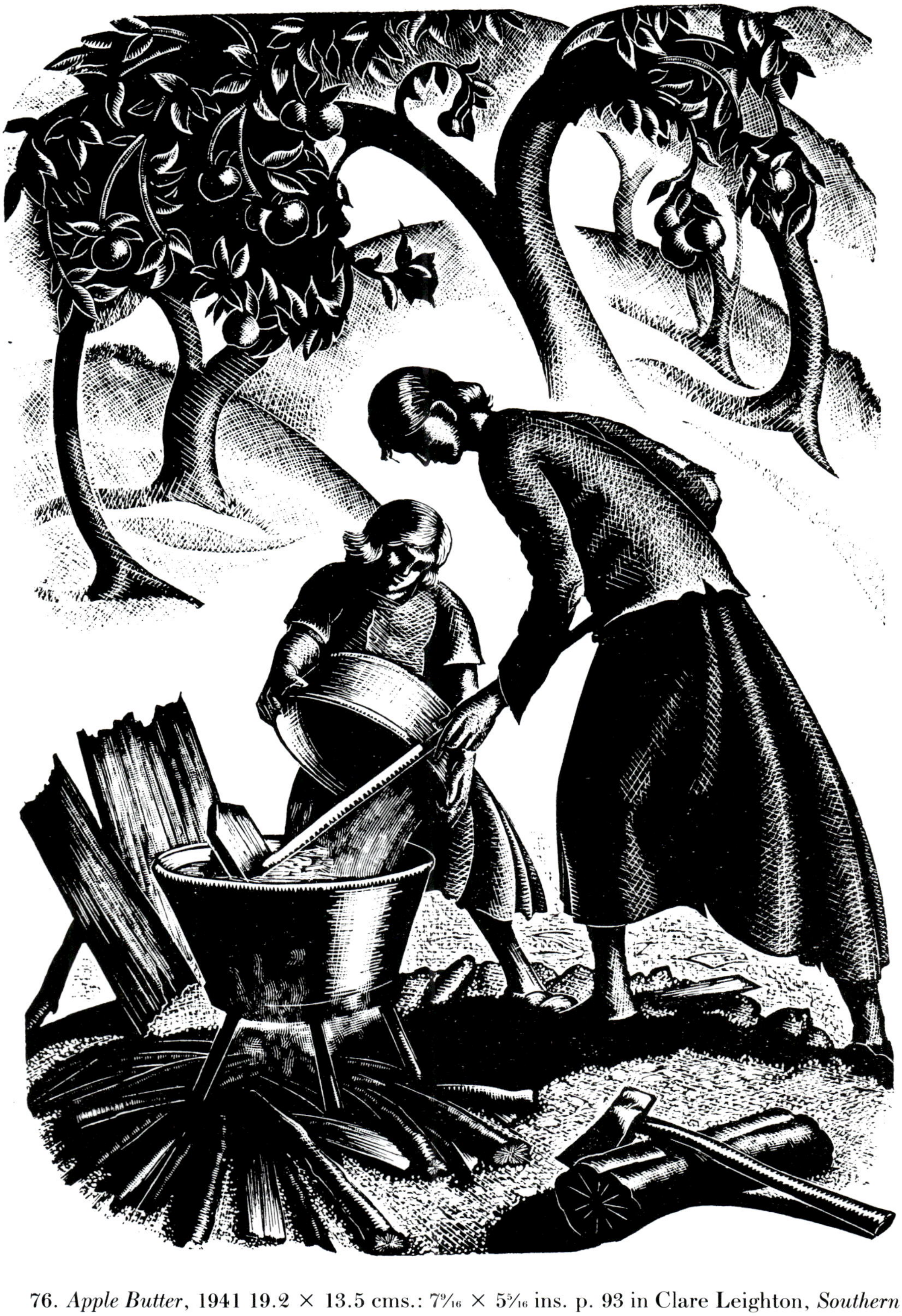

76. *Apple Butter*, 1941 19.2 × 13.5 cms.: 7⁷⁄₁₆ × 5⁵⁄₁₆ ins. p. 93 in Clare Leighton, *Southern Harvest*, London: Victor Gollancz Ltd., 1943

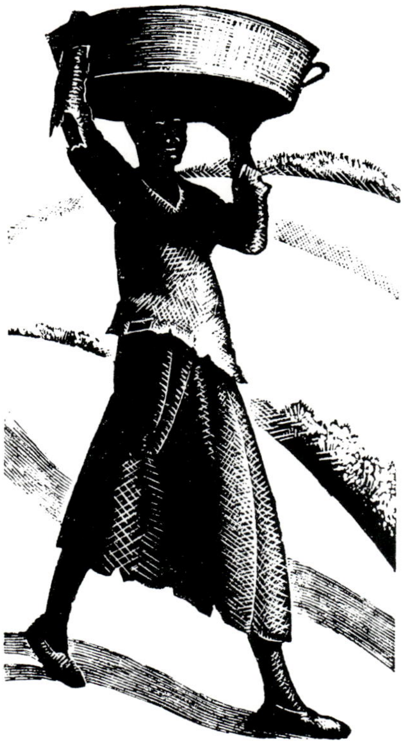

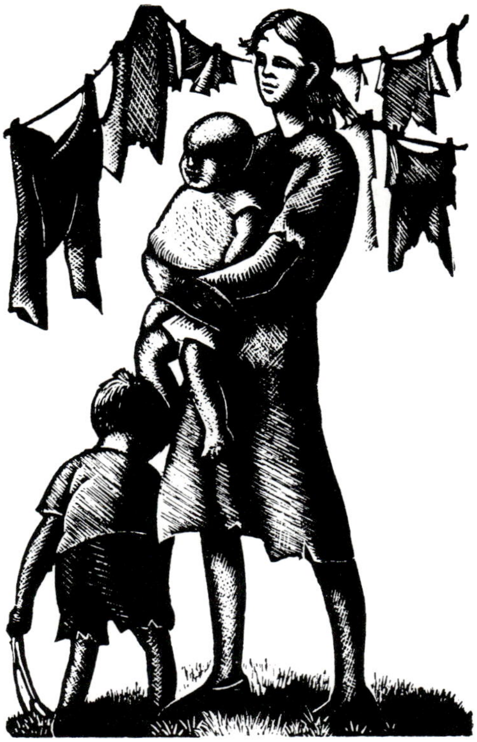

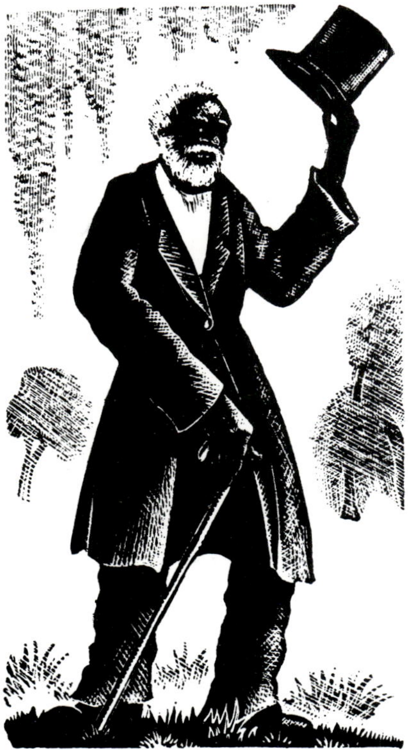

77a. *Woman Carrying Tin Bath*, 1941 9.7 × 5.2 cms.: 3 13/16 × 2 1/16 ins. p. 70 in Clare Leighton, *Southern Harvest*, London: Victor Gollancz Ltd., 1943

77b. *Po' White Woman*, 1941 9.7 × 6.2 cms.: 3 13/16 × 2 7/16 ins. p. 83 in Clare Leighton, *Southern Harvest*, London: Victor Gollancz Ltd., 1943

77c. *Old Sam*, 1941 9.7 × 5.4 cms.: 3 13/16 × 2 1/8 ins. p. 102 in Clare Leighton, *Southern Harvest*, London: Victor Gollancz Ltd., 1943

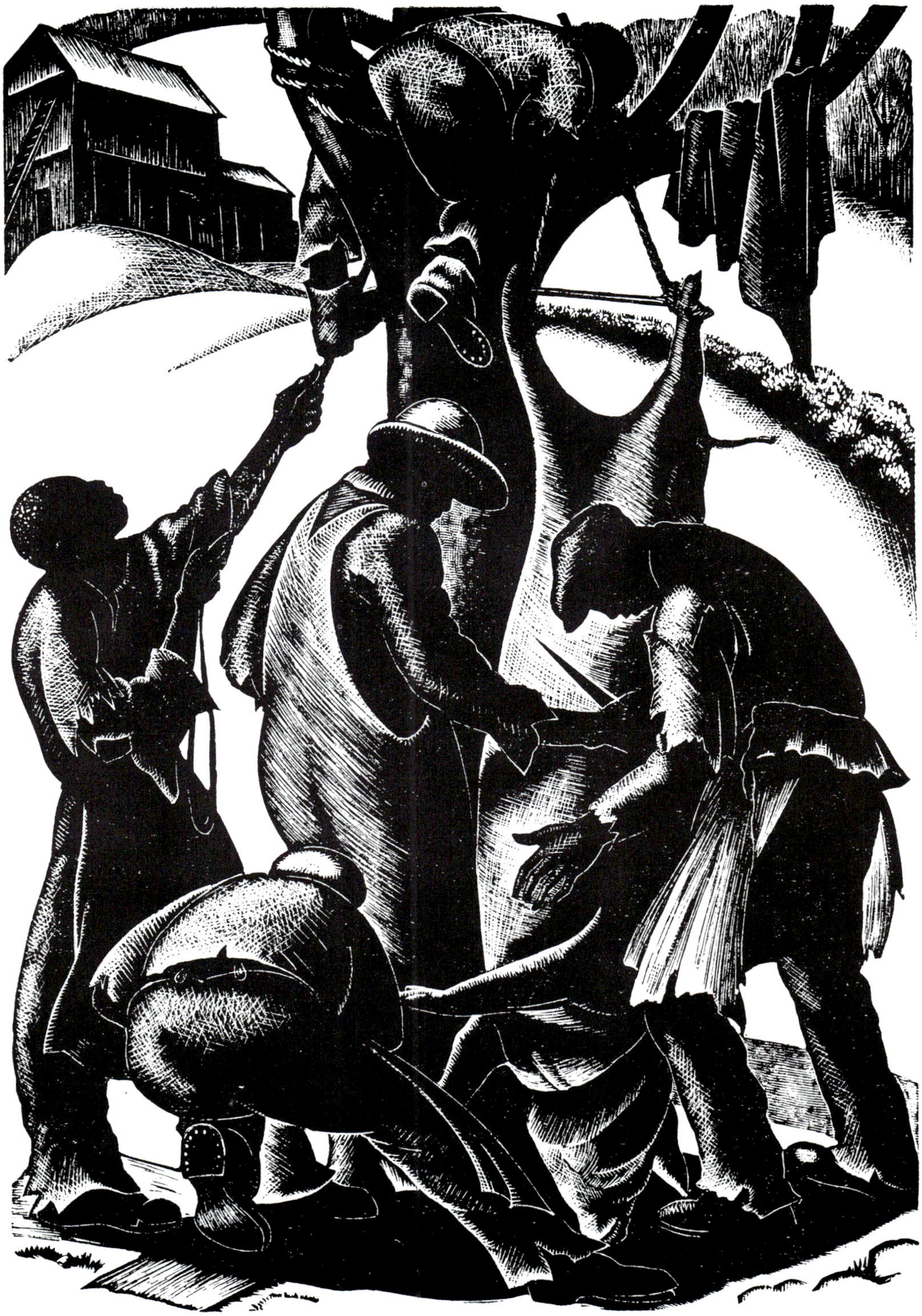

78. *Hog Killing*, 1941 19.4 × 13.5 cms.: 7⅝ × 5⁵⁄₁₆ ins. p. 69 in Clare Leighton, *Southern Harvest*, London: Victor Gollancz Ltd., 1943

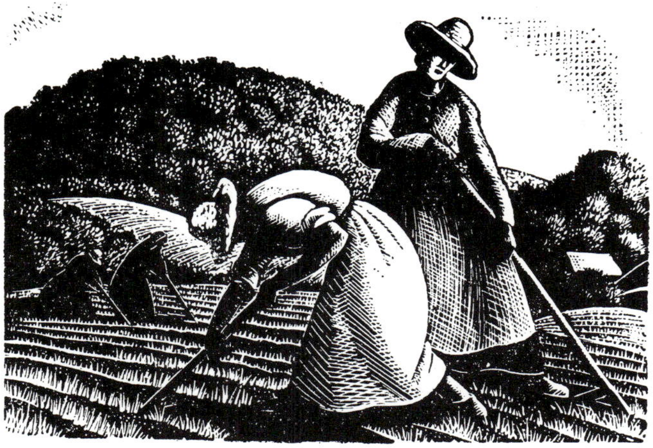

79a. *Women Hoeing*, 1941 5.7 × 8.4 cms.: 2¼ × 3⁵⁄₁₆ ins. p. 22 in Gilbert White, *Natural History of Selborne*, London: Penguin Books, 1941

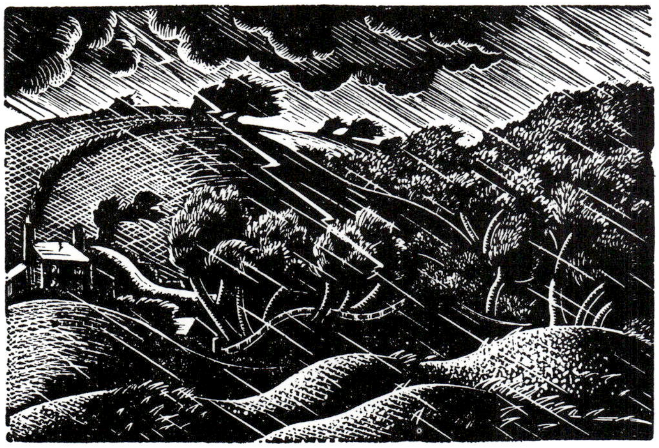

79b. *The Storm*, 1941 5.7 × 8.4 cms.: 2¼ × 3⁵⁄₁₆ ins. p. 71 in Gilbert White, *Natural History of Selborne*, London: Penguin Books, 1941

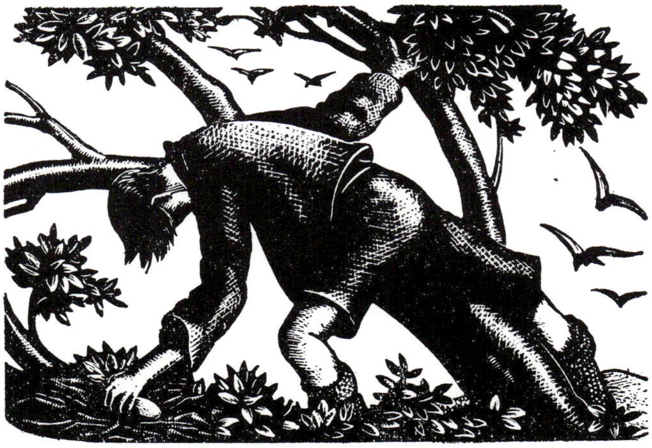

79c. *Boy Birdnesting*, 1941 5.9 × 8 cms.: 2⁵⁄₁₆ × 3⁵⁄₁₆ ins. p. 92 in Gilbert White, *Natural History of Selborne*, London: Penguin Books, 1941

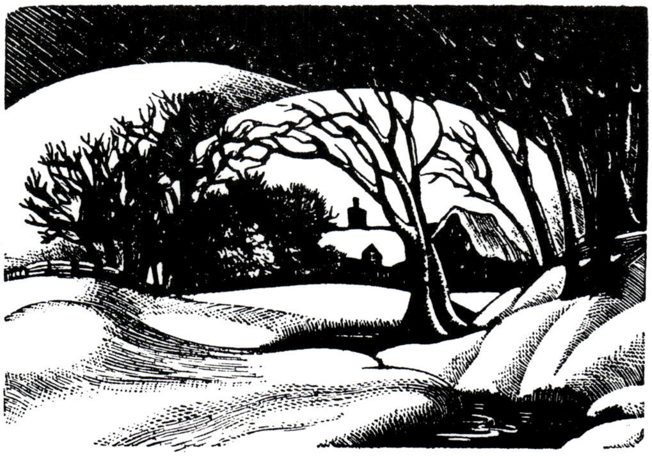

79d. *Snow Scene*, 1941 5.9 × 8 cms.: 2⁵⁄₁₆ × 3⁵⁄₁₆ ins. p. 225 in Gilbert White, *Natural History of Selborne*, London: Penguin Books, 1941

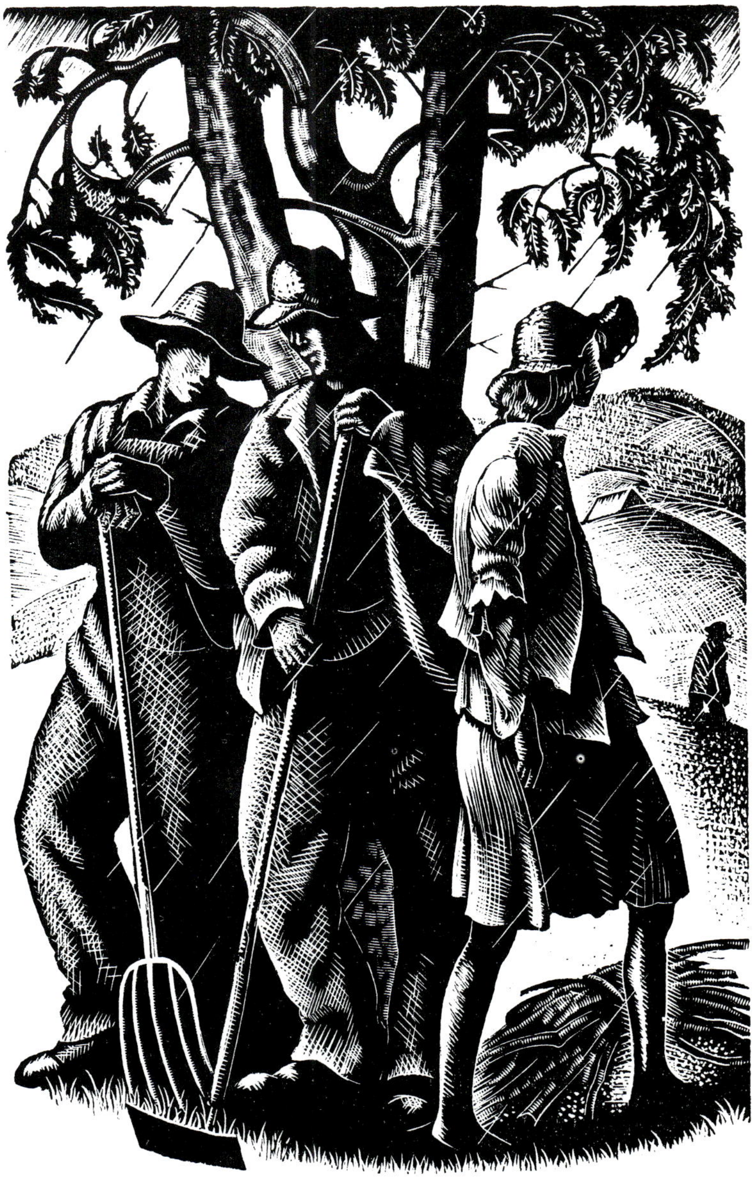

80. *Shelter from t' Rain*, 1944 15.6 × 9.8 cms.: 6⅛ × 3⅞ ins. p. 66 in Elizabeth Madox Roberts, *The Time of Man*, New York: Viking Press, 1944 D.L.

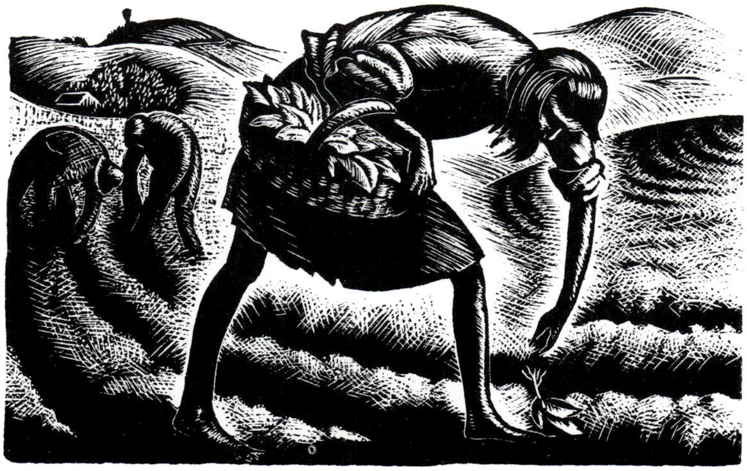

81a. *Ellen Planting Tobacco*, 1944 7.3 × 9.8 cms.: 2⅞ × 3⅞ ins. p. 9 in Elizabeth Madox Roberts, *The Time of Man*, New York: Viking Press, 1944 D.L.

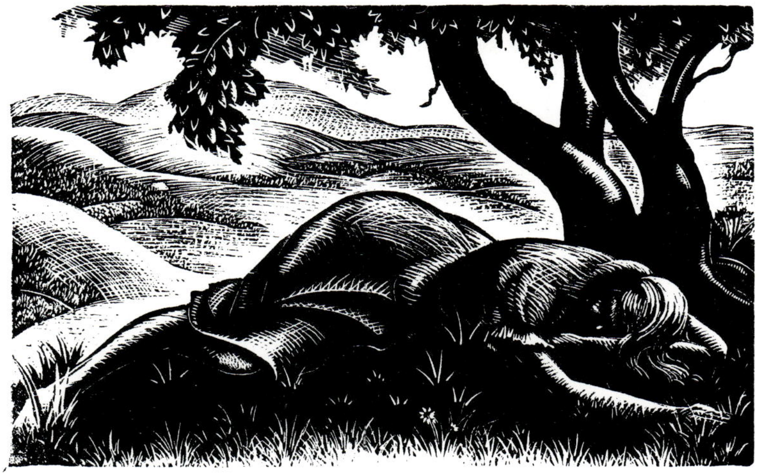

81b. *She Lay there all Day*, 1944 6.2 × 9.8 cms.: 2⁷⁄₁₆ × 3⅞ ins. p. 200 in Elizabeth Madox Roberts, *The Time of Man*, New York: Viking Press, 1944 D.L.

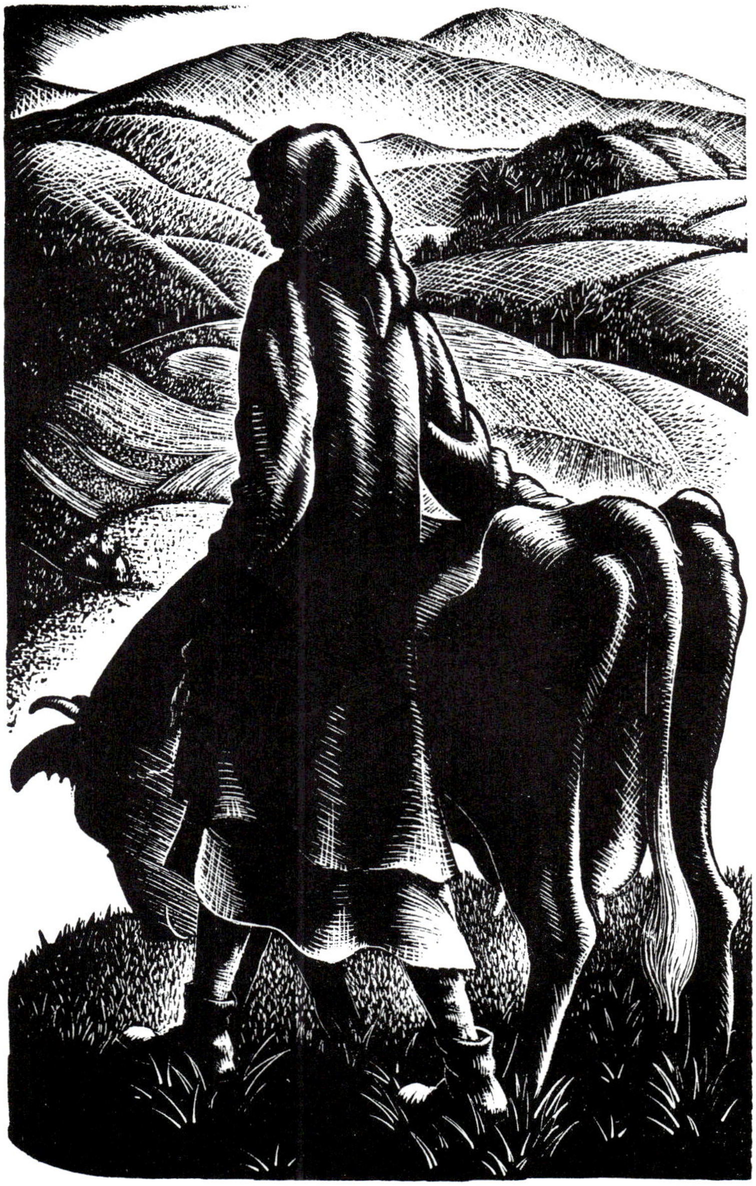

82. *T' Top of t' Rise*, 1944 15.7 × 9.8 cms.: 6³⁄₁₆ × 3⁷⁄₈ ins. p. 235 in Elizabeth Madox Roberts, *The Time of Man*, New York: Viking Press, 1944 D.L.

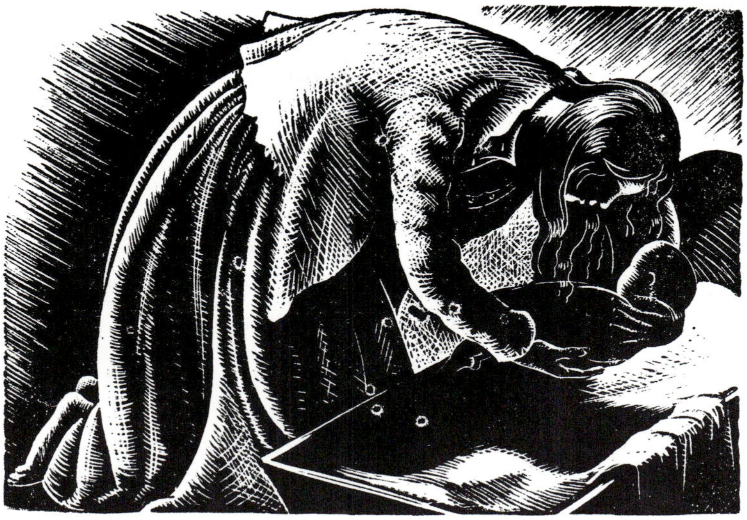

83a. *Ellen at t' Cradle*, 1944 6.9 × 9.7 cms.: $2\frac{11}{16} \times 3\frac{13}{16}$ ins. p. 298 in Elizabeth Madox Roberts, *The Time of Man*, New York: Viking Press, 1944 D.L.

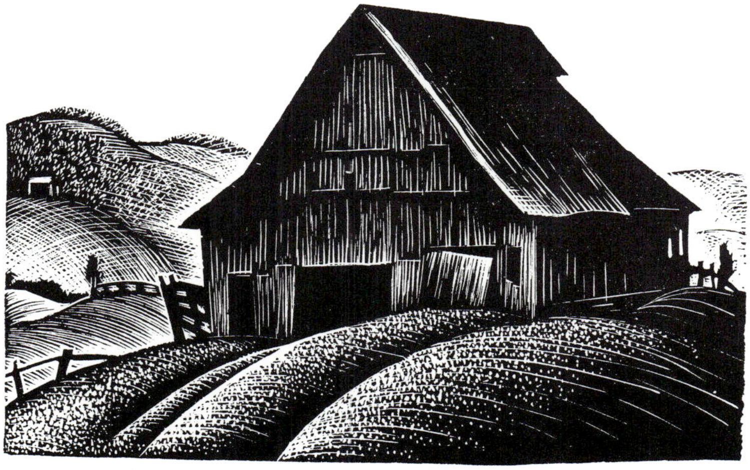

83b. *Tobacco Barn*, 1944 6 × 9.8 cms.: $2\frac{3}{8} \times 3\frac{7}{8}$ ins. p. 369 in Elizabeth Madox Roberts, *The Time of Man*, New York: Viking Press, 1944 D.L.

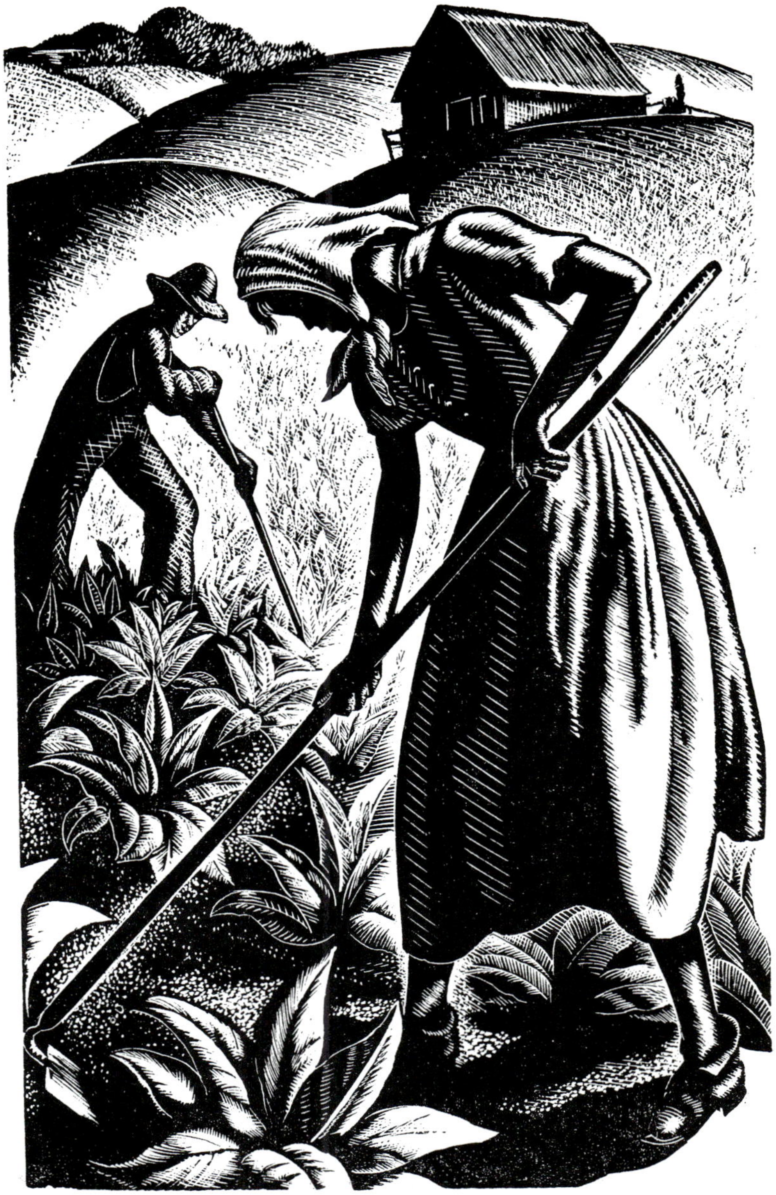

84. *Ellen Hoeing*, 1944 15.9 × 10 cms.: 6¼ × 3 15/16 ins. p. 26 in Elizabeth Madox Roberts, *The Time of Man*, New York: Viking Press, 1944 D.L.

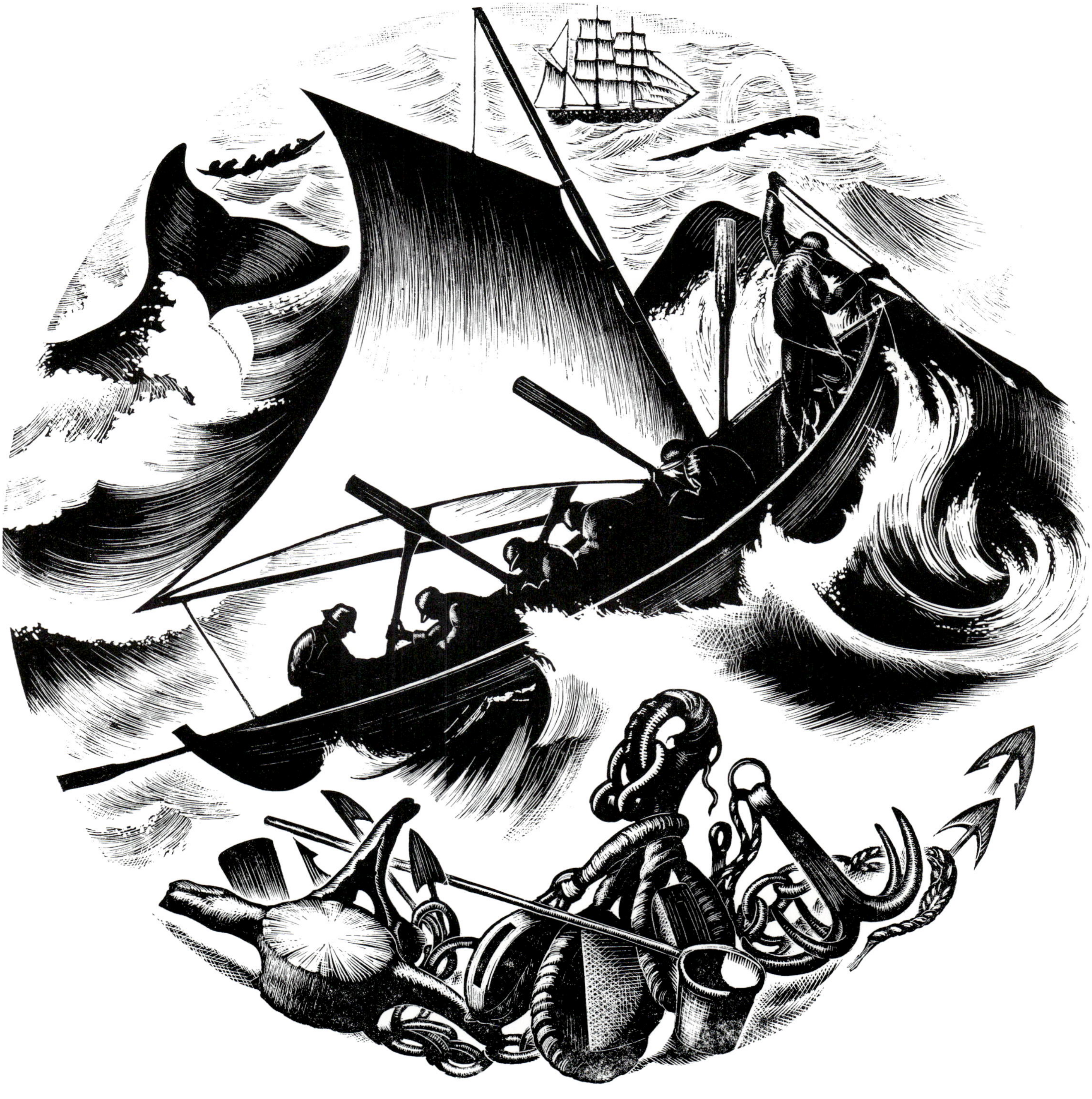

85. *Whaling*, 1949–50 24.1 cms.: 9½ ins. diameter, one of twelve New England Industries designs for Wedgwood Plates (here reduced to 79%) D.L.

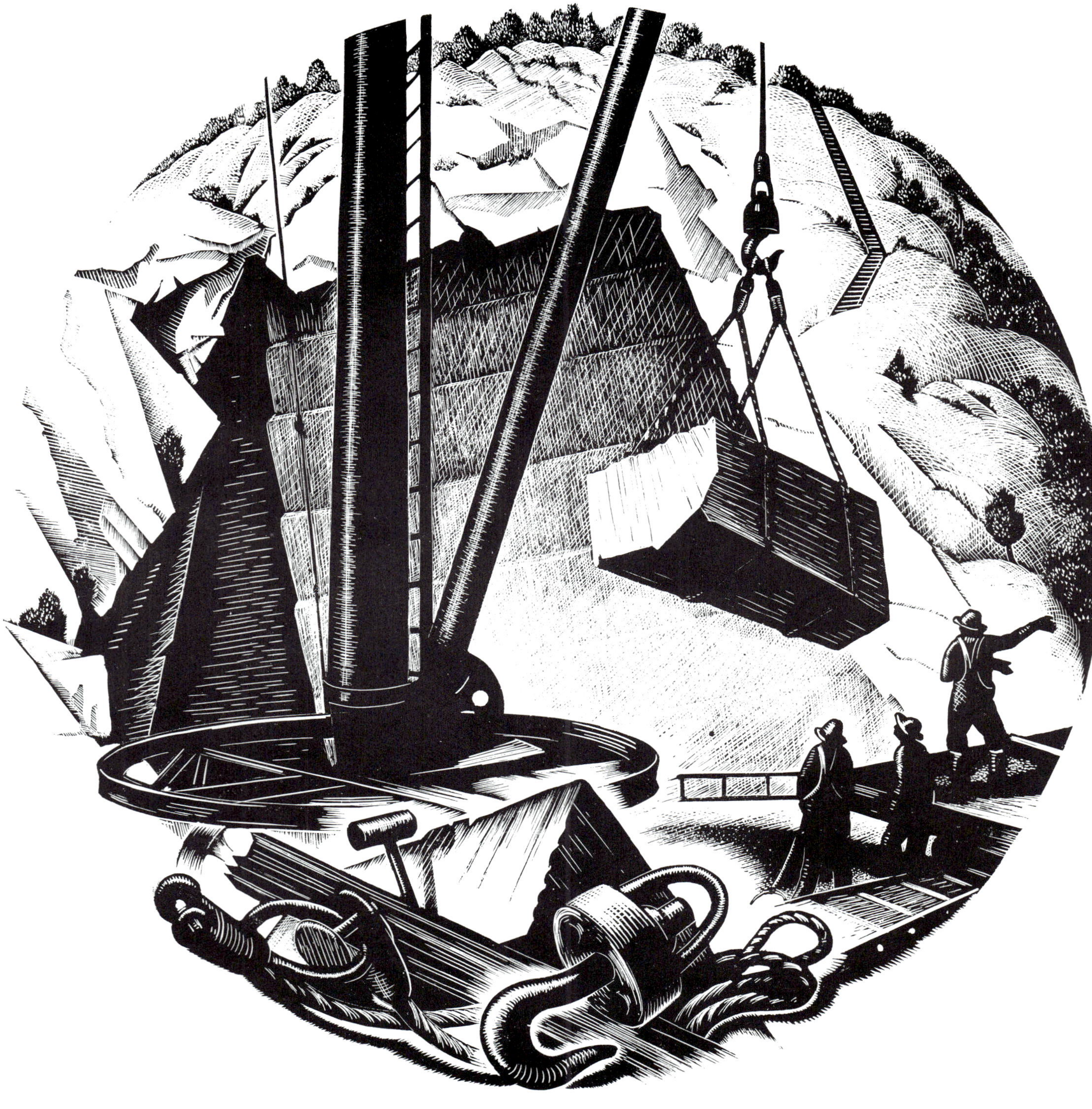

86. *Marble Quarrying*, 1949–50 24.1 cms.: 9½ ins. diameter, one of twelve New England Industries designs for Wedgwood Plates (here reduced to 79%) D.L.

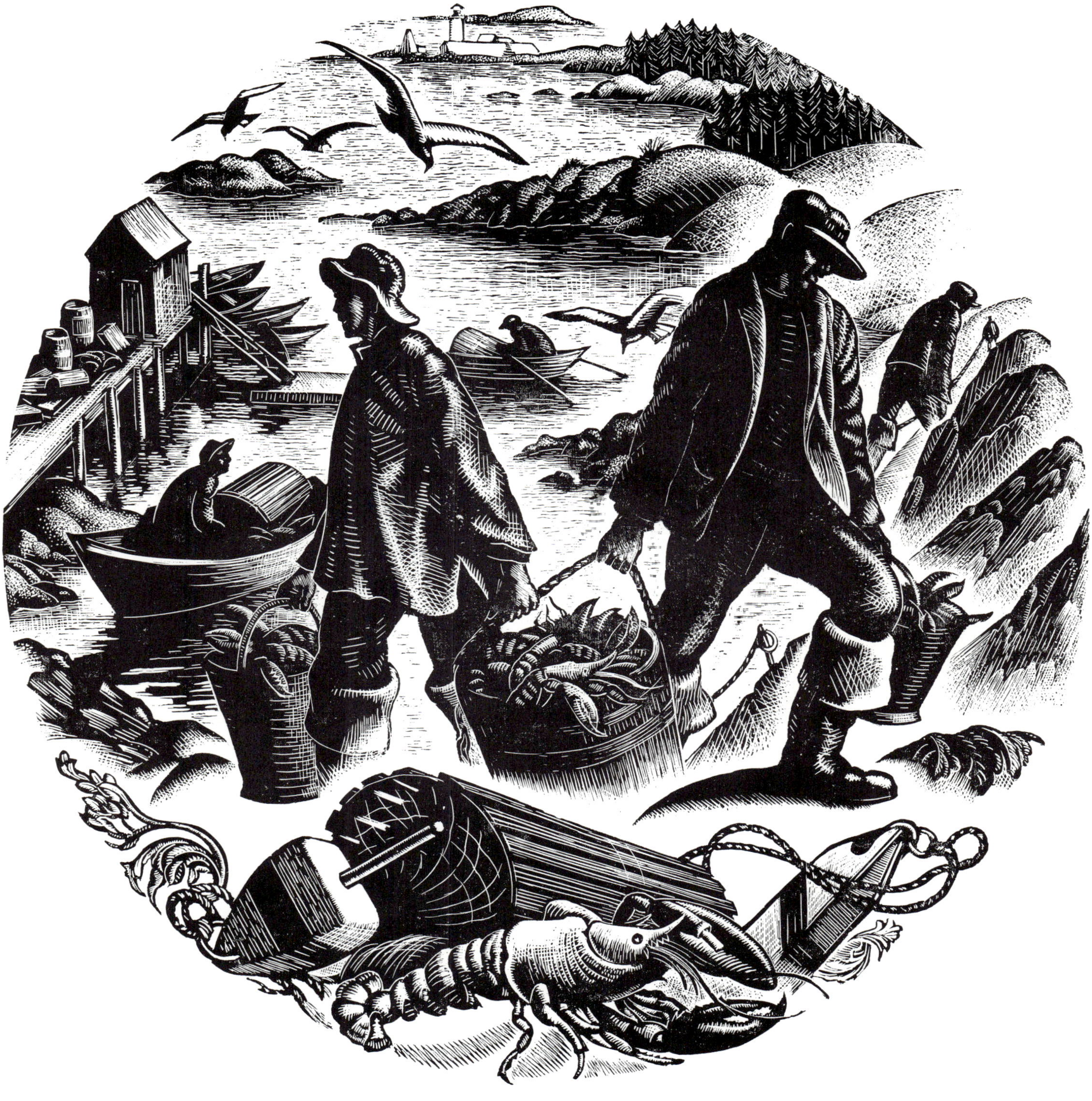

87. *Lobstering*, 1949–50 24.1 cms.: 9½ ins. diameter, one of twelve New England Industries designs for Wedgwood Plates (here reduced to 79%) D.L.

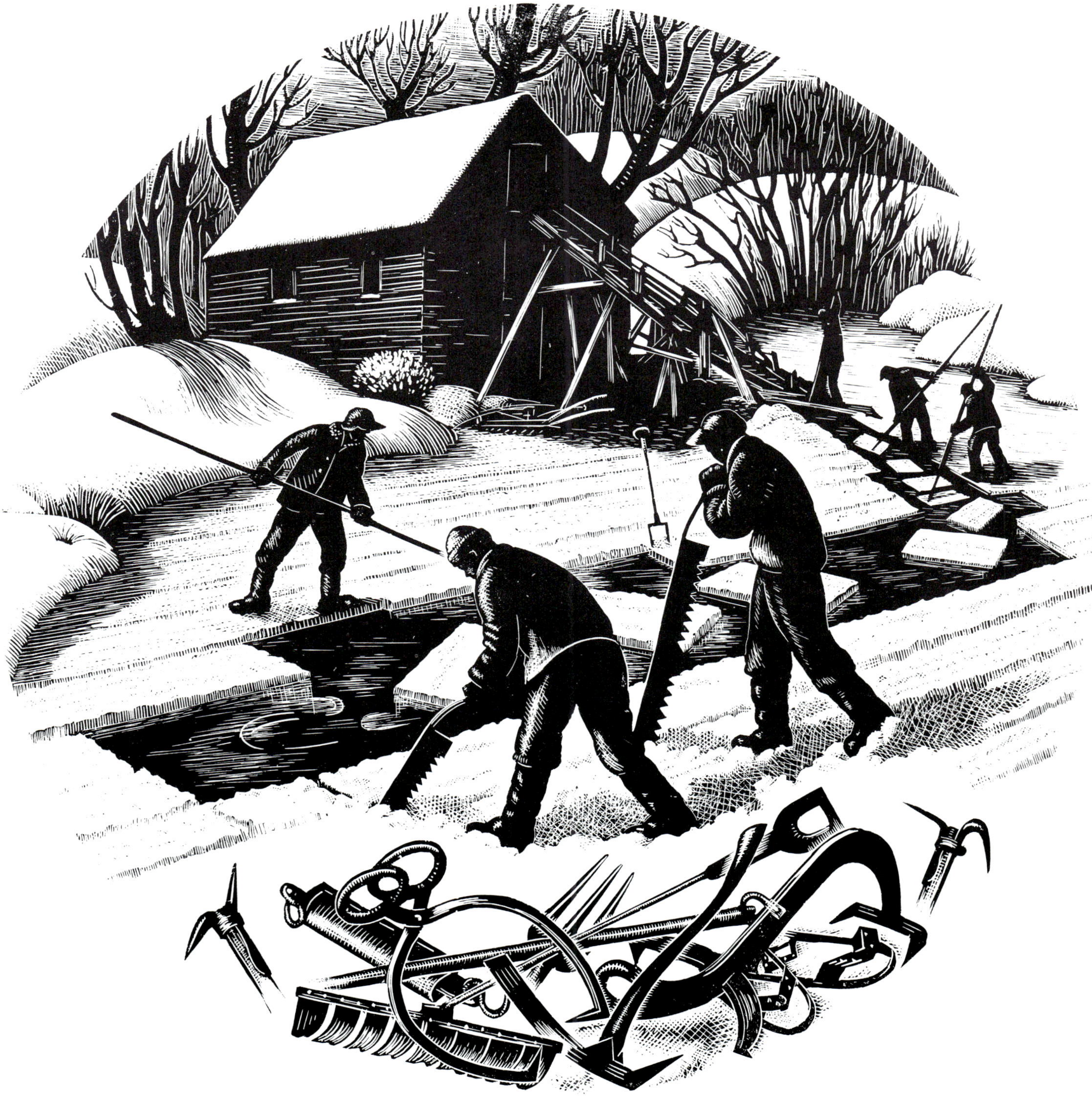

88. *Ice Cutting*, 1949–50 24.1 cms.: 9½ ins. diameter, one of twelve New England Industries designs for Wedgwood Plates (here reduced to 79%) D.L.

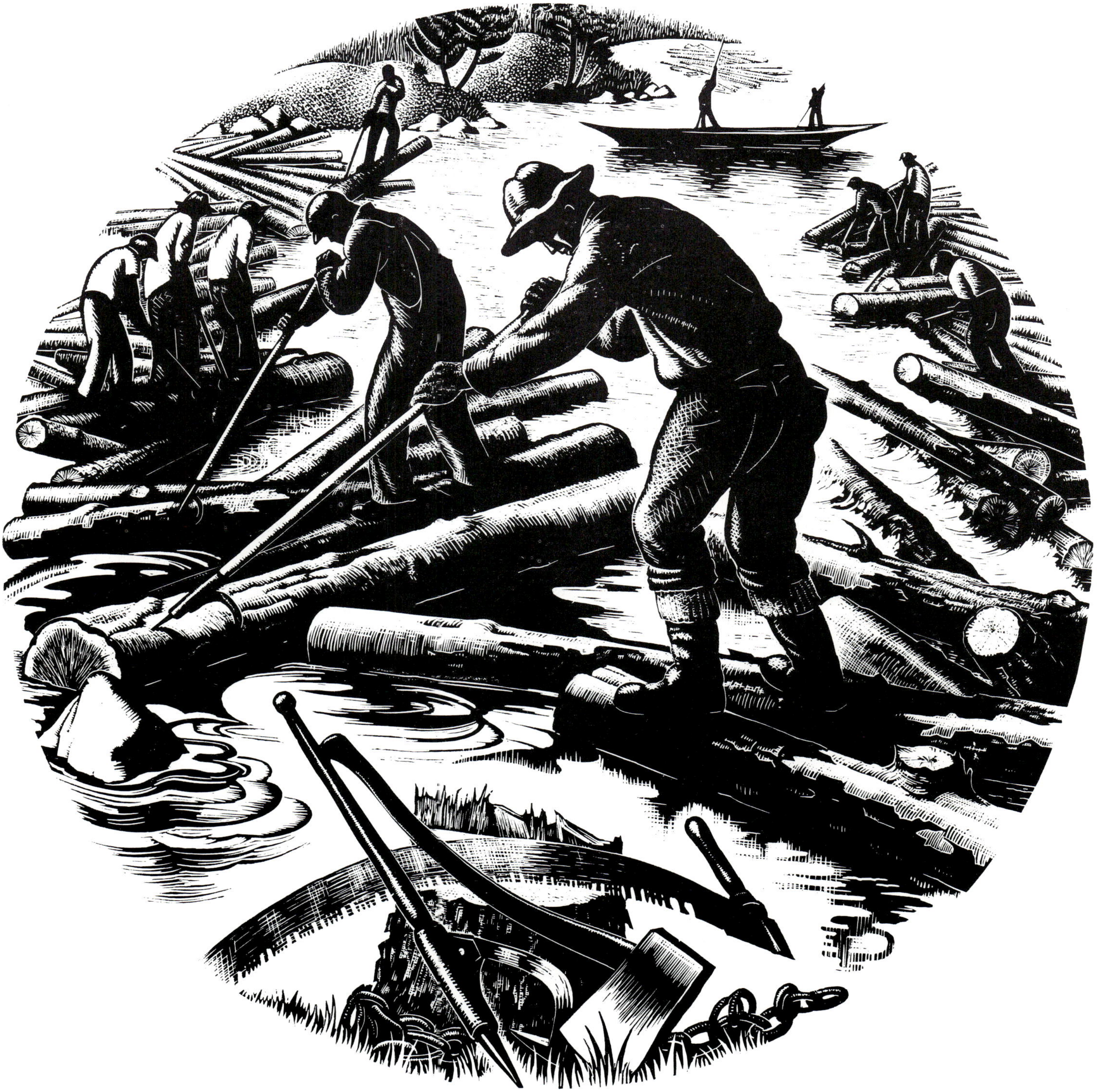

89. *Logging*, 1949–50 24.1 cms.: 9½ ins. diameter, one of twelve New England Industries designs for Wedgwood Plates (here reduced to 79%) D.L.

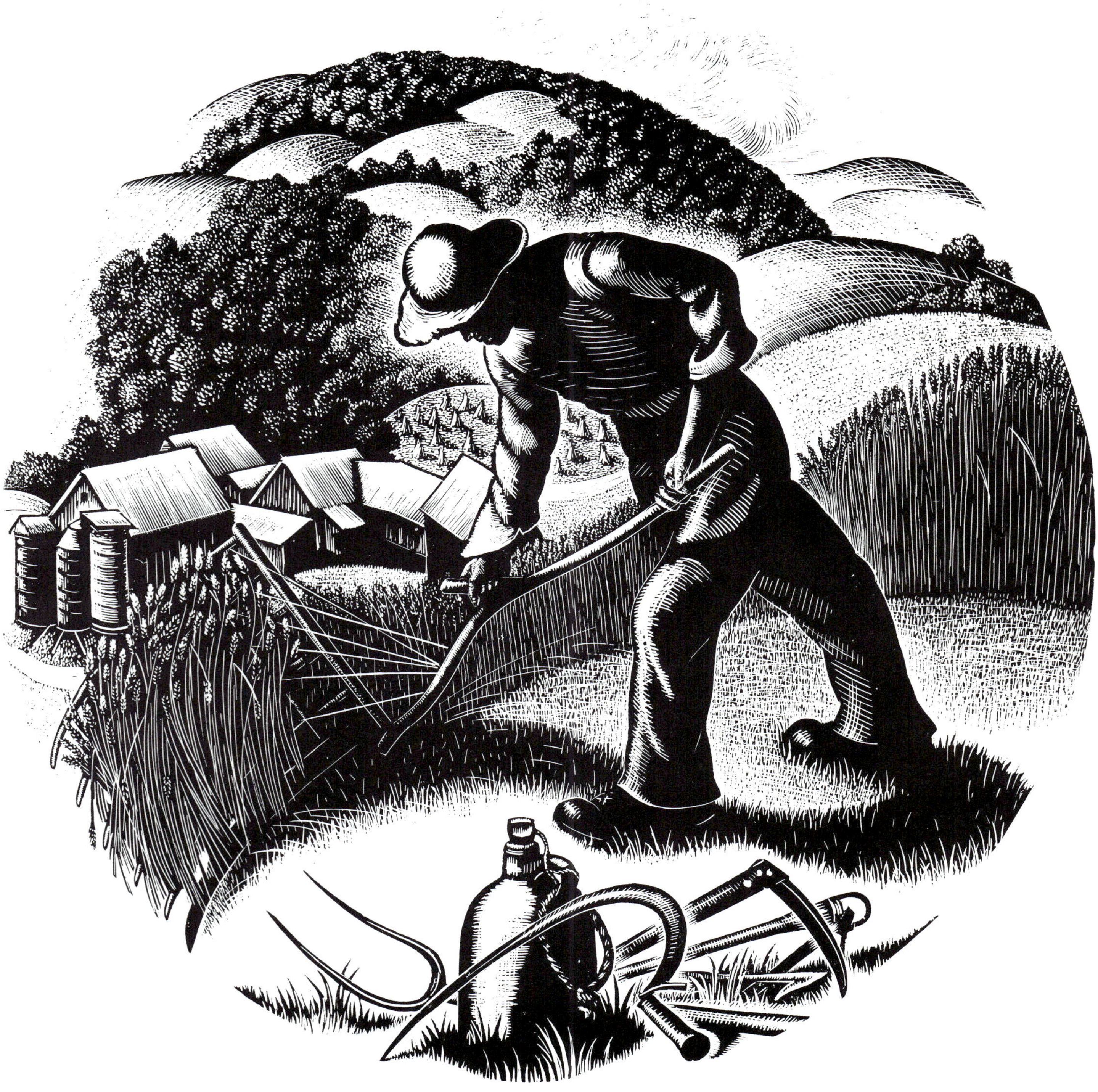

90. *Farming*, 1949–50 24.1 cms.: 9½ ins. diameter, one of twelve New England Industries designs for Wedgwood Plates (here reduced to 79%) D.L.

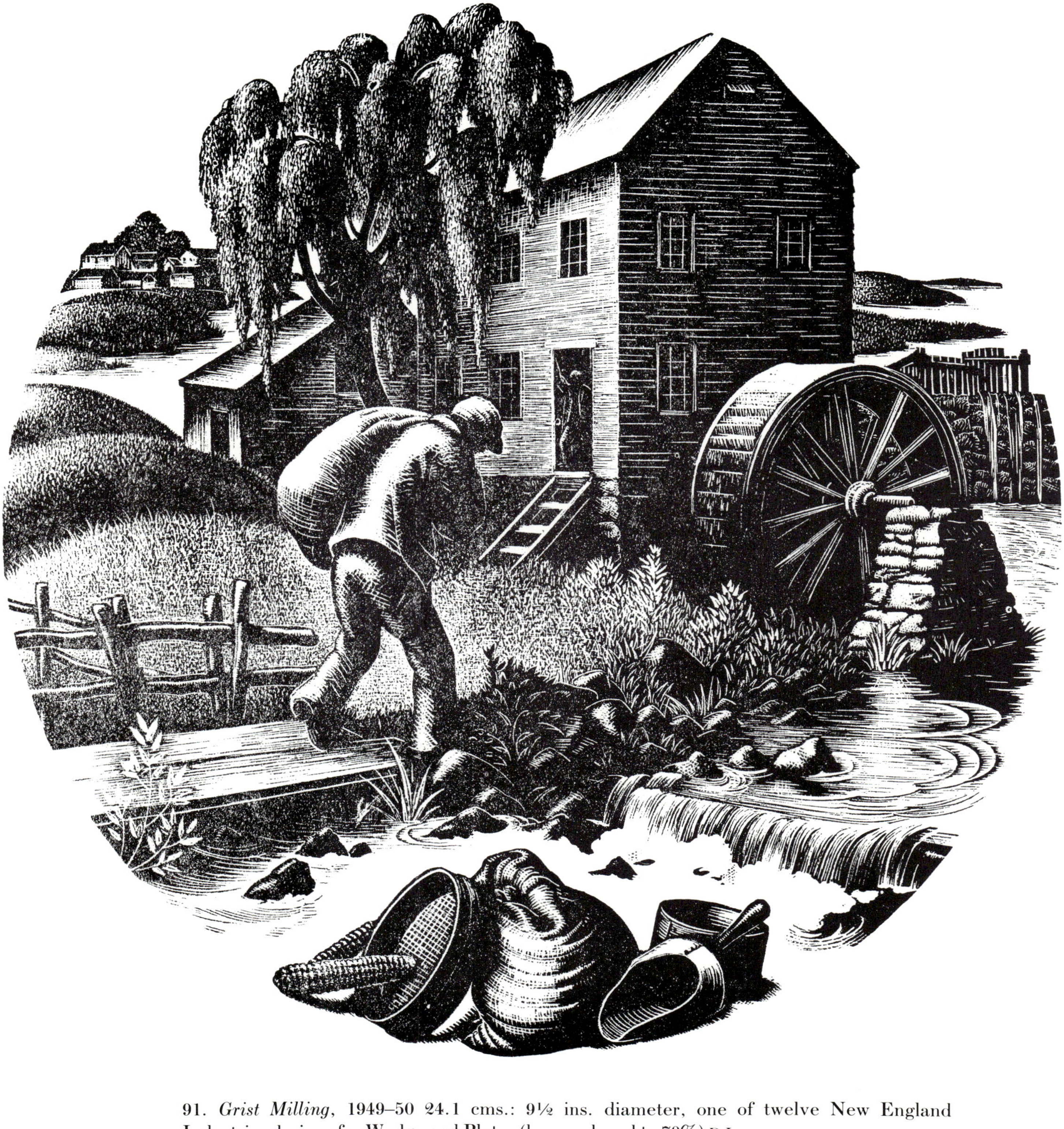

91. *Grist Milling*, 1949–50 24.1 cms.: 9½ ins. diameter, one of twelve New England Industries designs for Wedgwood Plates (here reduced to 79%) D.L.

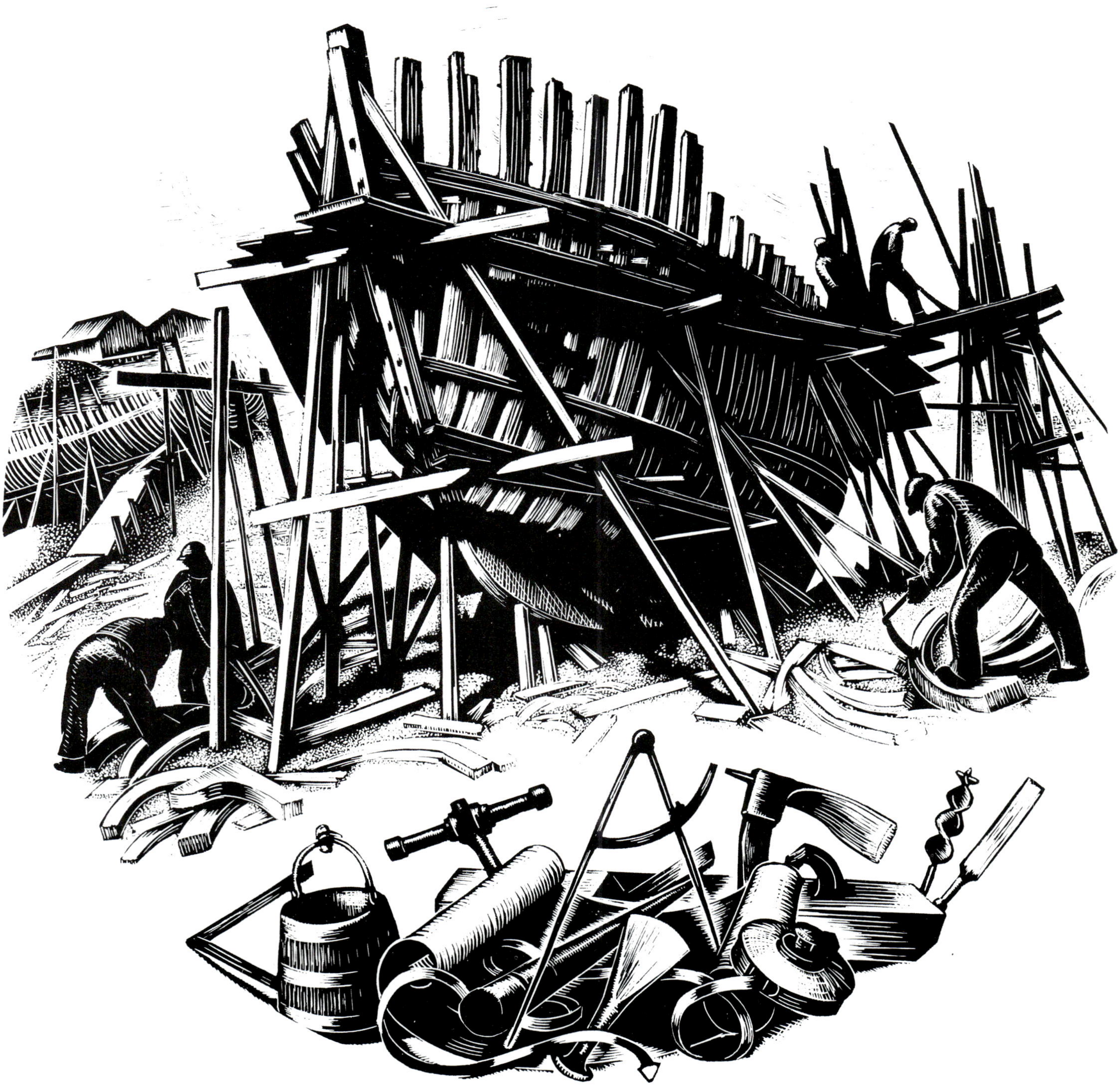

92. *Ship Building*, 1949–50 24.1 cms.: 9½ ins. diameter, one of twelve New England Industries designs for Wedgwood Plates (here reduced to 79%) D.L.

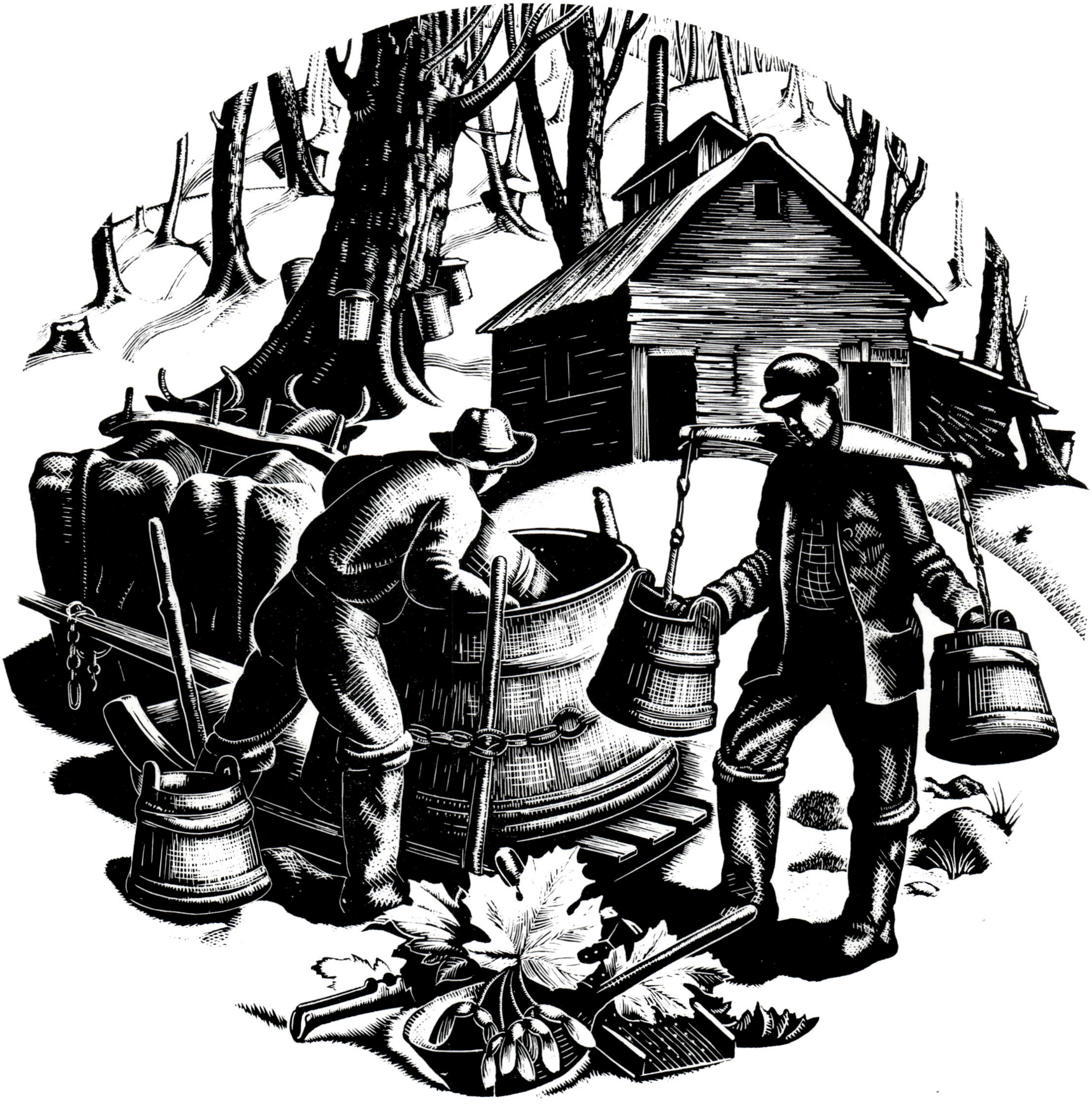

93. *Sugaring*, 1949–50 24.1 cms.: 9½ ins. diameter, one of twelve New England Industries designs for Wedgwood Plates (here reduced to 75%) D.L.

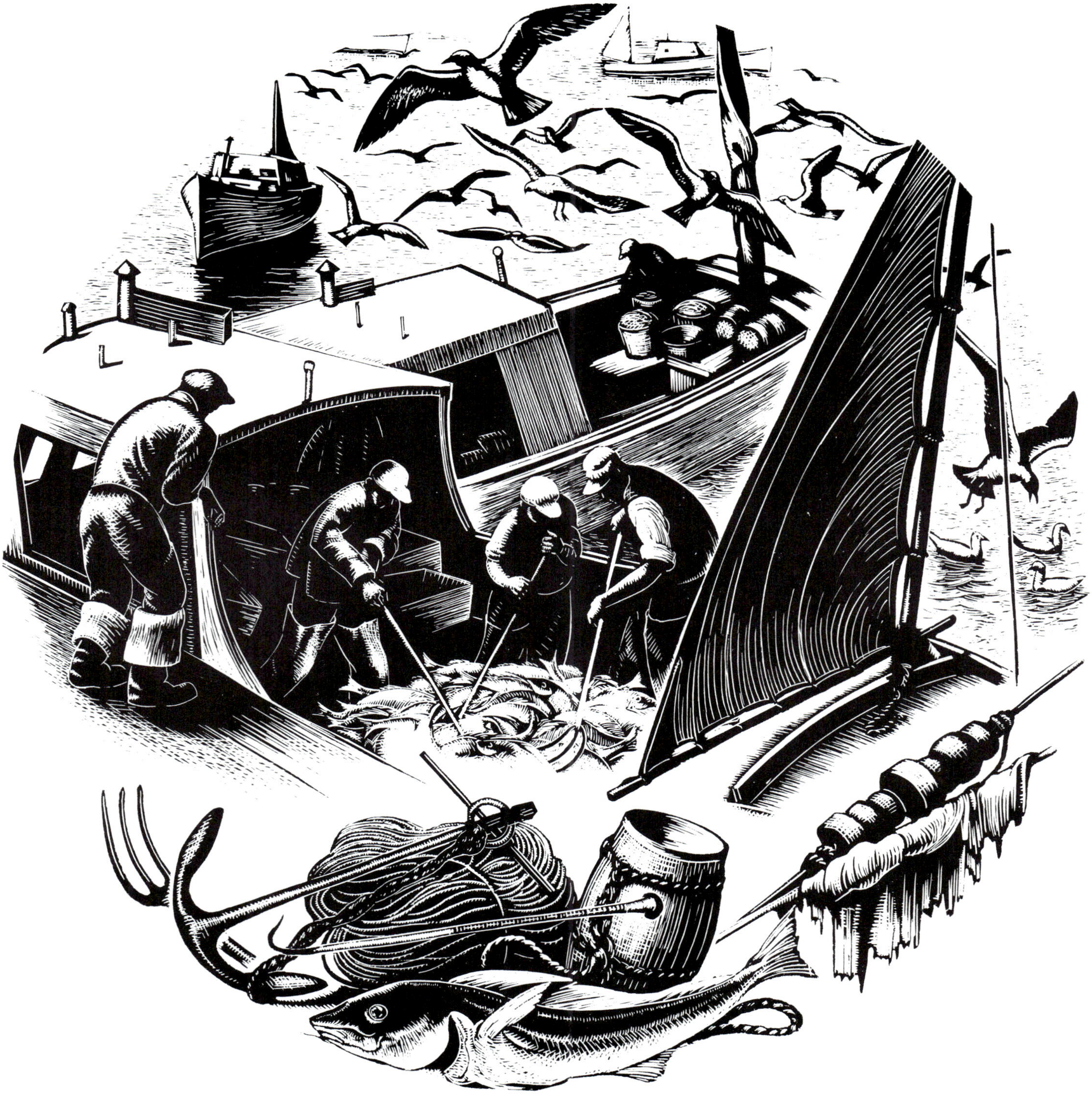

94. *Codfishing*, 1949–50 24.1 cms.: 9½ ins. diameter, one of twelve New England Industries designs for Wedgwood Plates (here reduced to 79%) D.L.

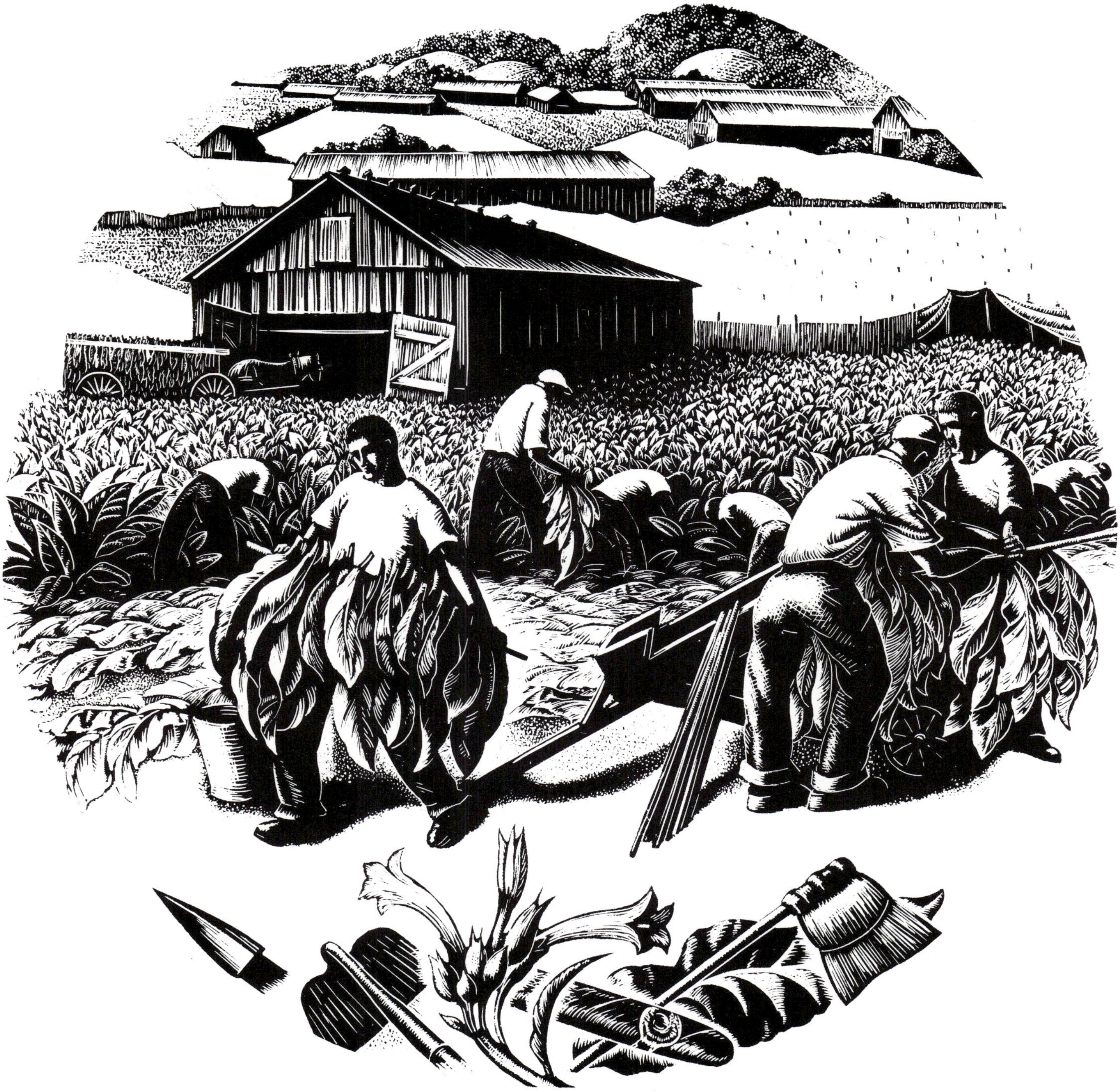

95. *Tobacco Growing*, 1949–50 24.1 cms.: 9½ ins. diameter, one of twelve New England Industries designs for Wedgwood Plates (here reduced to 79%) D.L.

96. *Cranberrying*, 1949–50 24.1 cms.: 9½ ins. diameter, Wedgwood Plate, one of twelve New England Industries designs (here reduced to 79%) D.L.

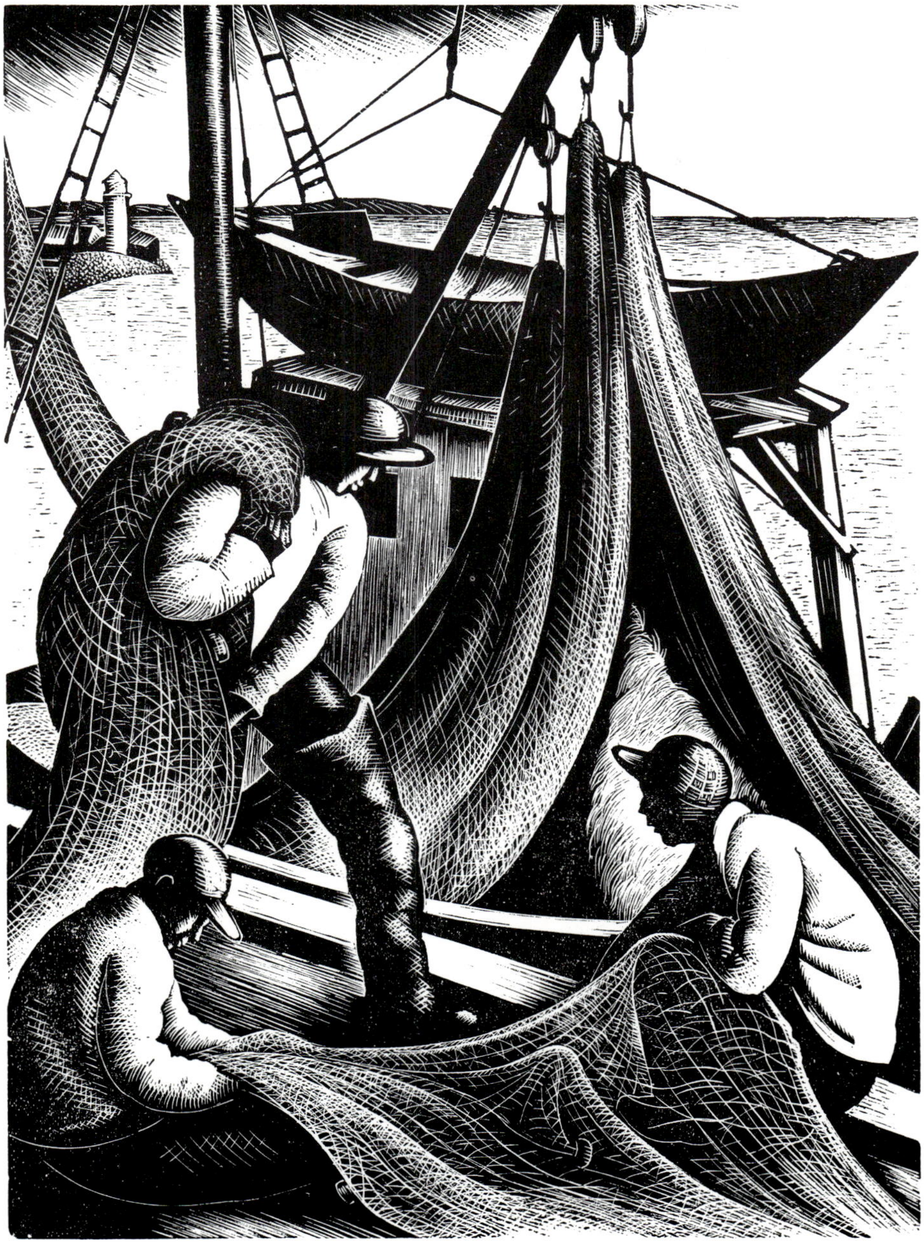

97. *Fishermen and Nets*, 1949–50 16.5 × 12.1 cms.: 6½ × 4¾ ins. commission for The Marblehead Art Association D.L.

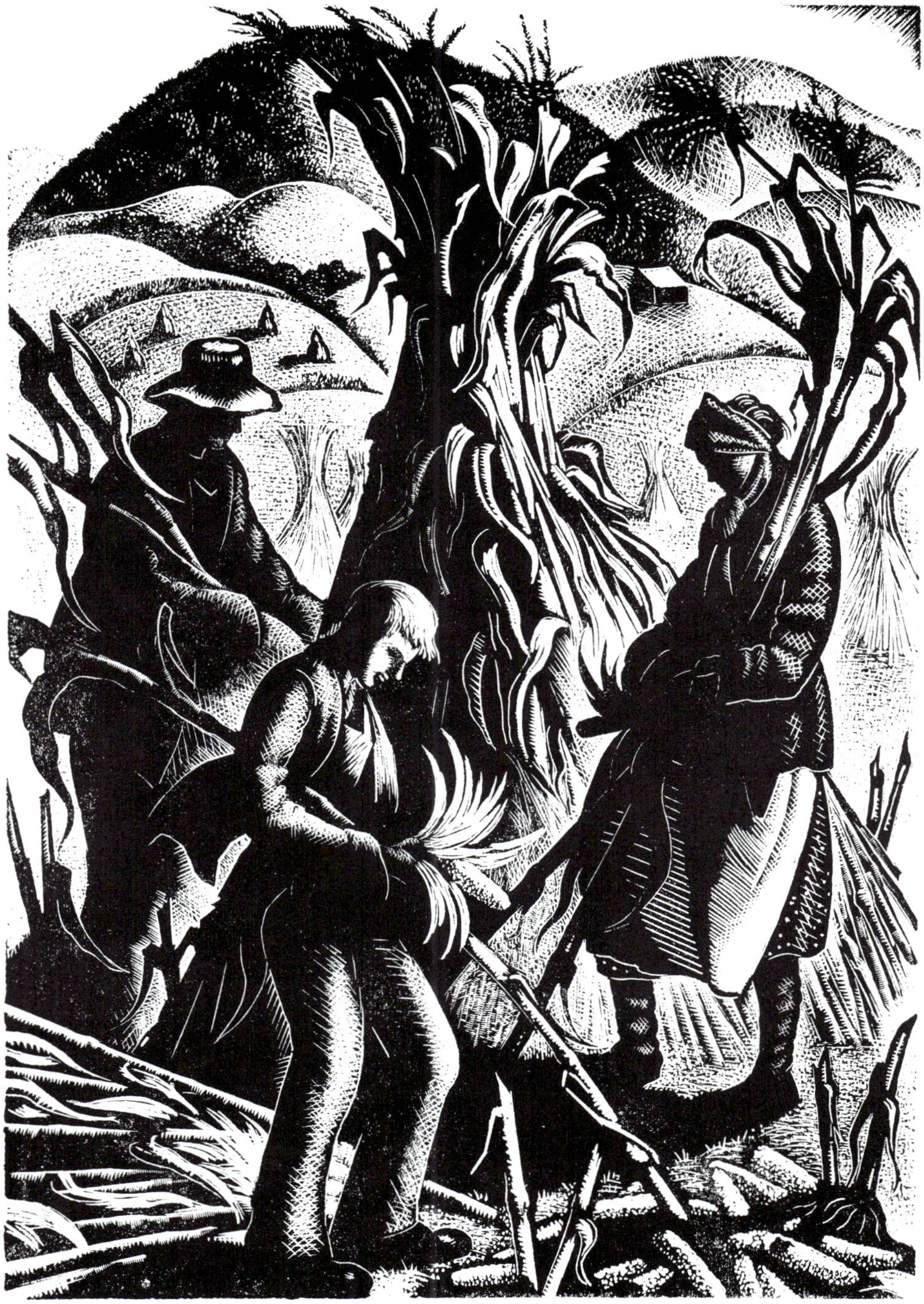

98. *Corn Shucking in the Mountains*, 1951–2 17.8 × 12.5 cms.: 7 × 4 15/16 ins. Vol. 1, p. 126 in *North Carolina Folklore*, Durham, N.C., Duke University Press, 1951 (7 Vols.) D.L.

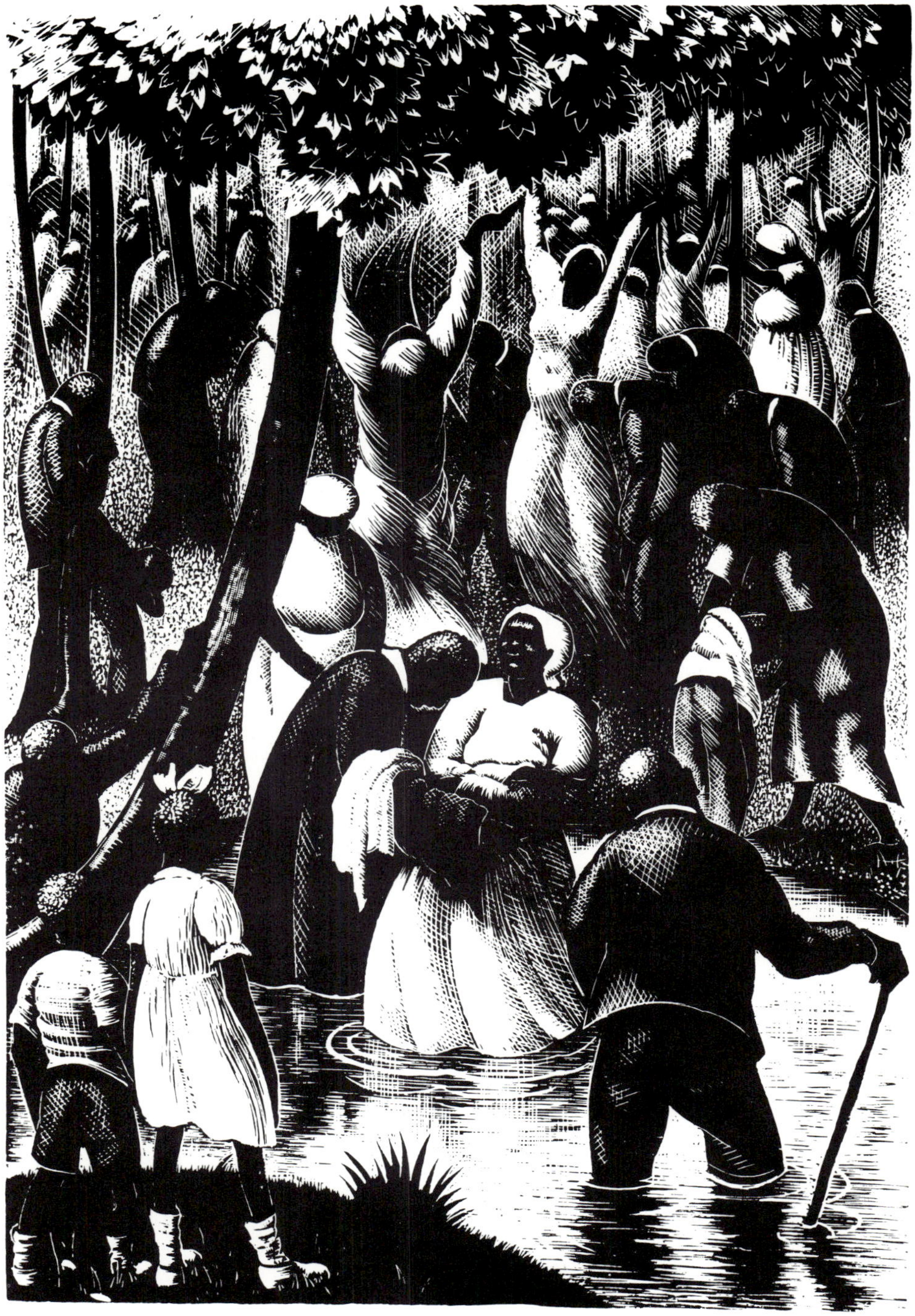

99. *The Baptizing*, 1951–2. 17.9 × 12.4 cms.: 7$\frac{1}{16}$ × 4$\frac{7}{8}$ ins. Vol. 1, p. 226 in *North Carolina Folklore*, Durham, N.C.: Duke University Press, 1951 (7 Vols.)

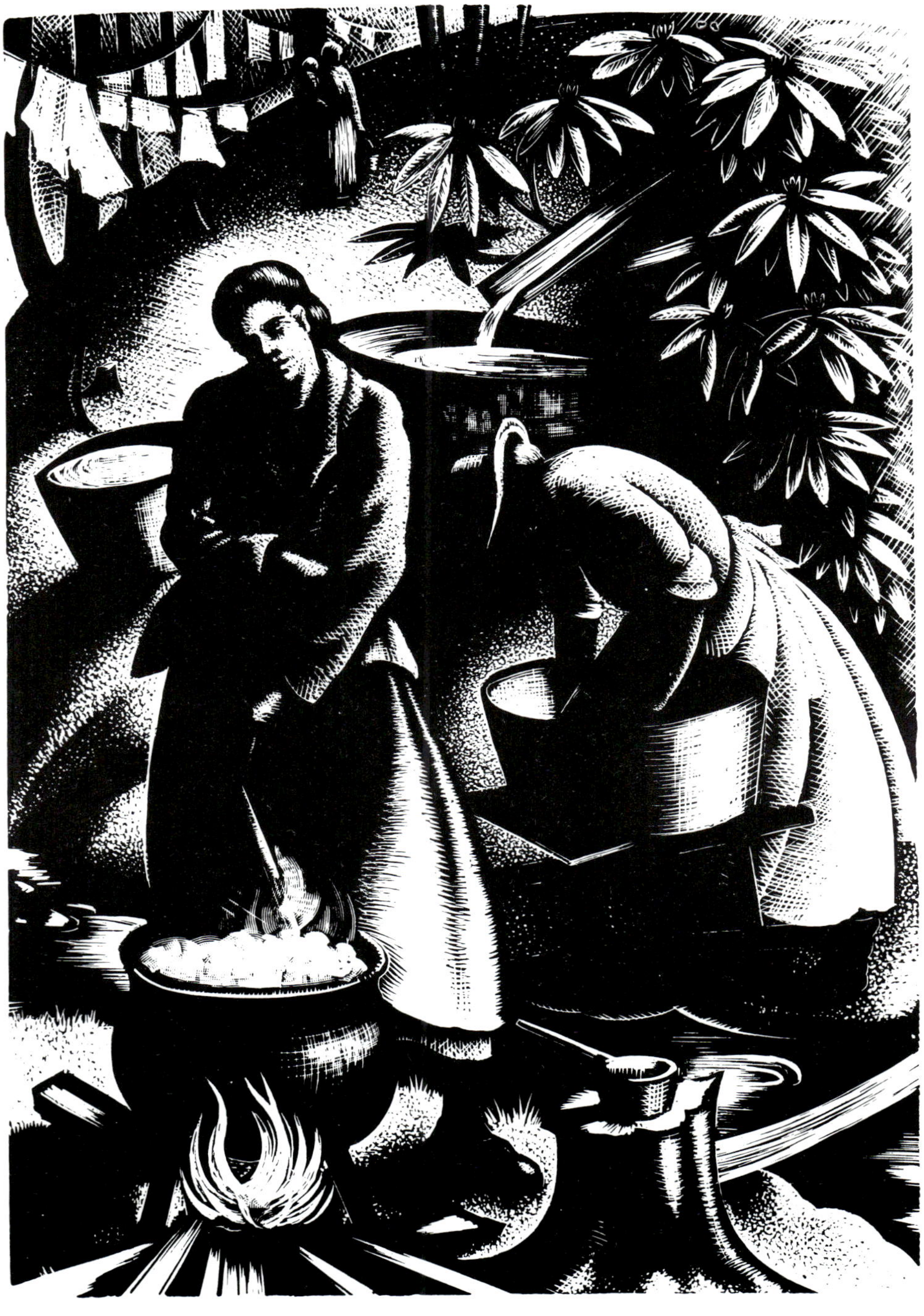

100. *Washing Clothes*, 1951–2. 17.8 × 12.5 cms.: 7 × 4¹⁵⁄₁₆ ins. Vol. 1, p. 456 in *North Carolina Folklore*, Durham, N.C.: Duke University Press, 1952 (7 Vols.) A.M.

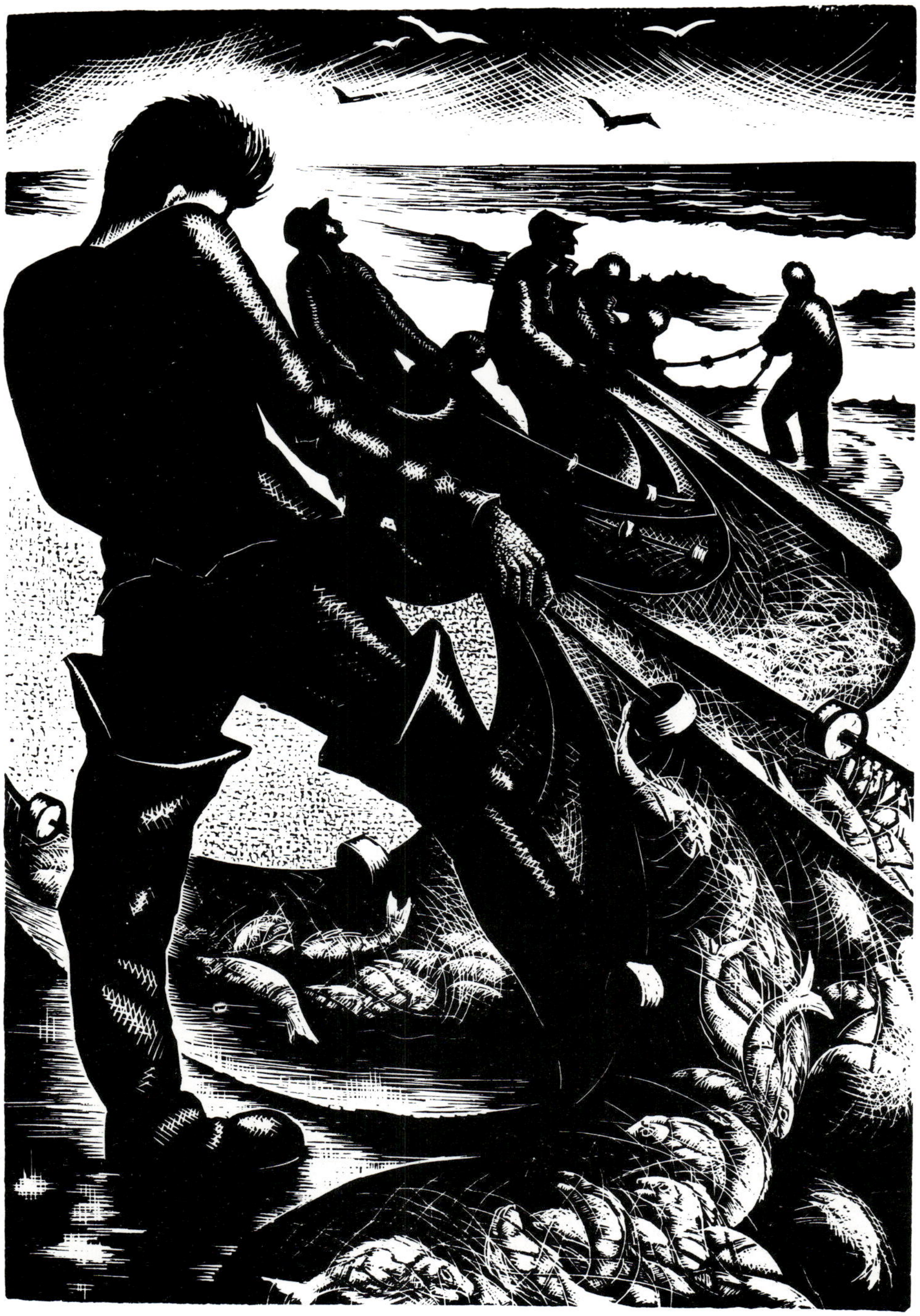

101. *Dragging Nets*, 1951–2 17.9 × 12.4 cms.: 7¹⁄₁₆ × 4⅞ ins. Vol. 1, p. 632 in *North Carolina Folklore*, Durham, N.C.: Duke University Press, 1952 (7 Vols.) A.M.

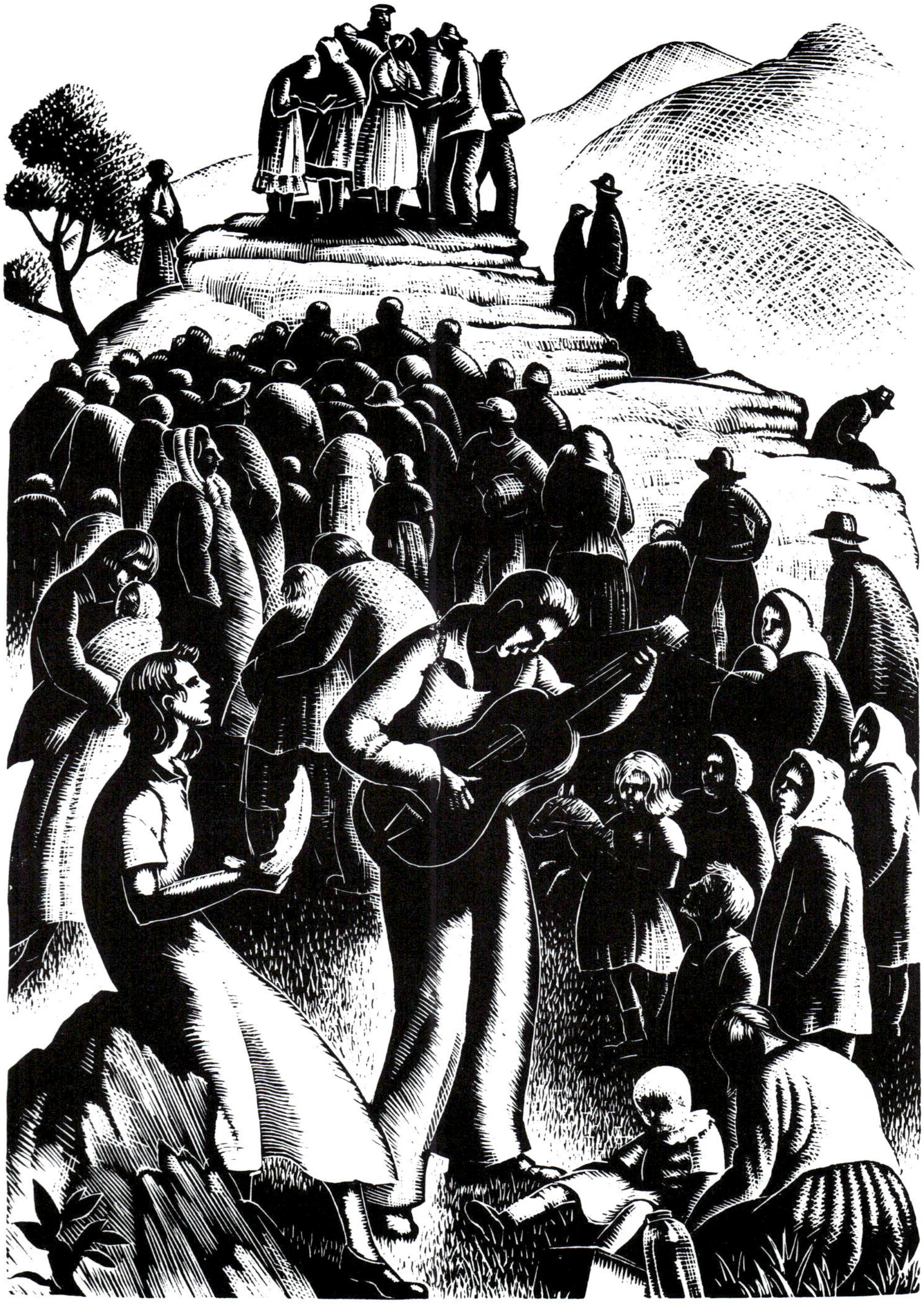

102. *All Day Singing*, 1951–2 17.6 × 12.4 cms.: 6$^{15}/_{16}$ × 4$^{7}/_{8}$ ins. Vol. II Frontispiece, repeated as Vol. IV frontispiece in *North Carolina Folklore*, Durham, N.C.: Duke University Press, 1952 (7 Vols.) A.M.

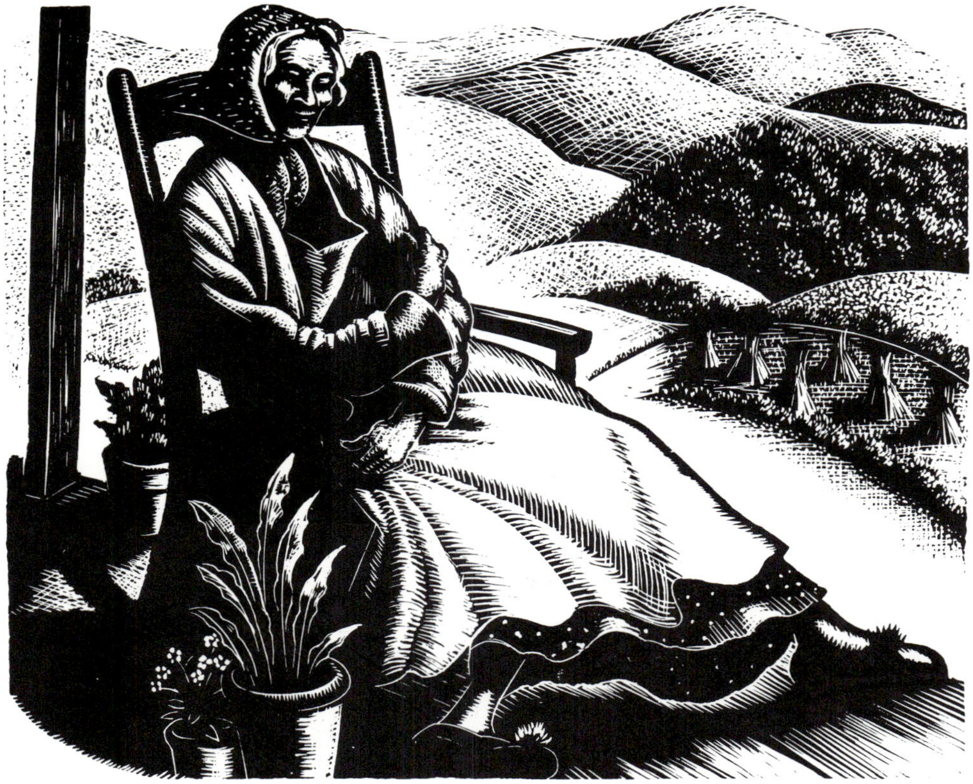

103a. *Centenarian*, 1951–2 10.3 × 12.7 cms.: 4¹⁄₁₆ × 5 ins. Vol. II, p. 142 in *North Carolina Folklore*, Durham, N.C.: Duke University Press, 1952 (7 Vols.) D.L.

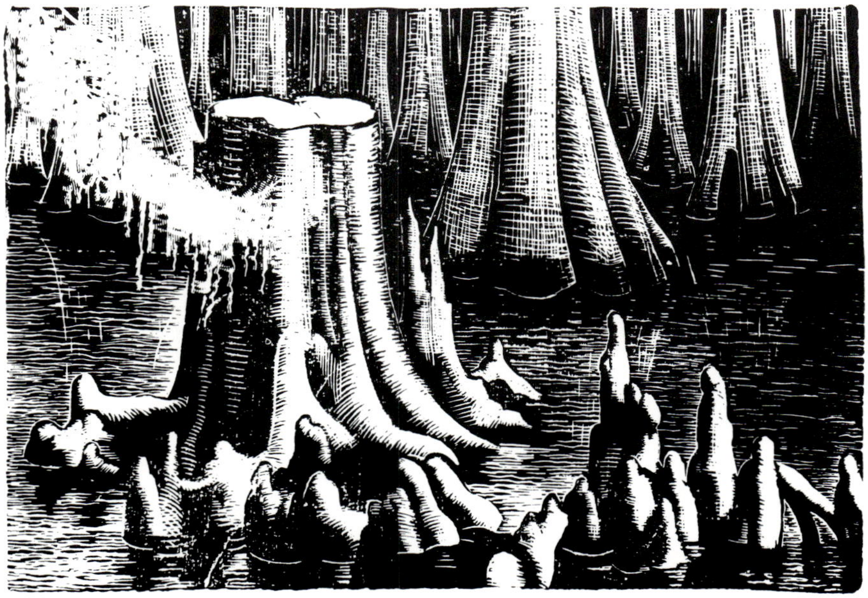

103b. *Cypress Knees*, 1951–2 7.6 × 11.3 cms.: 3 × 4⁷⁄₁₆ ins. Vol. III, p. 409 in *North Carolina Folklore*, Durham, N.C.: Duke University Press, 1952 (7 Vols.) A.M.

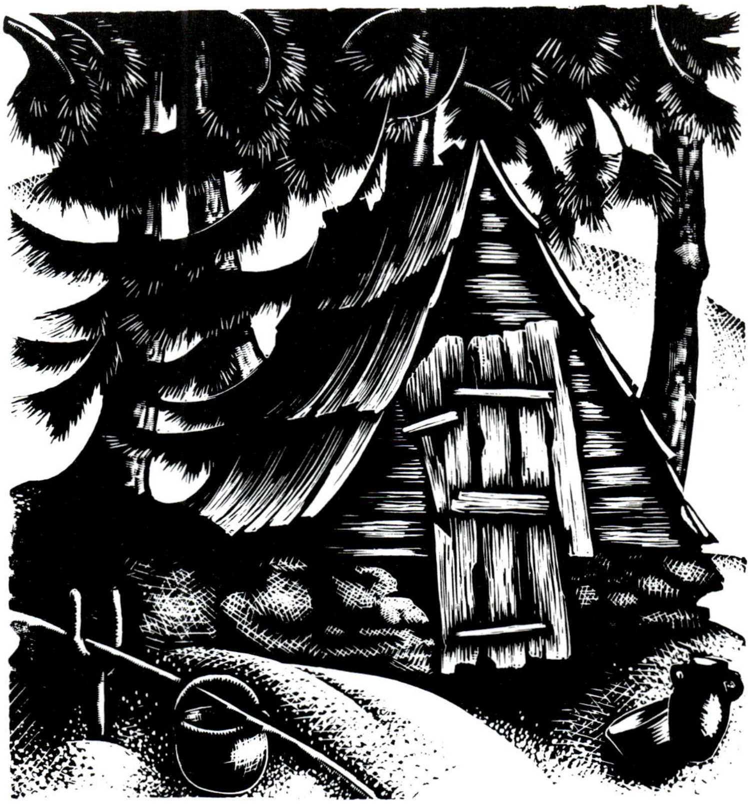

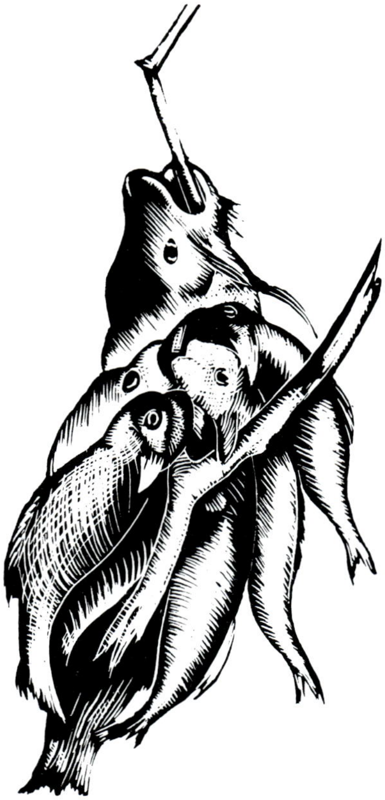

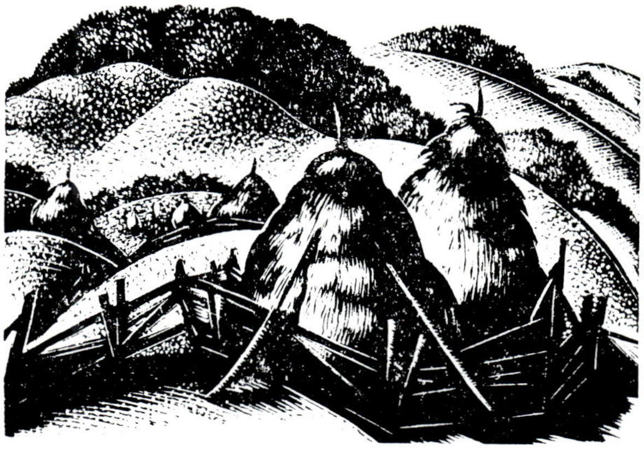

104a. *Spring House*, 1951–2 10.5 × 9.8 cms.: 4⅛ × 3⅞ ins. Vol. II, p. 310 in *North Carolina Folklore*, Durham, N.C.: Duke University Press, 1952 (7 Vols.) A.M.

104b. *Fish Caught*, 1951–2 10.5 × 5.1 cms.: 4⅛ × 2 ins. Vol. I, p. 354 in *North Carolina Folklore*, Durham, N.C.: Duke University Press, 1952 (7 Vols.) A.M.

104c. *Mountain Haystacks*, 1951–2 5.1 × 7.6 cms.: 2 × 3 ins. Vol. V, p. 366 in *North Carolina Folklore*, Durham, N.C.: Duke University Press, 1952 (7 Vols.) A.M.

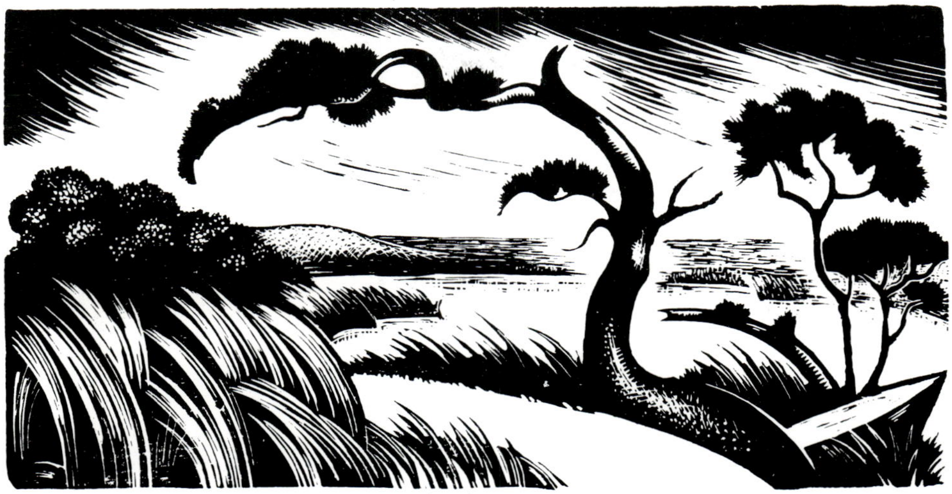

105a. *Wind and Pine*, 1951–2 6.4 × 12.4 cms.: 2½ × 4⅞ ins. Vol. II, p. 432 in *North Carolina Folklore*, Durham, N.C.: Duke University Press, 1952 (7 Vols.) A.M.

105b. *Mountain Girl*, 1951–2 12.4 × 7.9 cms.: 4⅞ × 3⅛ ins. Vol. VI, p. 166 in *North Carolina Folklore*, Durham, N.C.: Duke University Press, 1952 (7 Vols.) A.M.

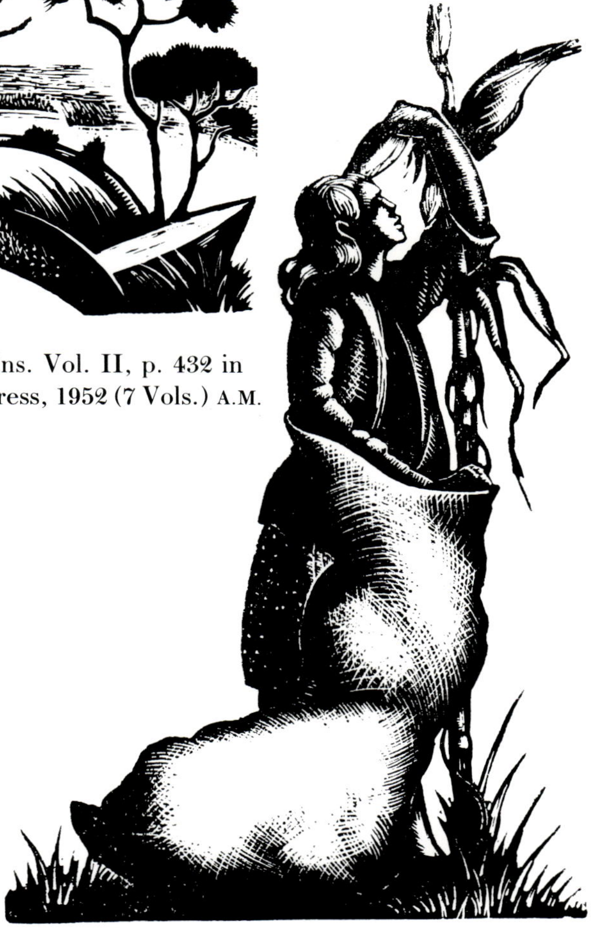

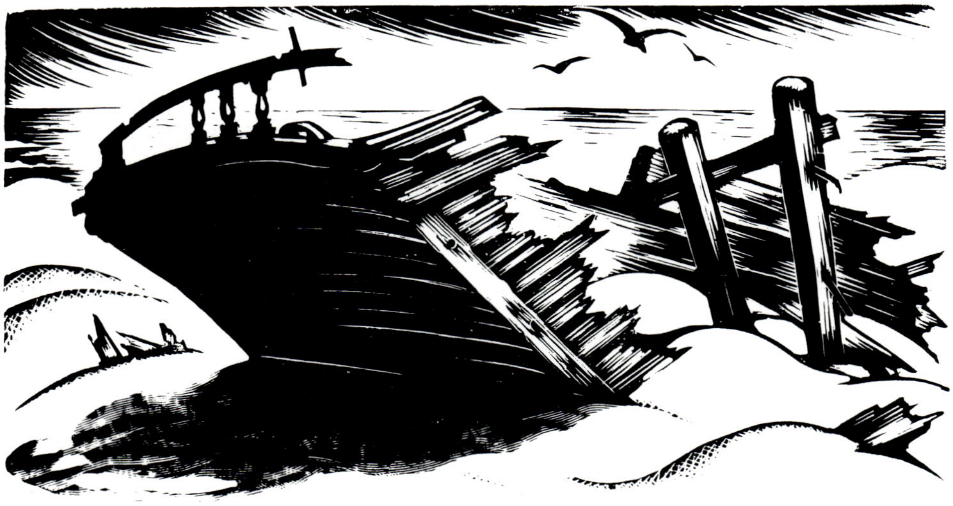

105c. *Hatteras Wreck*, 1951–2 6.5 × 12.5 cms.: 2⁹⁄₁₆ × 4¹⁵⁄₁₆ ins. Vol. II, p. 660 in *North Carolina Folklore*, Durham, N.C.: Duke University Press, 1952 (7 Vols.) A.M.

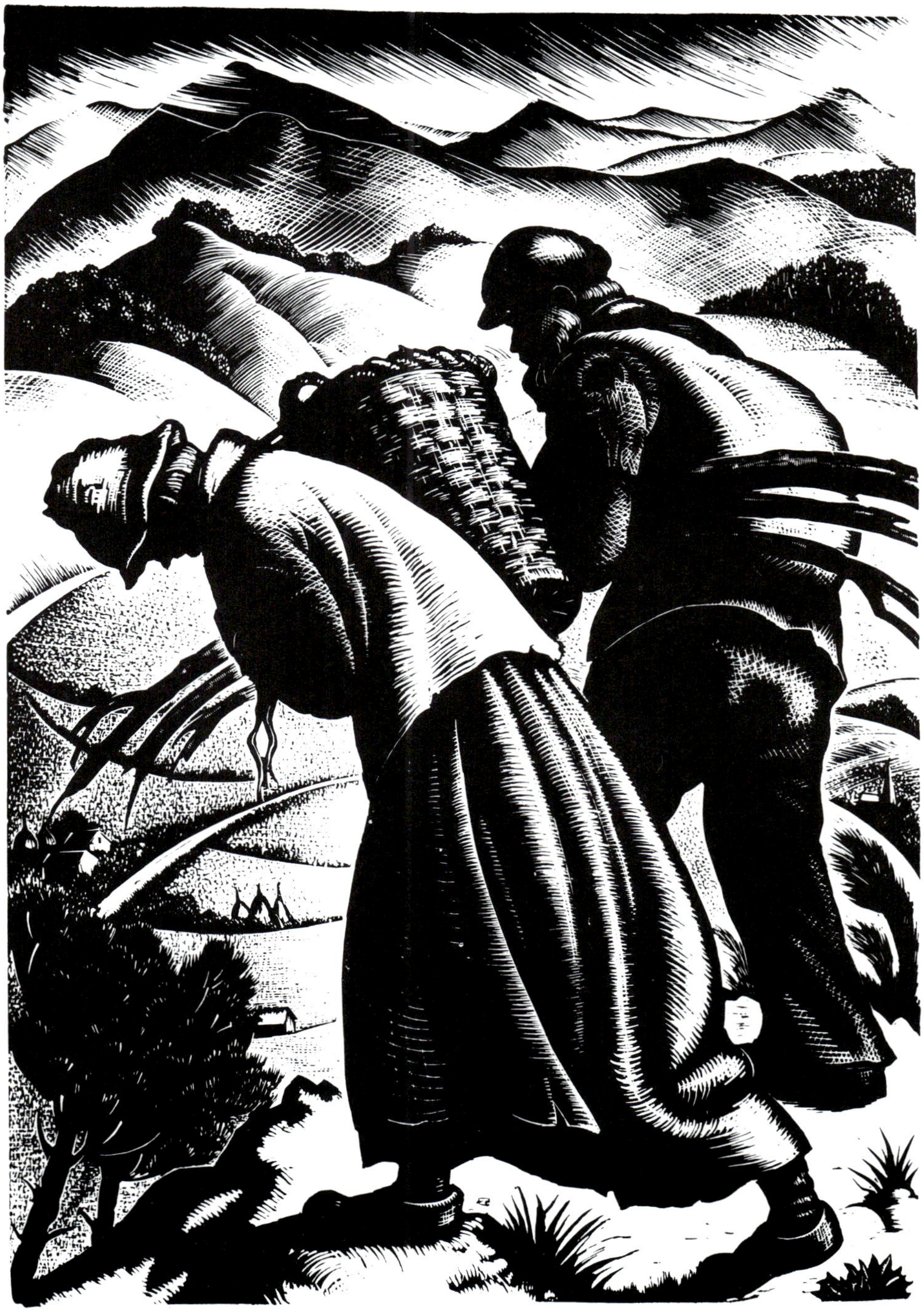

106. *Herb Gatherers*, 1951–2 17.8 × 12.7 cms.: 7 × 5 ins. Vol. III, frontispiece in *North Carolina Folklore*, Durham, N.C.: Duke University Press, 1952 (7 Vols.) A.M.

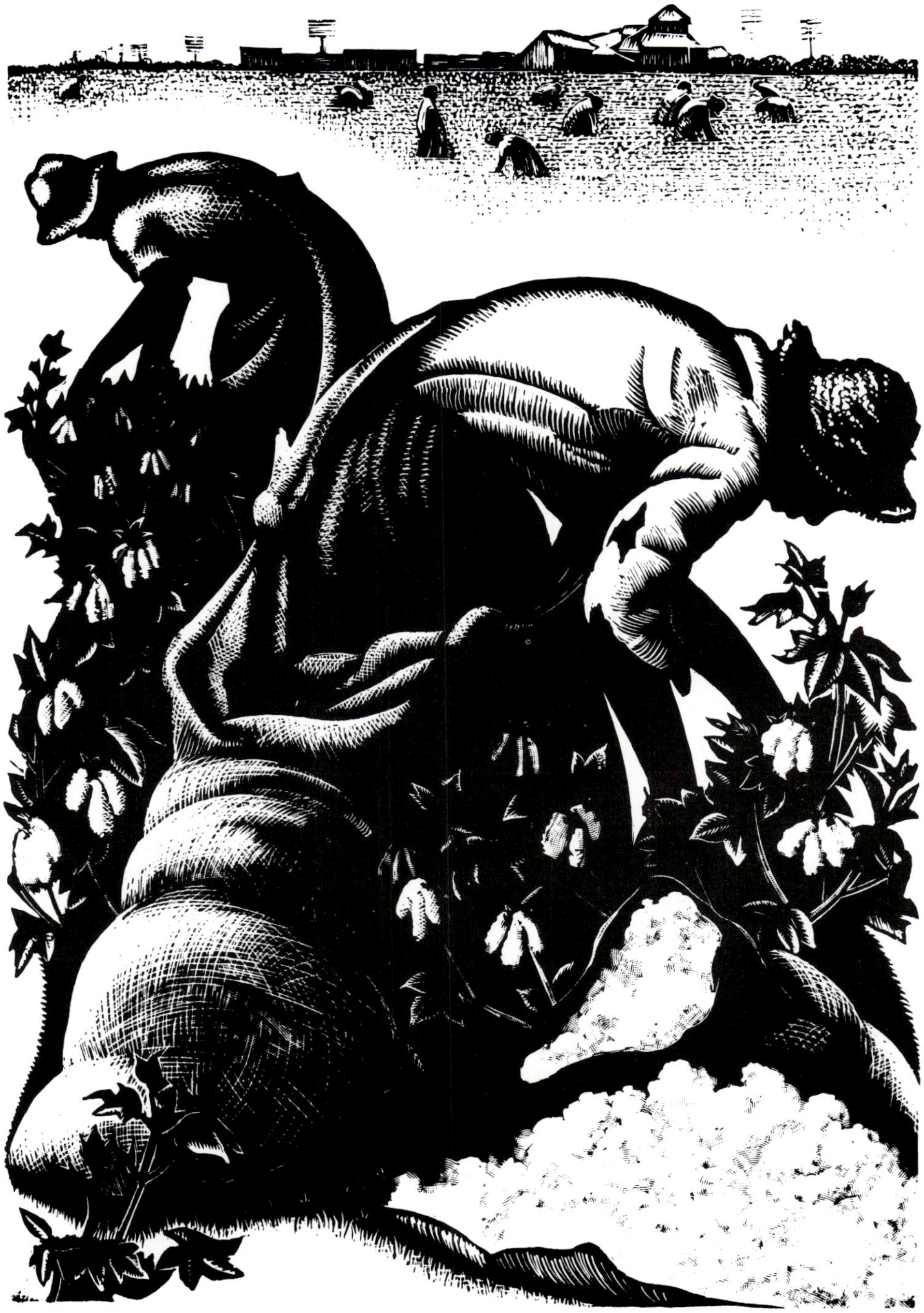

107. *Cotton Pickers*, 1951–2 17.8 × 12.5 cms.: 7 × 4 15/16 ins. Vol. III, p. 224 in *North Carolina Folklore*, Durham, N.C.: Duke University Press, 1952 (7 Vols.) A.M.

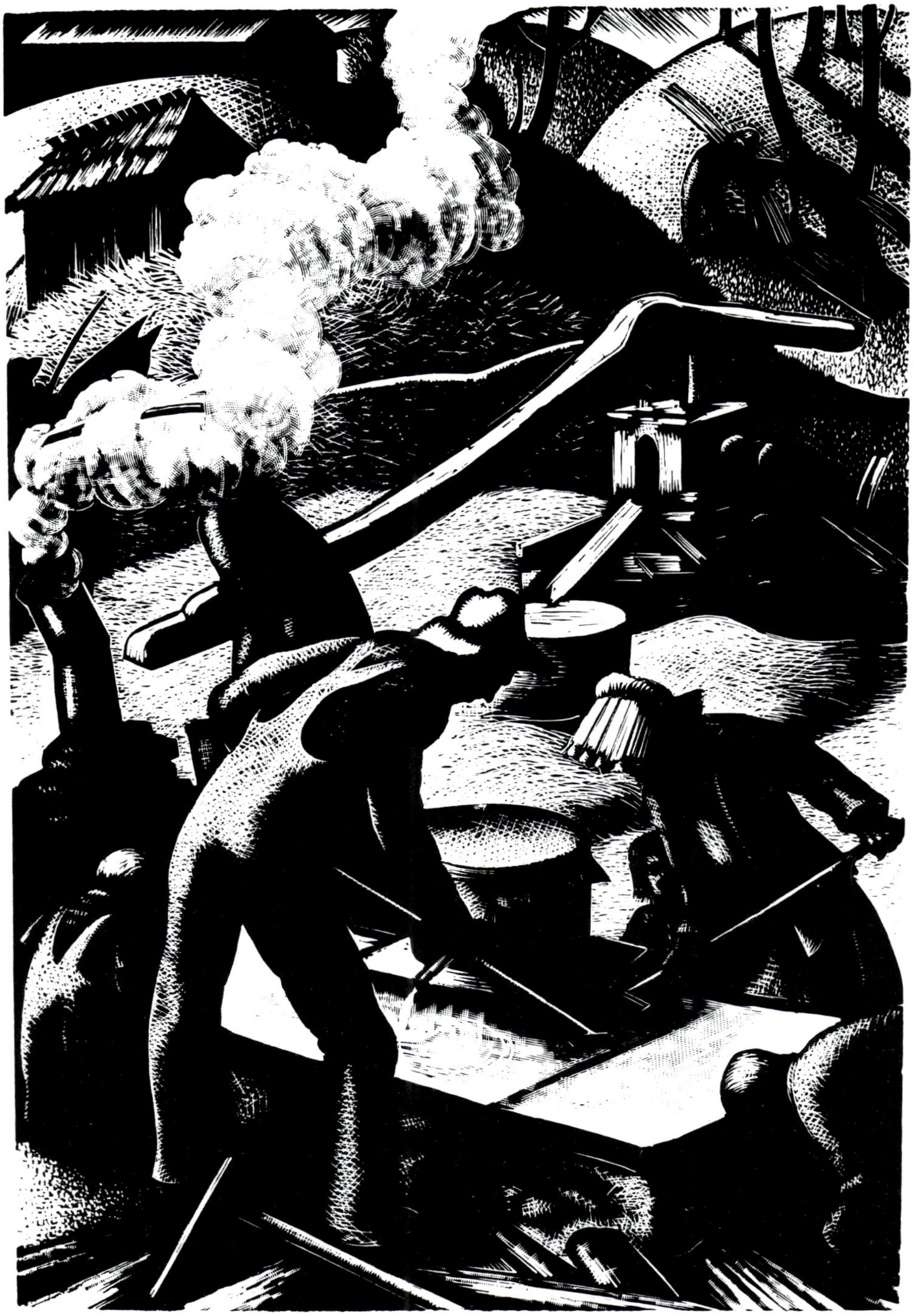

108. *Sorghum Boiling*, 1951–2 17.8 × 12.5 cms.: 7 × 4 15/16 ins. Vol. III, p. 460 in *North Carolina Folklore*, Durham, N.C.: Duke University Press, 1952 (7 Vols.) A.M.

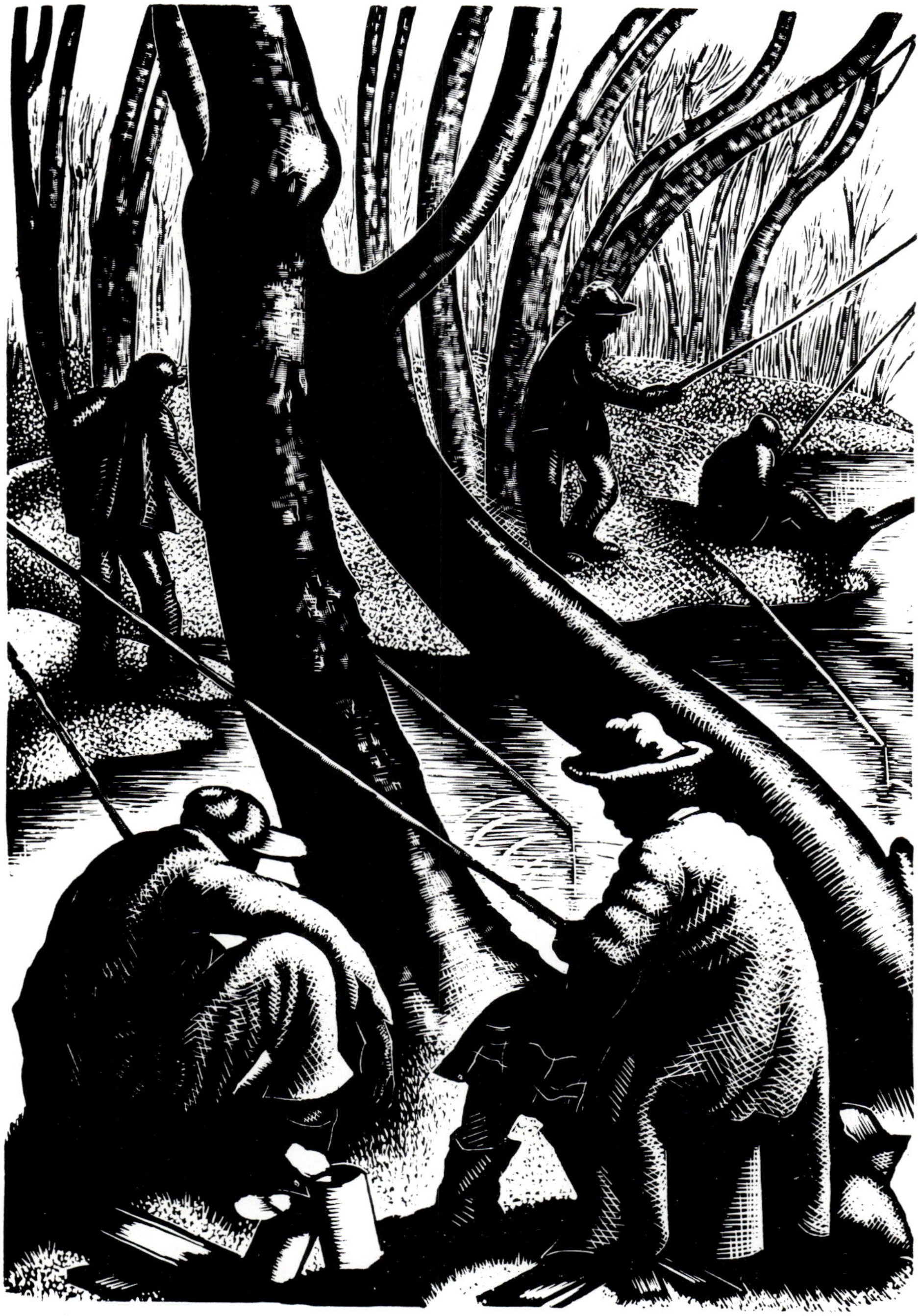

109. *Fishing in the Creek*, 1951–2 17.8 × 12.4 cms.: 7 × 4⅞ ins. Vol. III, p. 600 in *North Carolina Folklore*, Durham, N.C.: Duke University Press, 1952 (7 Vols.) A.M.

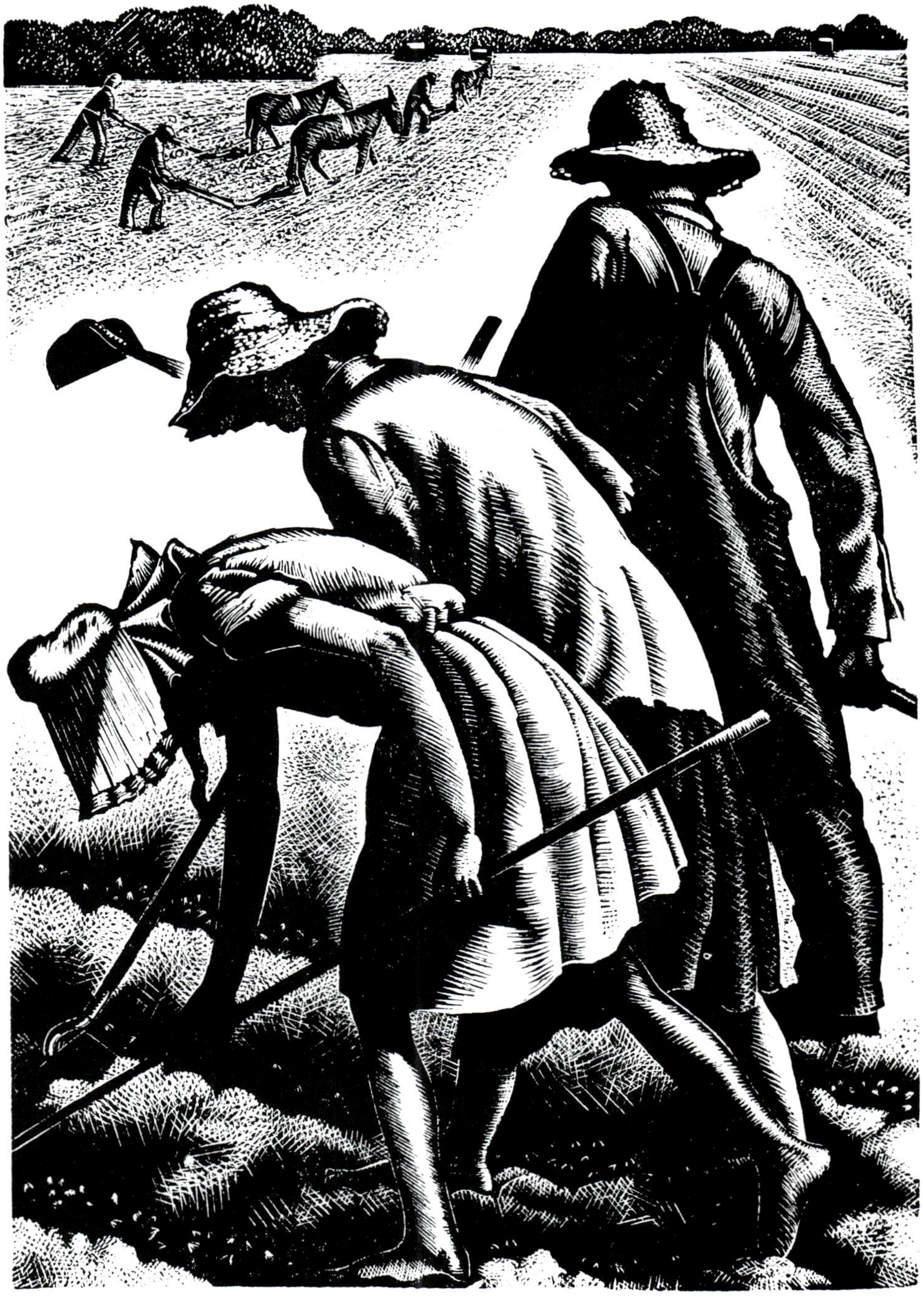

110. *Cotton Choppers*, 1951–2 17.6 × 12.4 cms.: 6 15/16 × 4 7/8 ins. Vol. V, frontispiece in *North Carolina Folklore*, Durham, N.C.: Duke University Press, 1952 (7 Vols.) A.M.

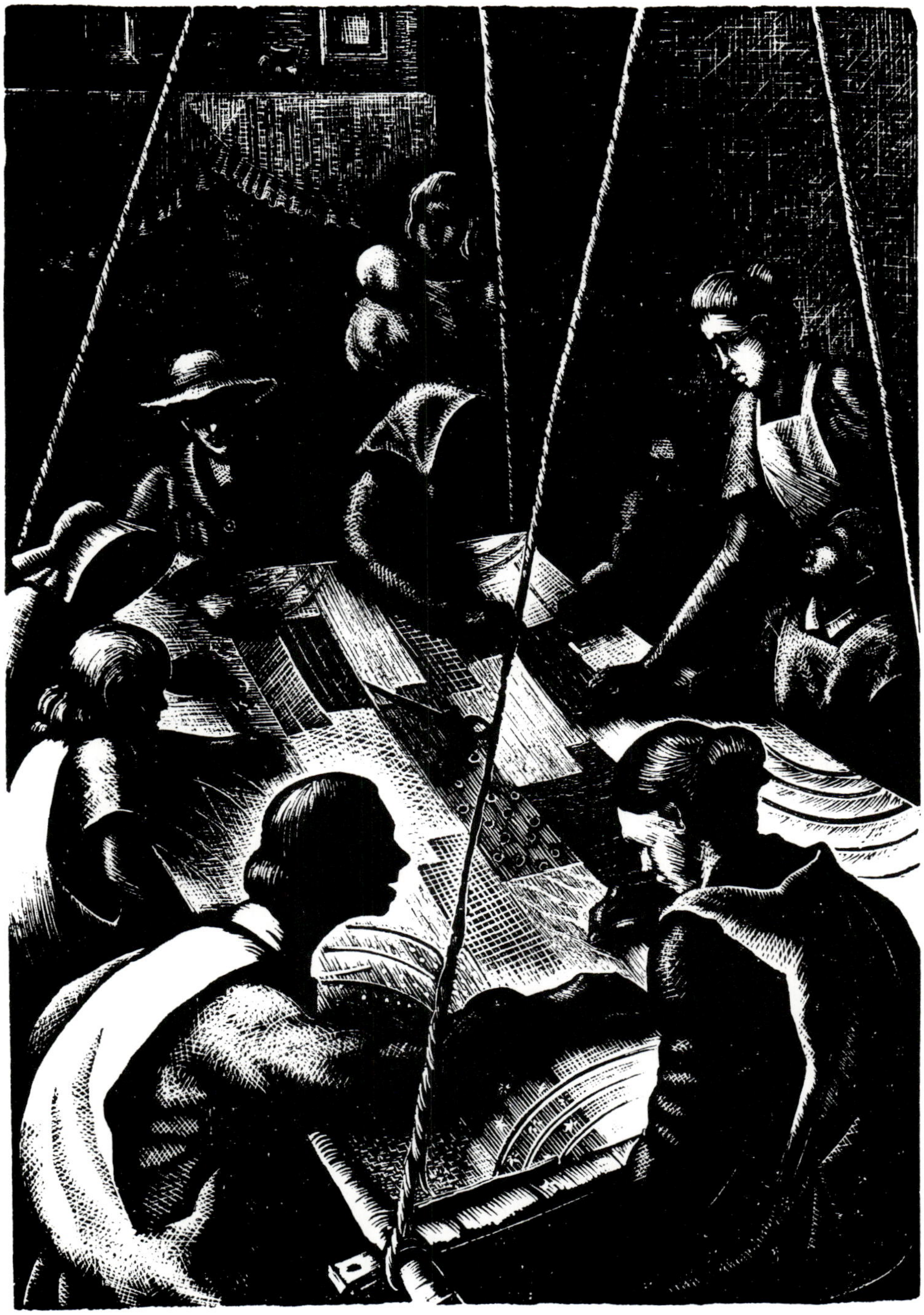

111. *Quilting Party*, 1951–2 17.8 × 12.5 cms.: 7 × 4$^{15}/_{16}$ ins. Vol. VI, frontispiece in *North Carolina Folklore*, Durham, N.C.: Duke University Press, 1952 (7 Vols.) A.M.

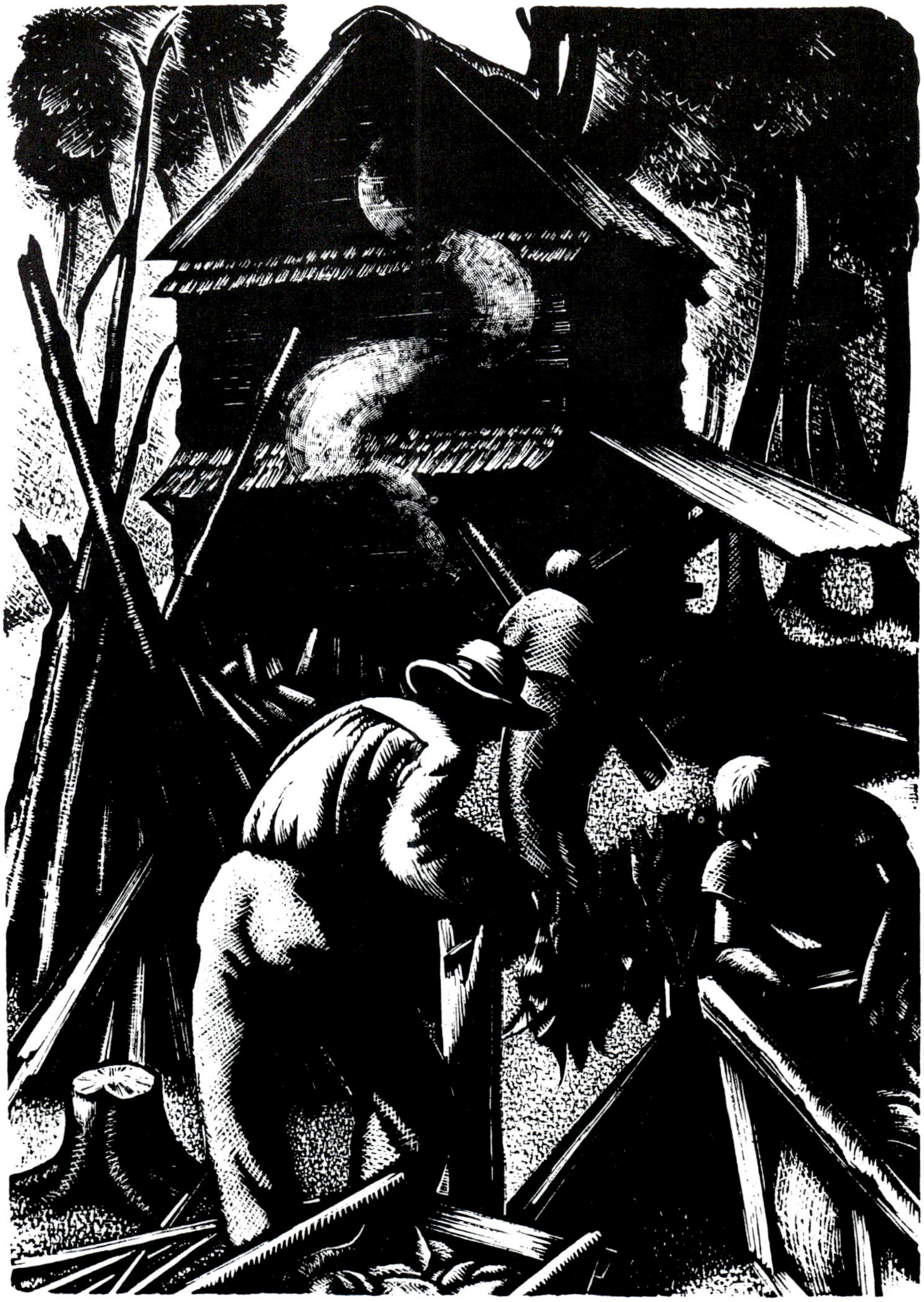

112. *Flue-curing Barn*, 1951–2 17.8 × 12.5 cms.: 7 × 4 15/16 ins. Vol. VI, p. 498 in *North Carolina Folklore*, Durham, N.C.: Duke University Press, 1952 (7 Vols.) A.M.

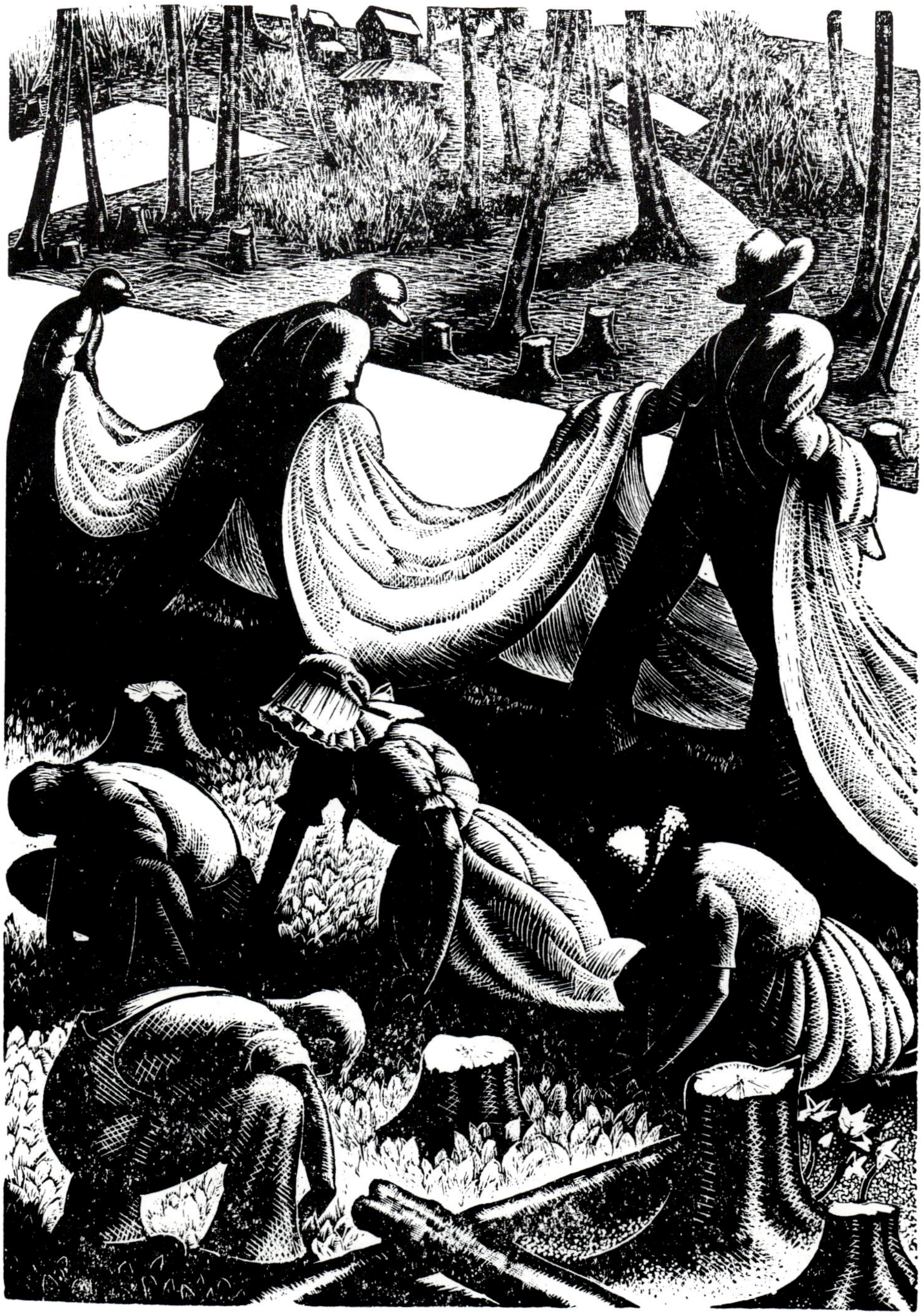

113. *Weeding the Tobacco Seed Bed*, 1951–2 17.9 × 12.5 cms.: 7¹⁄₁₆ × 4¹⁵⁄₁₆ ins. Vol. V, p. 152 in *North Carolina Folklore*, Durham, N.C.: Duke University Press, 1952 (7 Vols.) A.M.

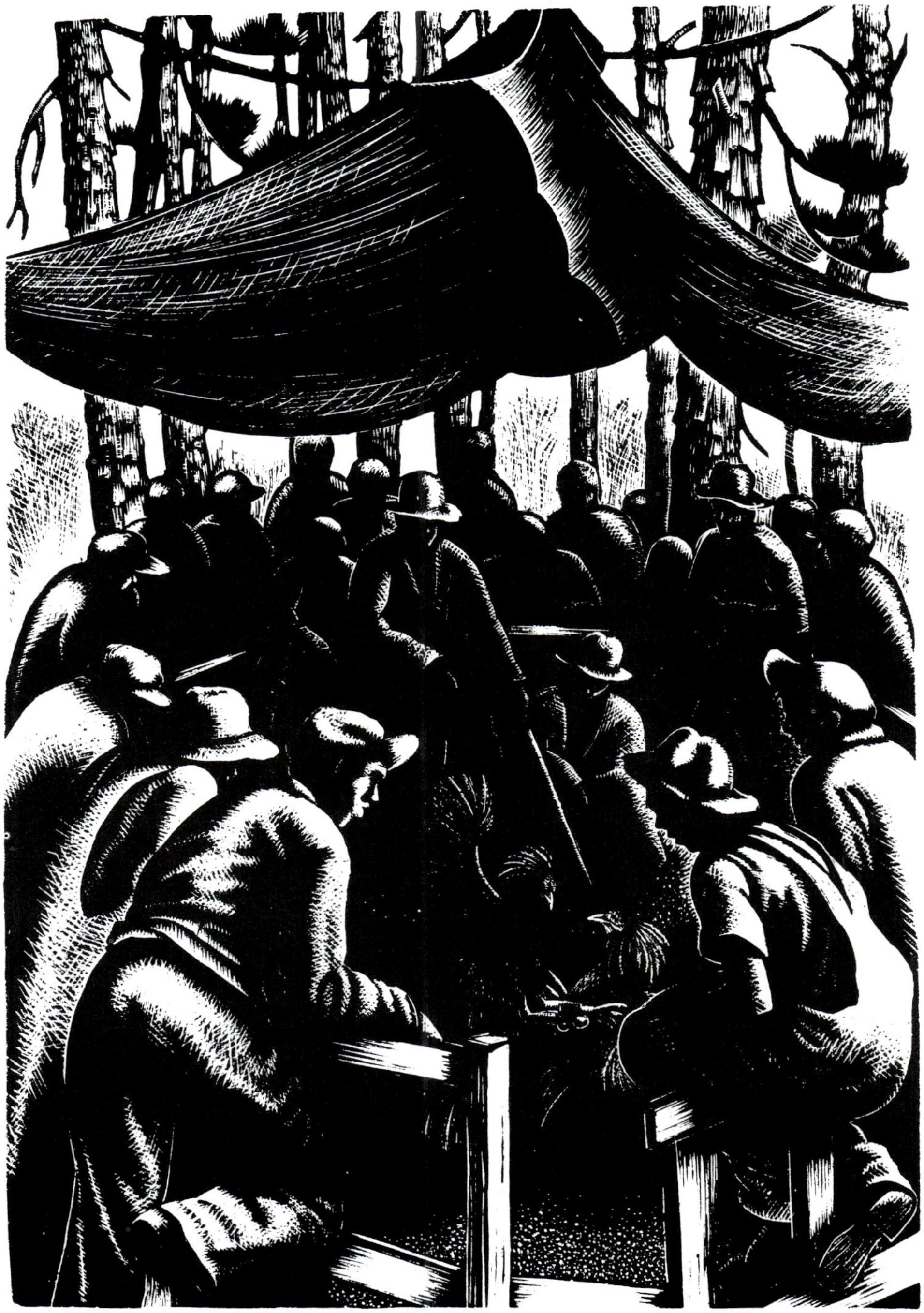

114. *Cock Fight*, 1951–2 17.8 × 12.4 cms.: 7 × 4⅞ ins. Vol. VII, p. 486 in *North Carolina Folklore*, Durham, N.C.: Duke University Press, 1952 (7 Vols.) A.M.

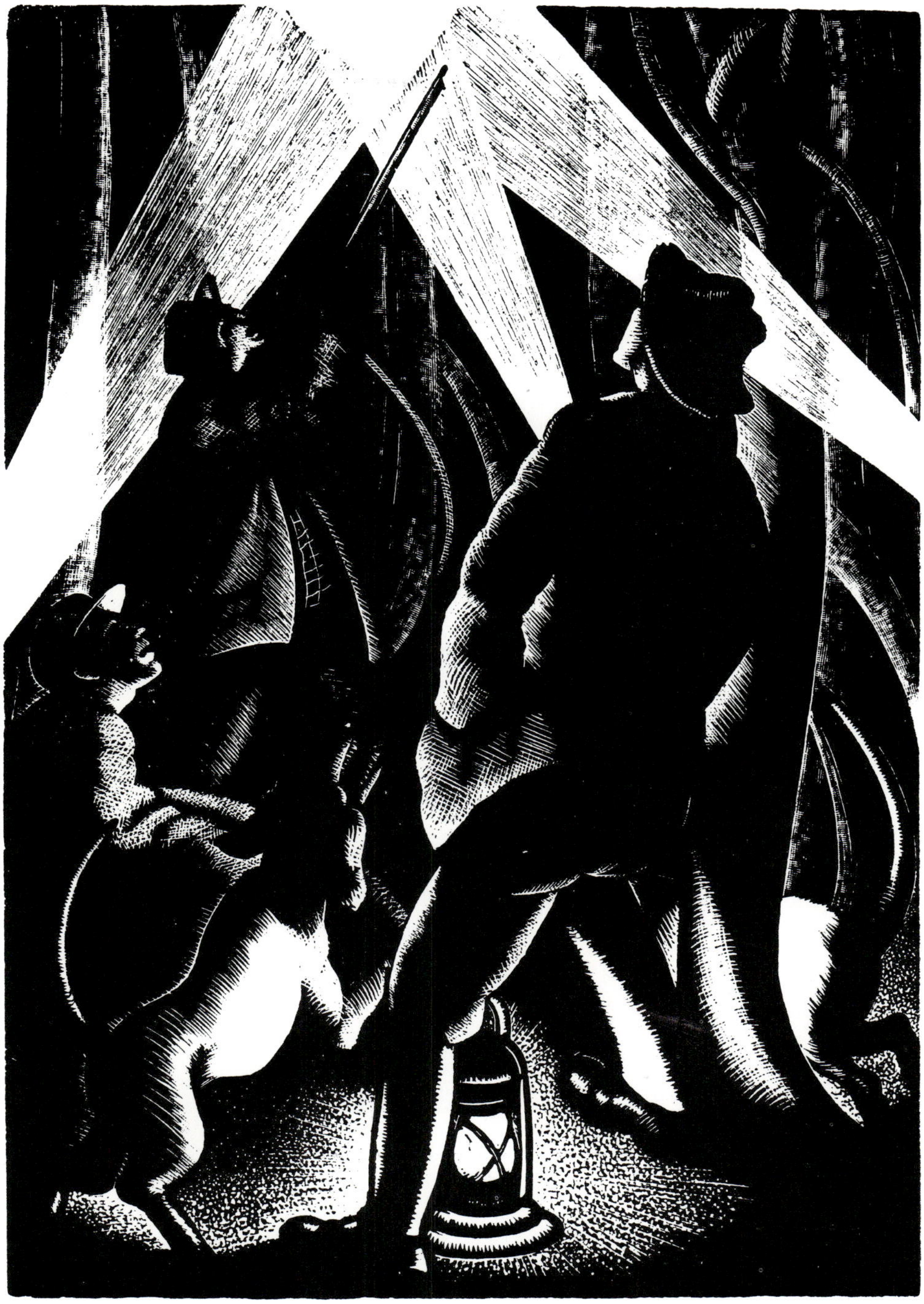

115. *The Coon Hunt*, 1951–2 17.8 × 12.5 cms.: 7 × 4 15/16 ins. Vol. VII, frontispiece in *North Carolina Folklore*, Durham, N.C.: Duke University Press, 1952 (7 Vols.) A.M.

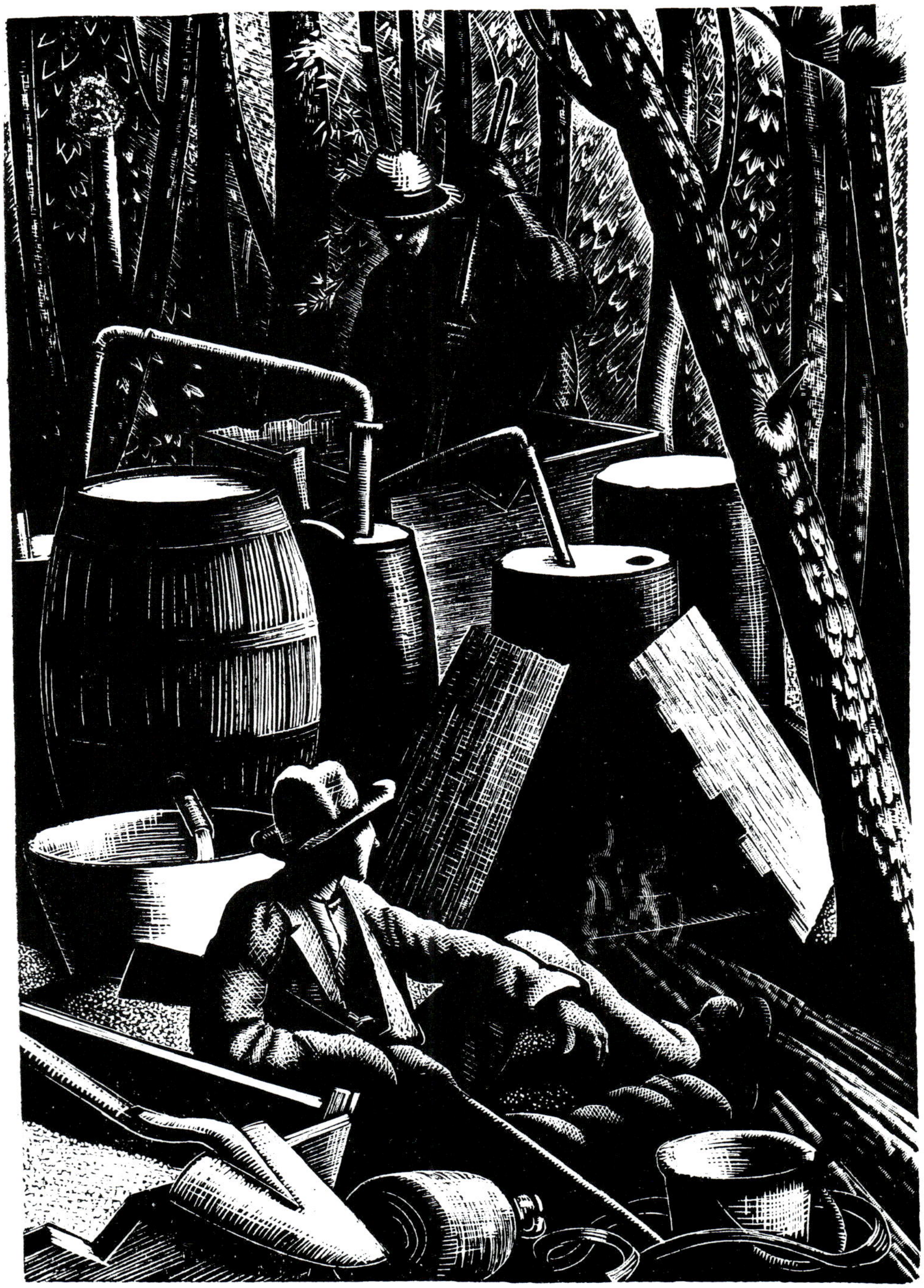

116. *Moonshine*, 1951–2 18.1 × 11.6 cms.: 7⅛ × 4⁹⁄₁₆ ins. Vol. VII, p. 190 in *North Carolina Folklore*, Durham, N.C.: Duke University Press, 1952 (7 Vols.) A.M.

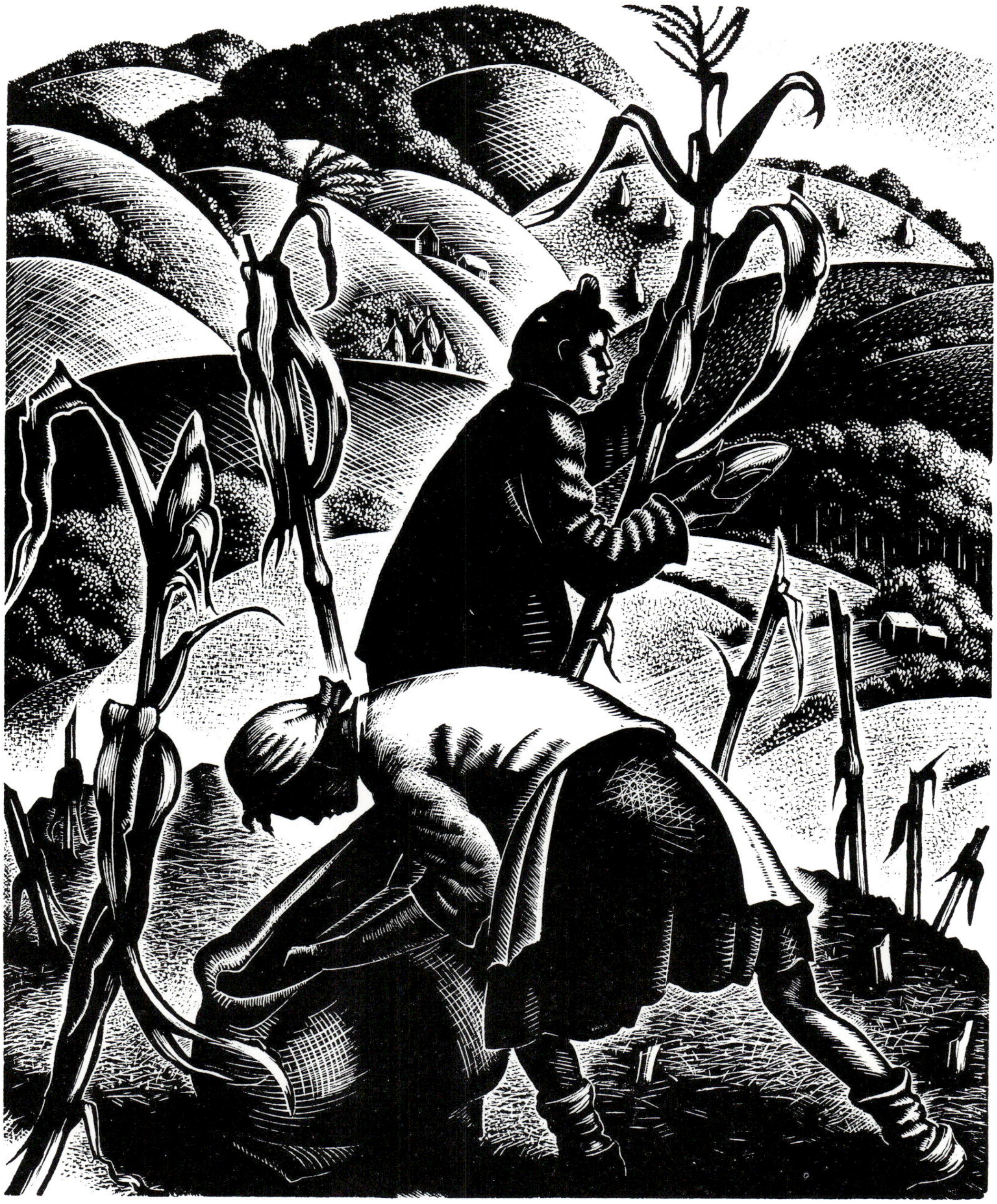

117. *Corn Pulling*, 1951–2 16.4 × 13.8 cms.: 6⁷⁄₁₆ × 5⁷⁄₁₆ ins., commission for The Prairie Print Makers, Chicago, Illinois, 1952 D.L.

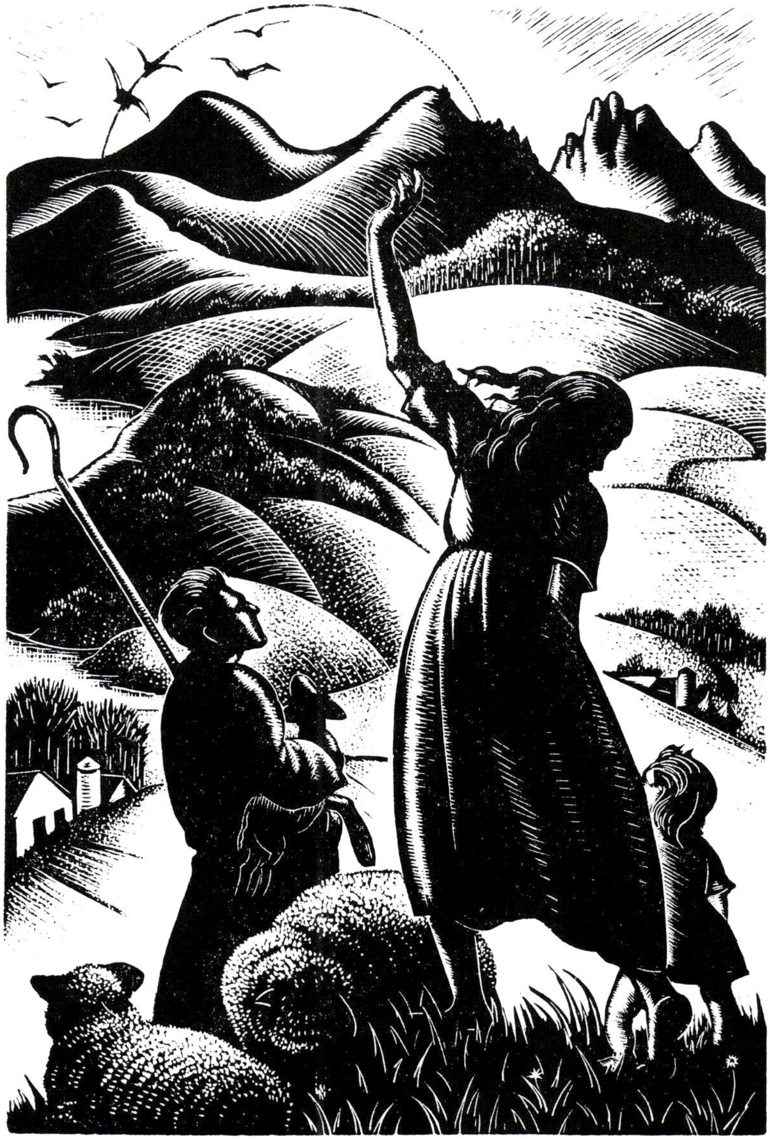

118. *Unto the Hills*, 1951–2 15.1 × 10 cms.: $5\frac{15}{16}$ × $3\frac{15}{16}$ ins. p. 2. Psalm 1, in *The Book of Psalms etc.*, New York: Doubleday Co., Inc., 1952

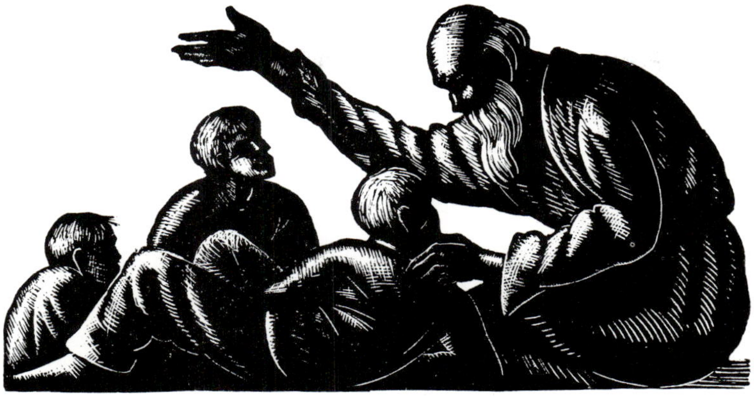

119a. *Hear ye children, the instruction of a father*, 1951–2 5.2 × 10 cms.: 2¹⁄₁₆ × 3¹⁵⁄₁₆ ins. p. 217 Proverbs, chapter 4, in *The Book of Psalms etc.*, New York: Doubleday Co., Inc., 1952

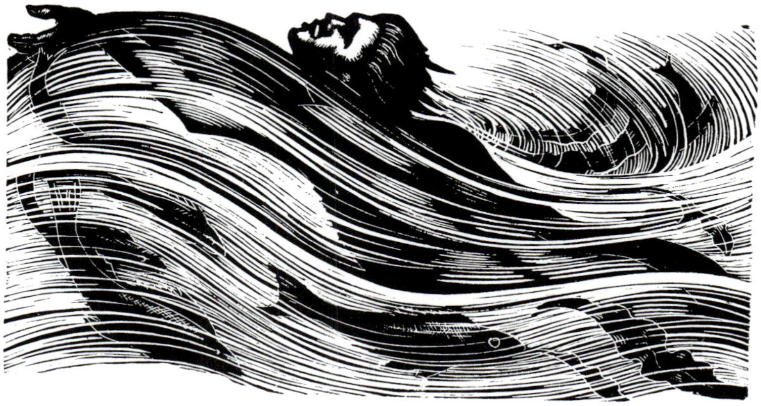

119b. *He sent from above, he took me, he drew me out of many waters.* 1951–2 5.2 × 10 cms.: 2¹⁄₁₆ × 3¹⁵⁄₁₆ ins. p. 21 Psalm 18, in *The Book of Psalms etc.*, New York: Doubleday Co., Inc., 1952

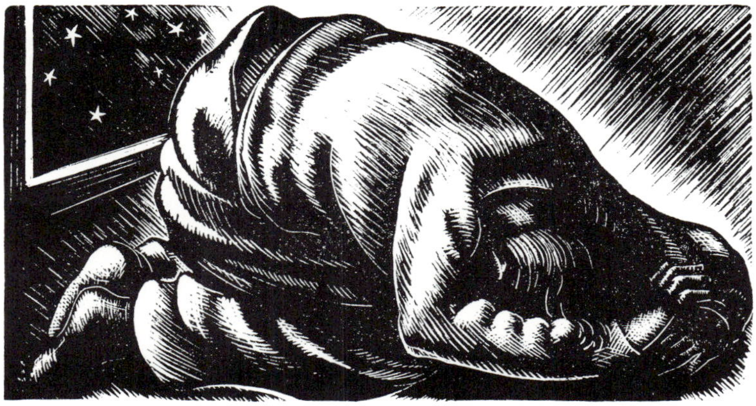

119c. *I cried with my whole heart*, 1951–2 5.2 × 10 cms.: 2¹⁄₁₆ × 3¹⁵⁄₁₆ ins., p. 176 Psalm 119, Koph, in *The Book of Psalms etc.*, New York: Doubleday Co., Inc., 1952

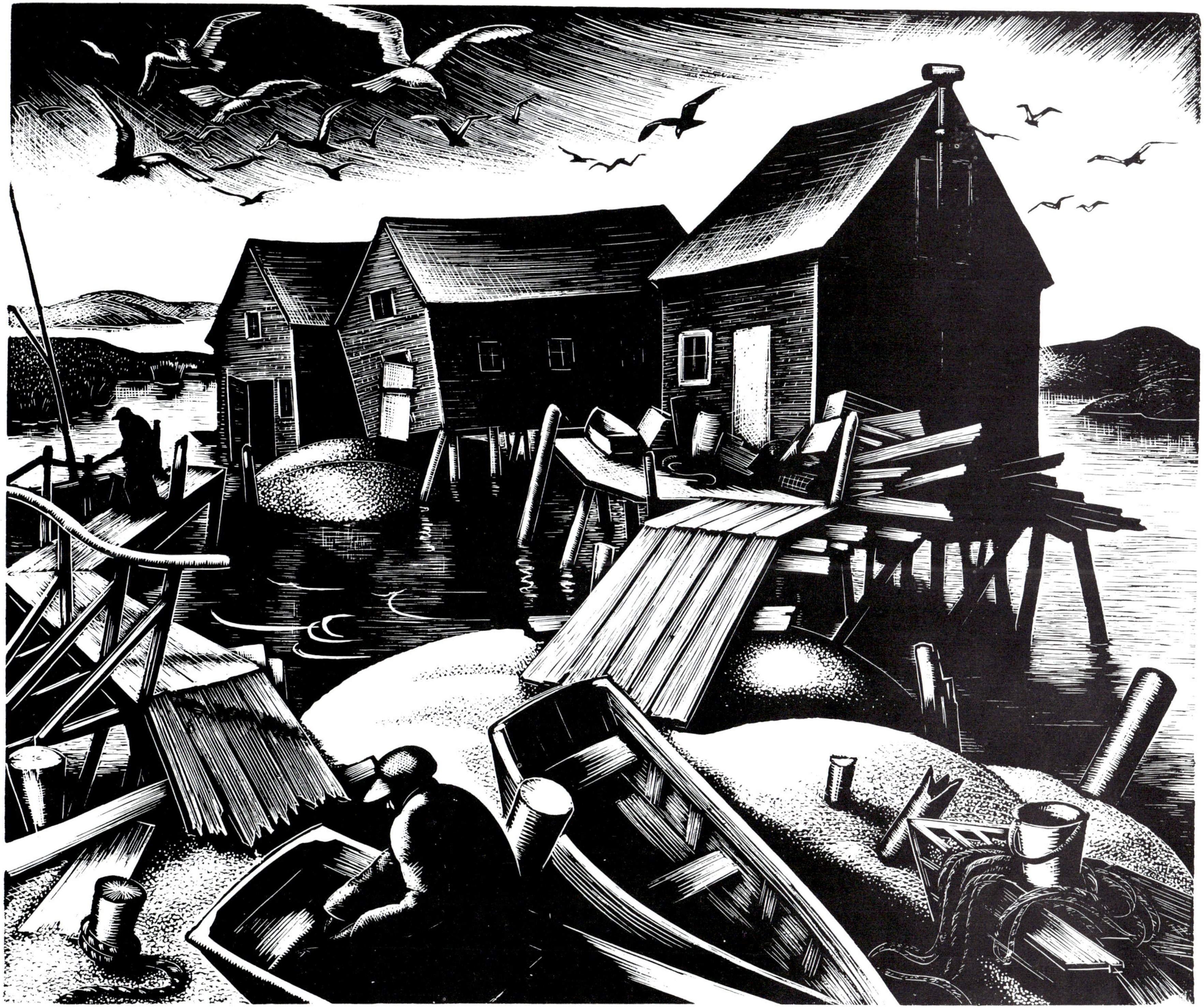

120. *Oysterhouses*, 1948–53 20.8 × 25.1 cms.: 8$^{3}/_{16}$ × 9⅞ ins., here reproduced from an impression in the Department of Western Art, Ashmolean Museum, Oxford

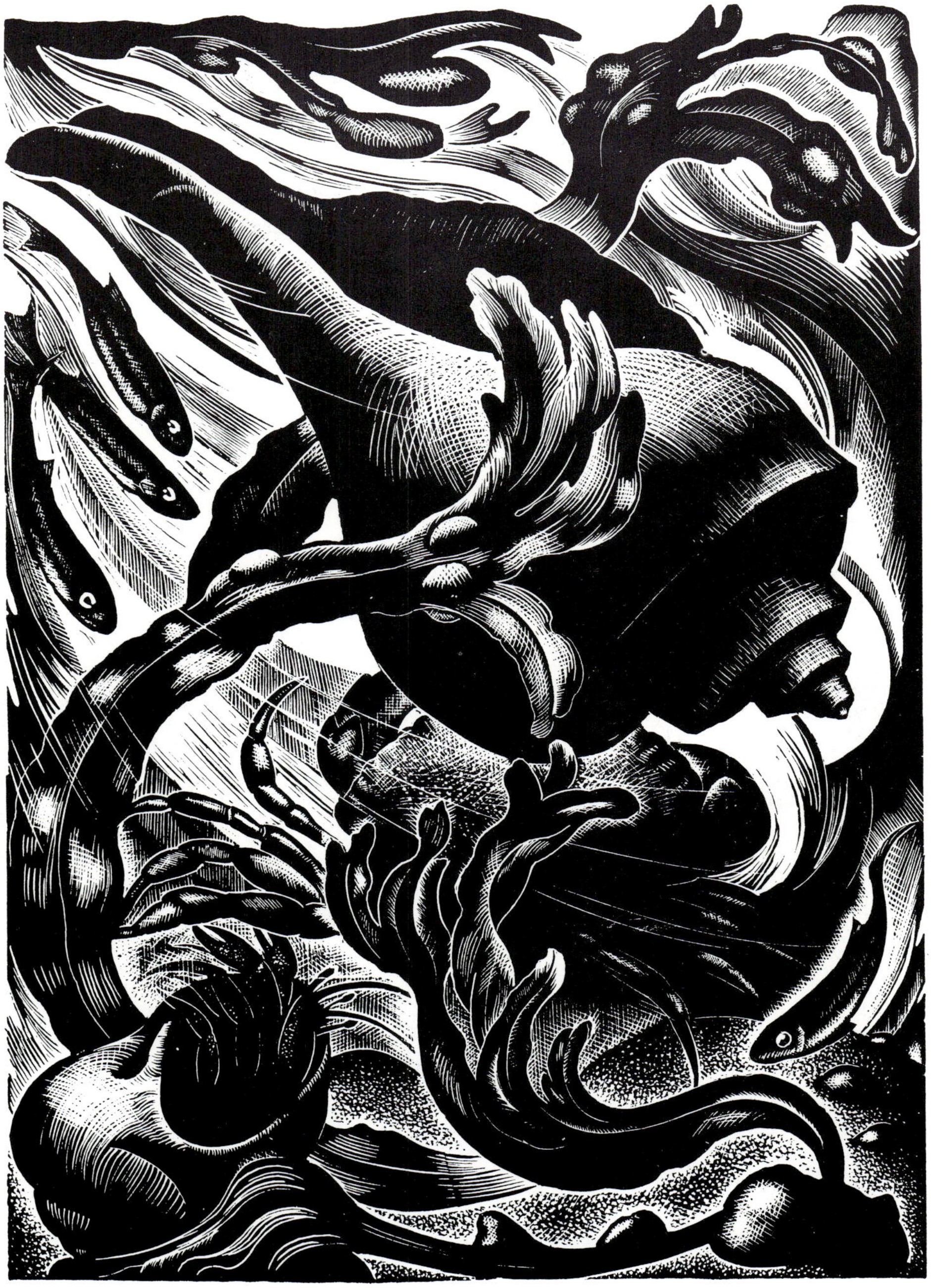

121. *Shells and Seaweed*, 1953 17 × 12.3 cms.: 6¹¹⁄₁₆ × 4¹³⁄₁₆ ins., p. 45 in Clare Leighton, *Where Land meets Sea*, New York: Rinehart & Co., 1954

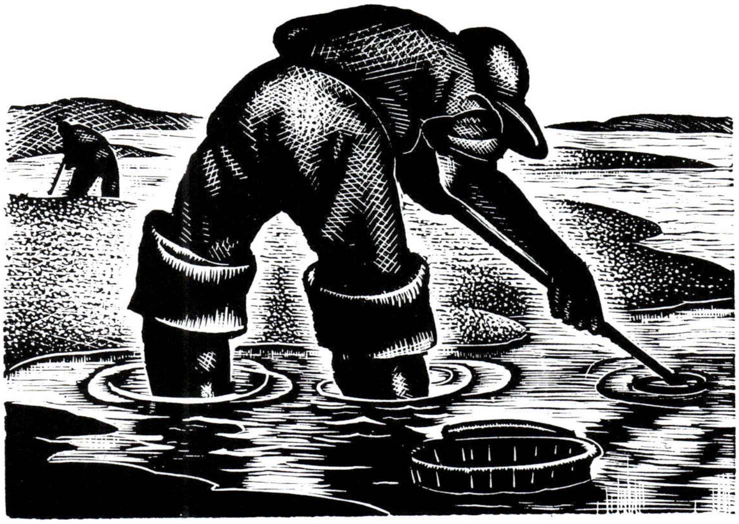

122a. *The Magic of the Flats*, 1953 6.8 × 9.5 cms.: 2¹¹⁄₁₆ × 3¾ ins. p. 41 in Clare Leighton, *Where Land meets Sea*, New York: Rinehart & Co., 1954

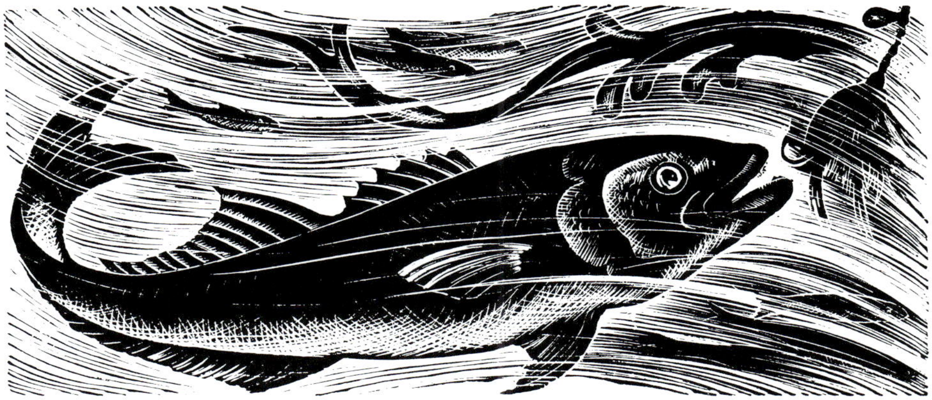

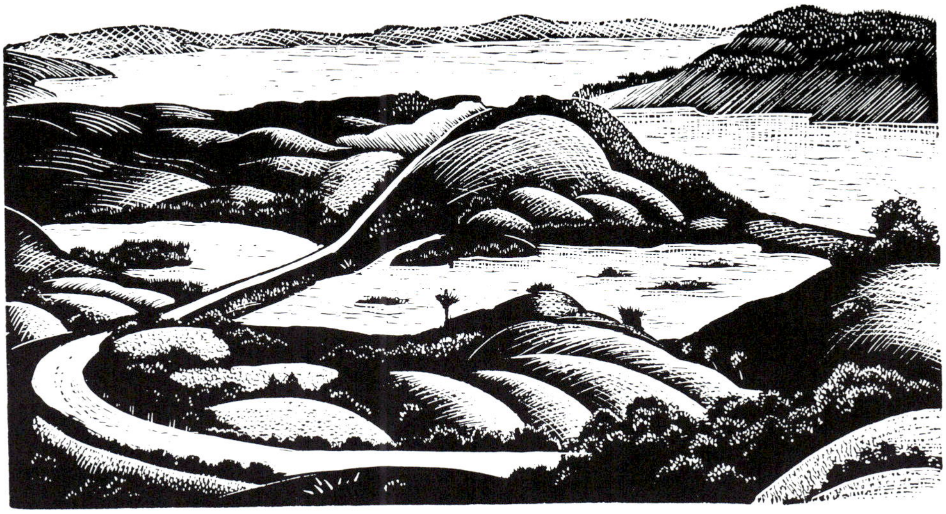

122b. *Bluefish*, 1953 5.2 × 12.3 cms.: 2¹⁄₁₆ × 4¹³⁄₁₆ ins., p. 57 in Clare Leighton, *Where Land meets Sea*, New York: Rinehart & Co., 1954

122c. *Cape Cod Road*, 1953 6.7 × 12.3 cms.: 2⅝ × 4¹³⁄₁₆ ins., p. 3 in Clare Leighton, *Where Land meets Sea*, New York: Rinehart & Co., 1954

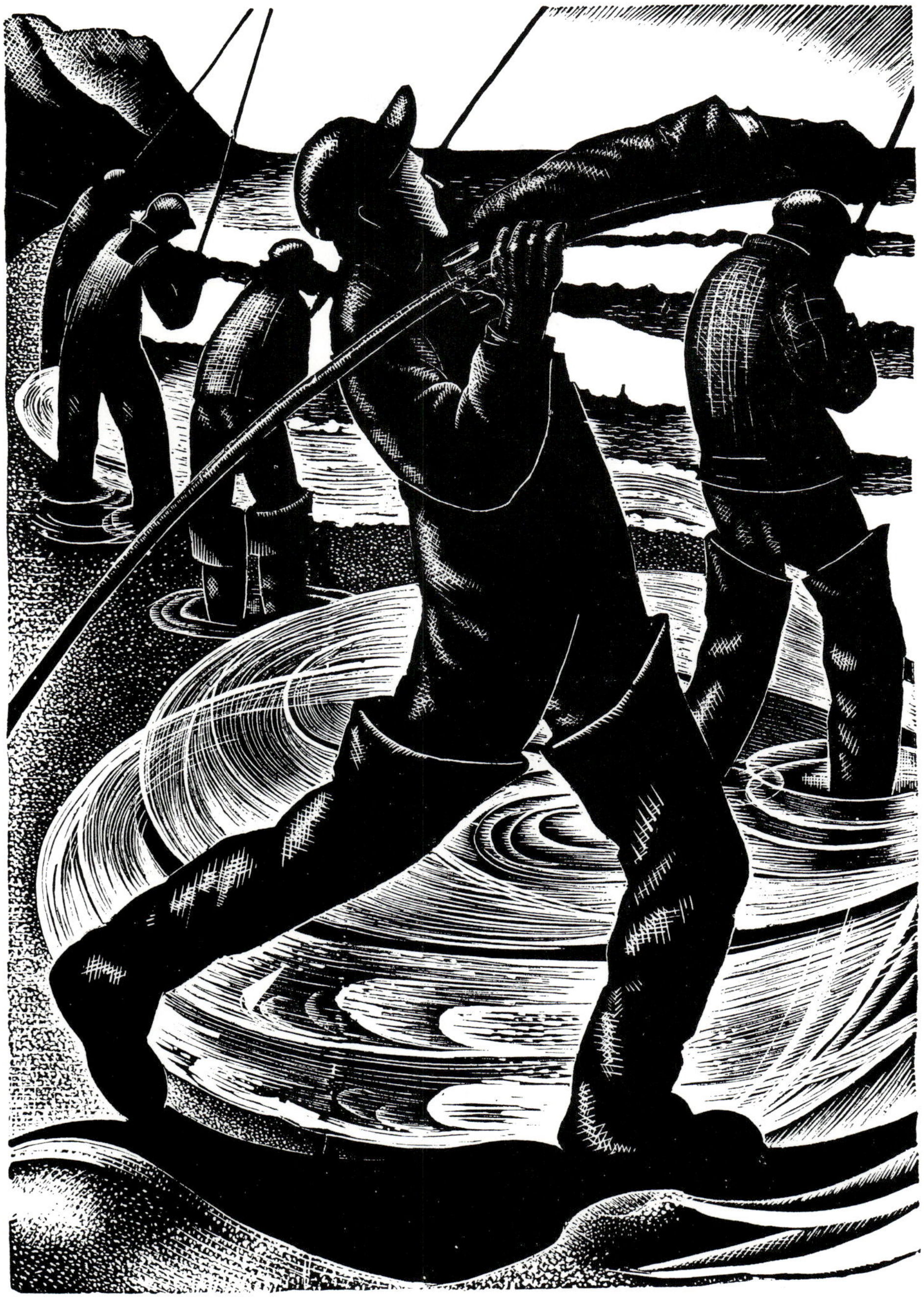

123. *Casting*, 1953 17.3 × 12.4 cms.: $6^{13}/_{16}$ × $4^{3}/_{4}$ ins., p. 95 in Clare Leighton, *Where Land meets Sea*, New York: Rinehart & Co., 1954

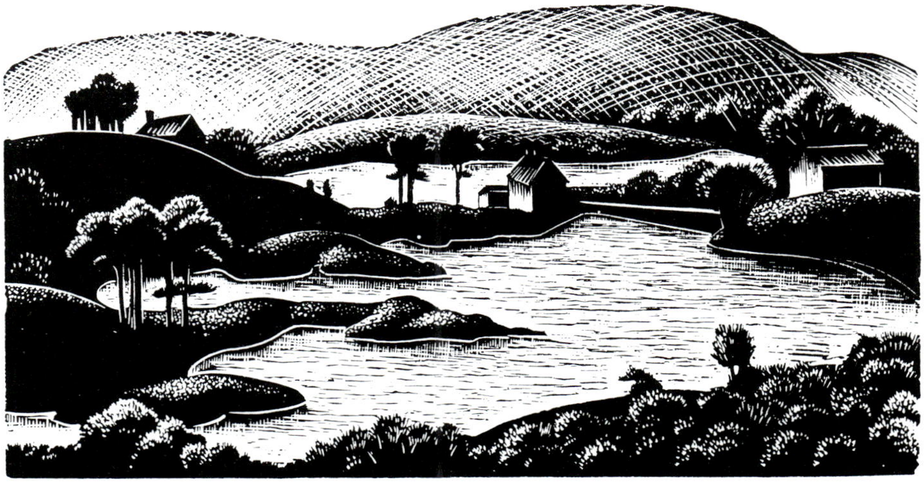

124a. *The Bay*, 1953 6.4 × 12.4 cms.: 2½ × 4¾ ins., p. 67 in Clare Leighton, *Where Land meets Sea*, New York: Rinehart & Co., 1954

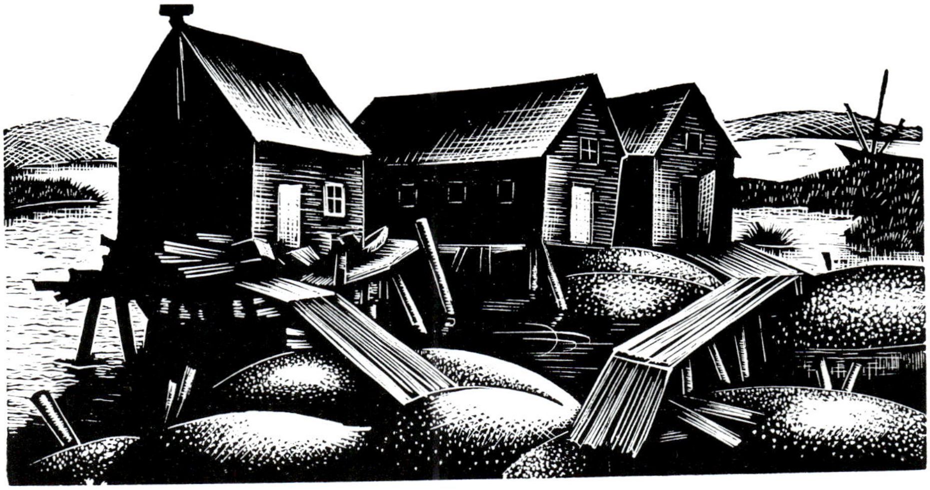

124b. *The Wellfleet Oysterhouses*, 1953 6.5 × 12.4 cms.: 2⁹⁄₁₆ × 4¾ ins., p. 117 in Clare Leighton, *Where Land meets Sea*, New York: Rinehart & Co., 1954

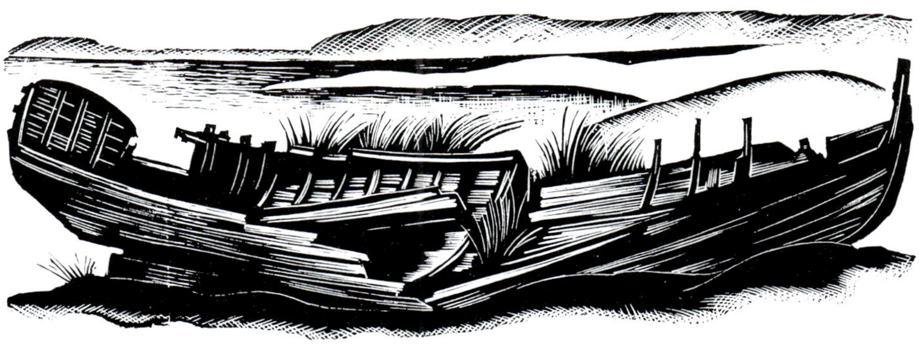

124c. *Wrecked Boat*, 1953 4.5 × 12.4 cms.: 1¾ × 4¾ ins., p. 127 in Clare Leighton, *Where Land meets Sea*, New York: Rinehart & Co., 1954

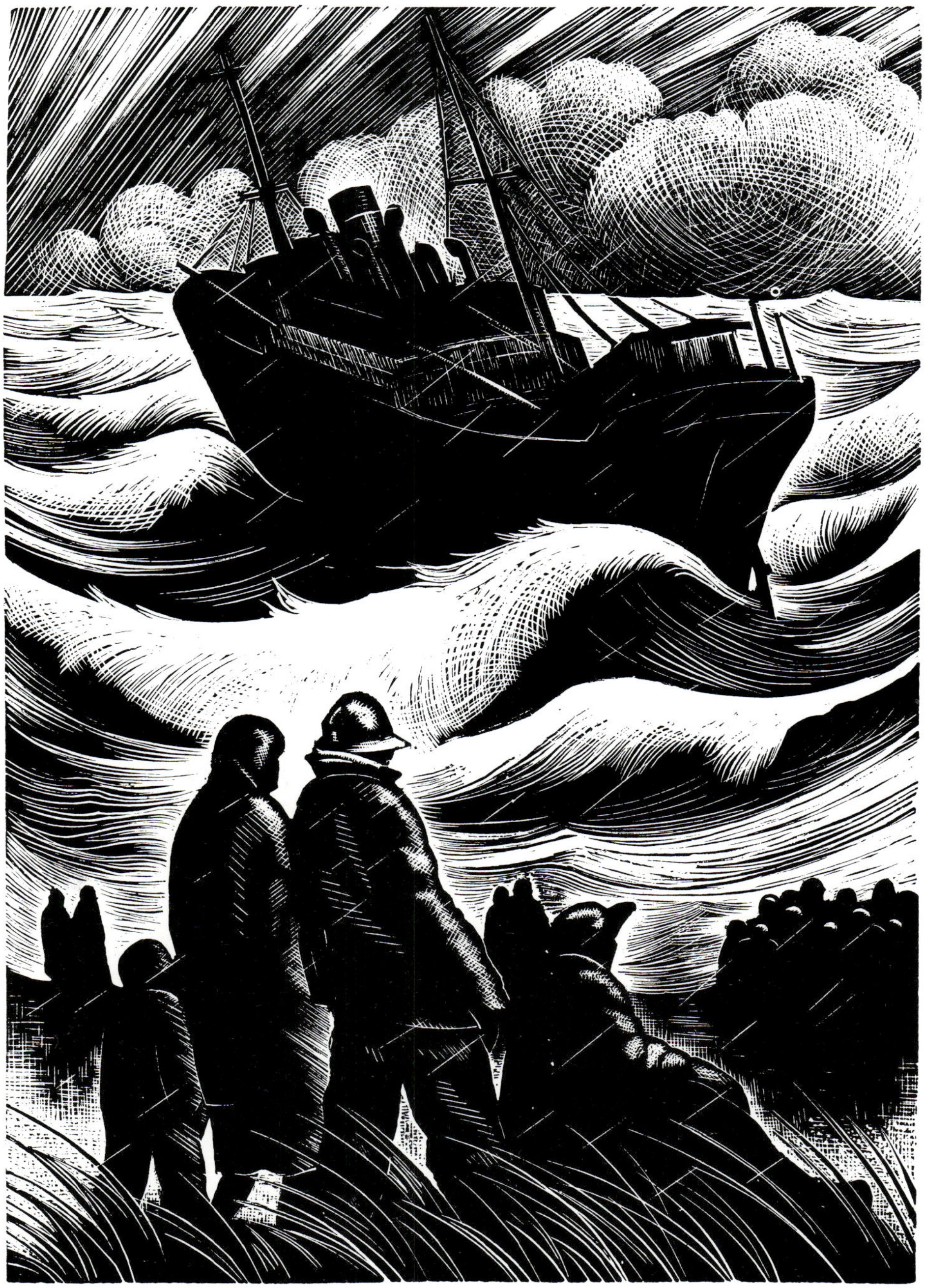

125. *Ship Wreck*, 1953 17.2 × 12.3 cms.: 6¾ × 4$^{13}/_{16}$ ins., p. 131 in Clare Leighton, *Where Land meets Sea*, New York: Rinehart & Co., 1954

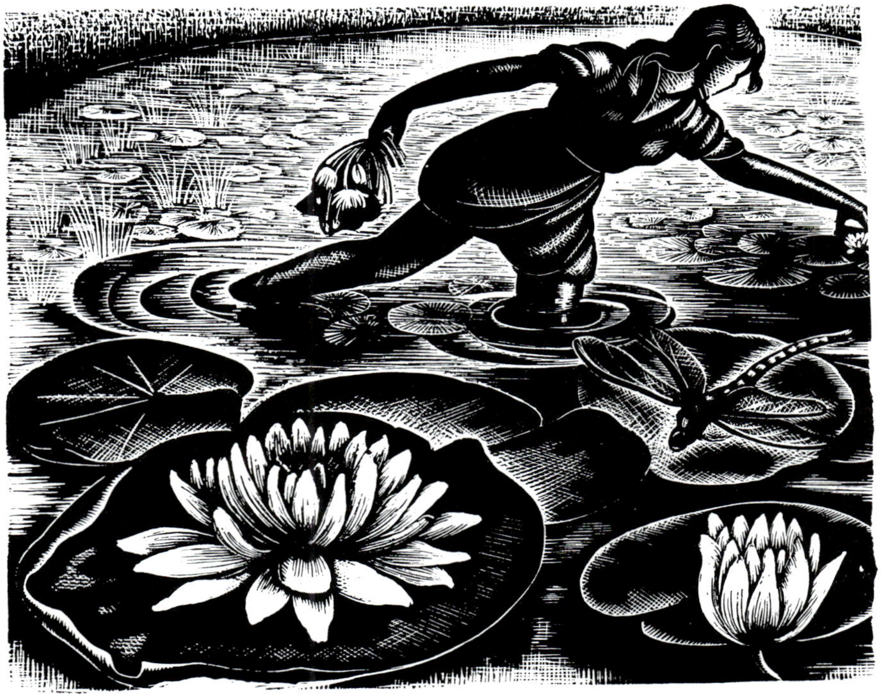

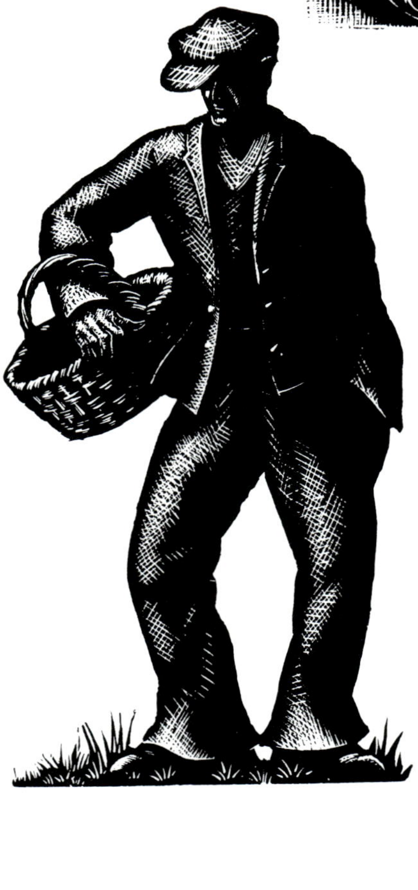

126a. *Gathering Water Lilies*, 1953 9.1 × 12.4 cms.: $3\frac{9}{16} \times 4\frac{3}{4}$ ins., p. 167 in Clare Leighton, *Where Land meets Sea*, New York: Rinehart & Co., 1954

126b. *The Berry Picker*, 1953 10.3 × 5.4 cms.: $4\frac{1}{16} \times 2\frac{1}{8}$ ins., p. 166 in Clare Leighton, *Where Land meets Sea*, New York: Rinehart & Co., 1954

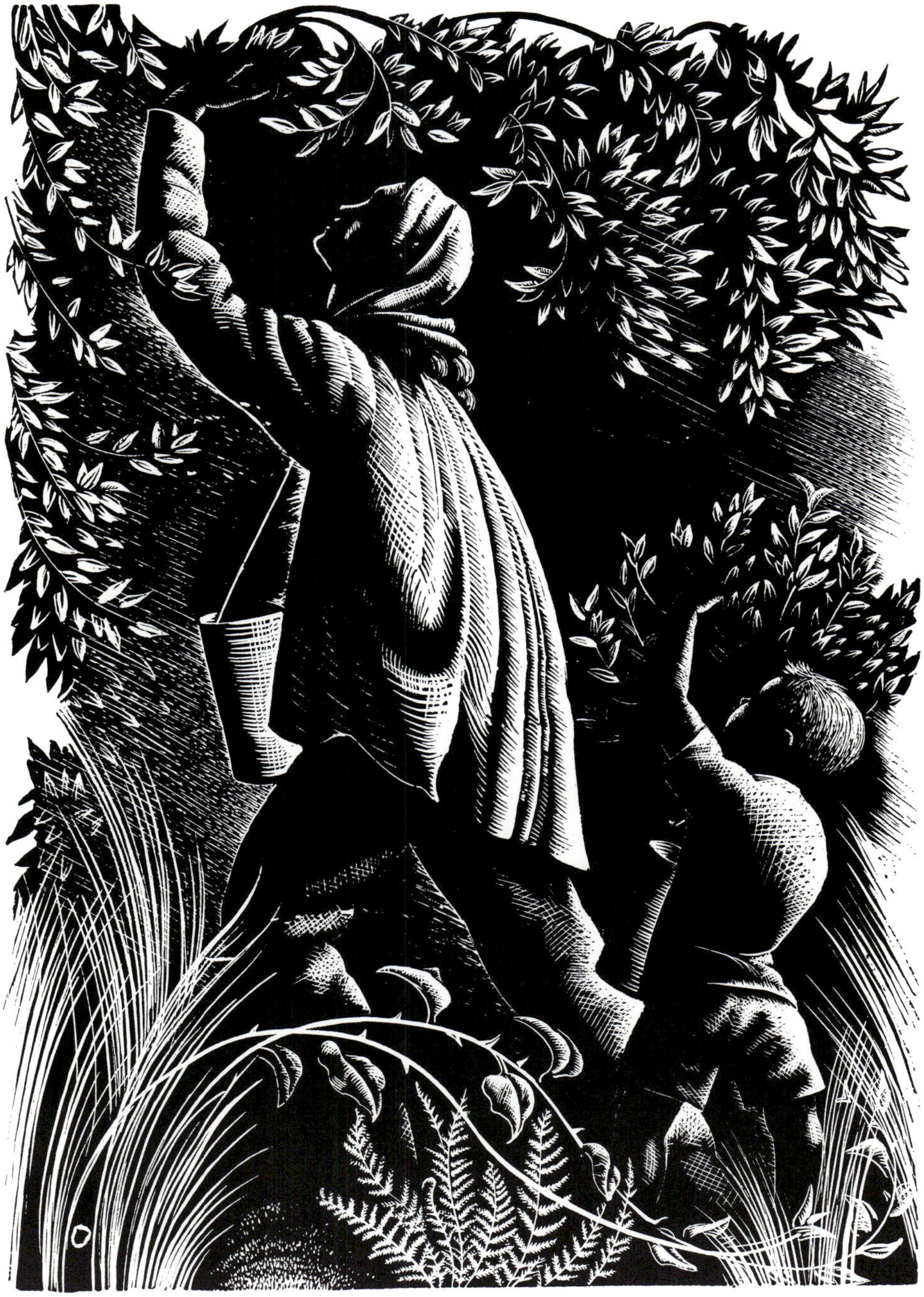

127. *Picking Blueberries*, 1953 17.2 × 12.4 cms.: 6¾ × 4¾ ins., p. 155 in Clare Leighton, *Where Land meets Sea*, New York: Rinehart & Co., 1954

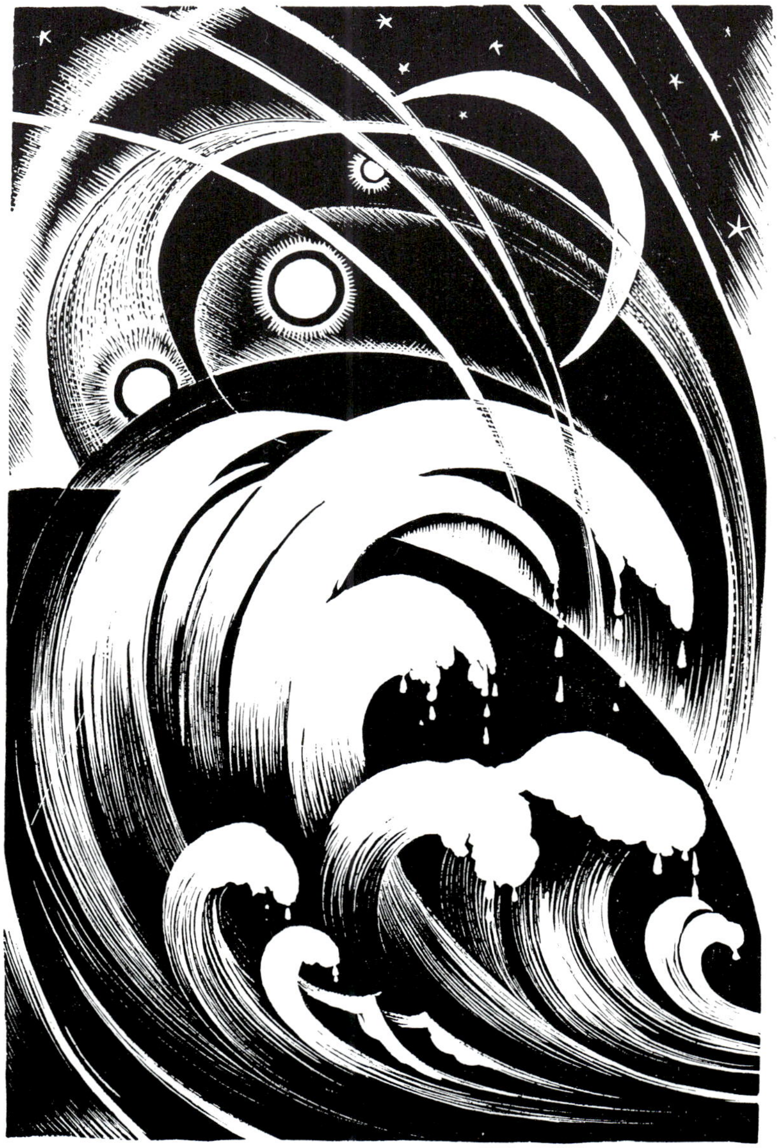

128. *In the Beginning*, 1953. 15.3 × 10.2 cms.: 6 × 4 ins., p. 2 in *Imagination's Other Place*, edited by Helen Plotz, New York: Thomas Y. Crowell, 1955

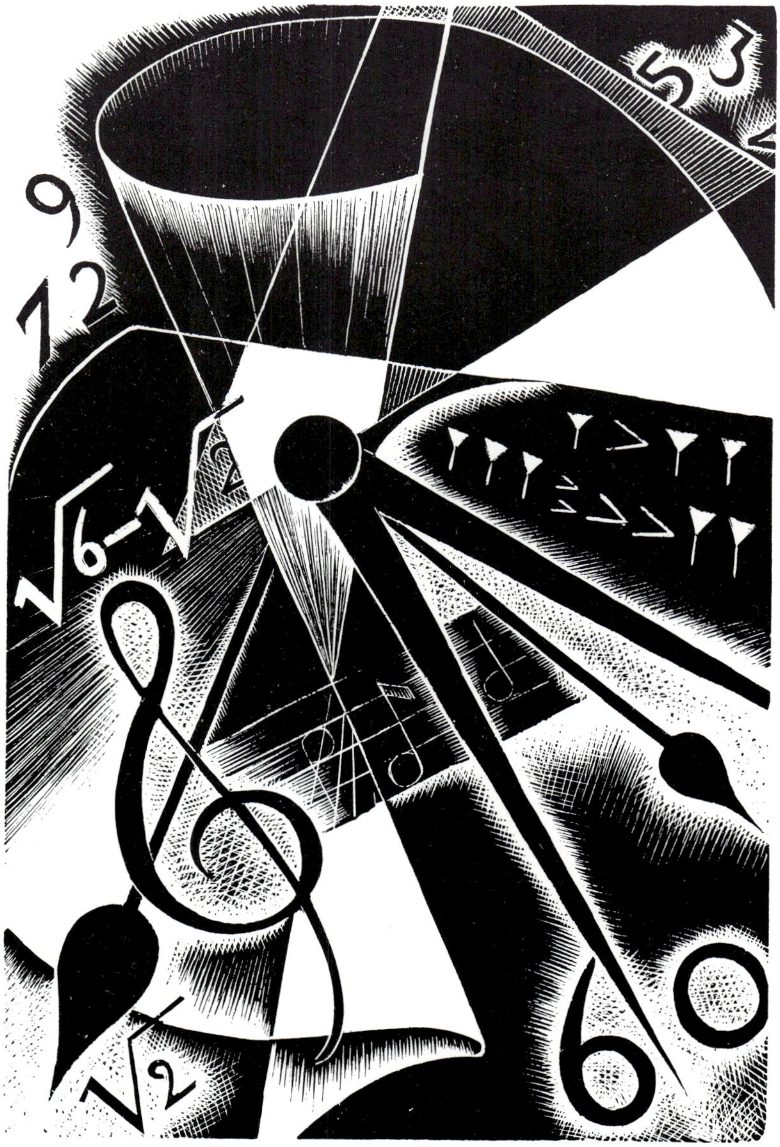

129. *Euclid*, 1953 15.3 × 10.2 cms.: 6 × 4 ins., p. 58 in *Imagination's Other Place*, edited by Helen Plotz, New York: Thomas Y. Crowell, 1955.

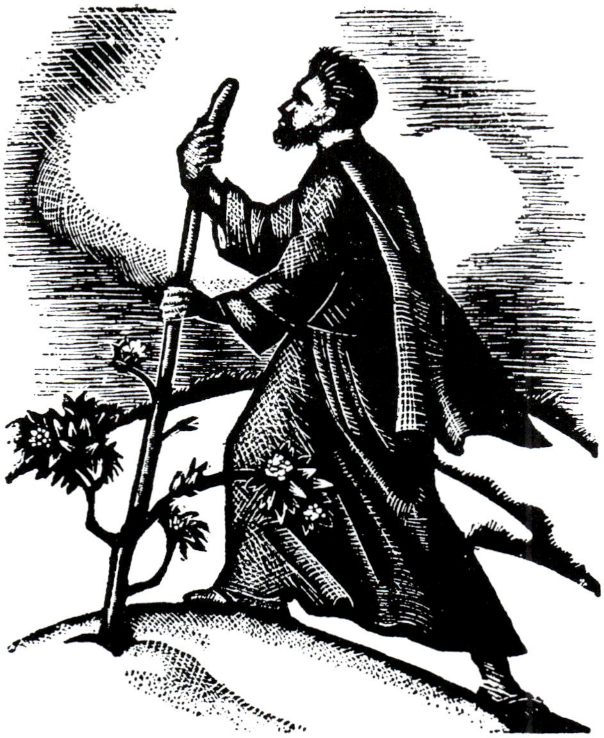

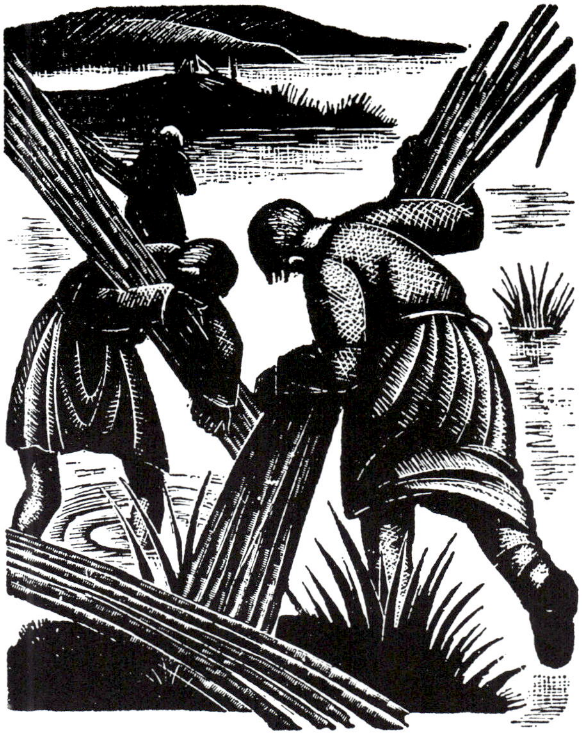

130a. *Joseph of Arimathea*, 1960 9.8 × 7.8 cms.: 3⅞ × 3¹⁄₁₆ ins., p. 5 in Hugh Ross Williamson, *The Flowering Hawthorn*, London: Peter Davies; New York: Hawthorn Books, 1962

130b. *'And there he built with wattles from the marsh/A little lonely church in days of yore'*, 1960 9.8 × 7.6 cms.: 3⅞ × 3 ins., p. 36 in Hugh Ross Williamson, *The Flowering Hawthorn*, London: Peter Davies; New York: Hawthorn Books, 1962

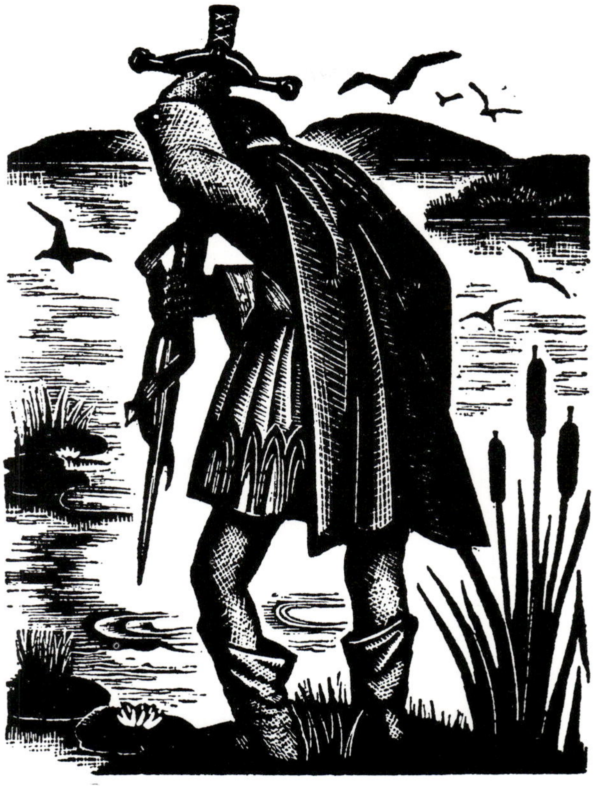

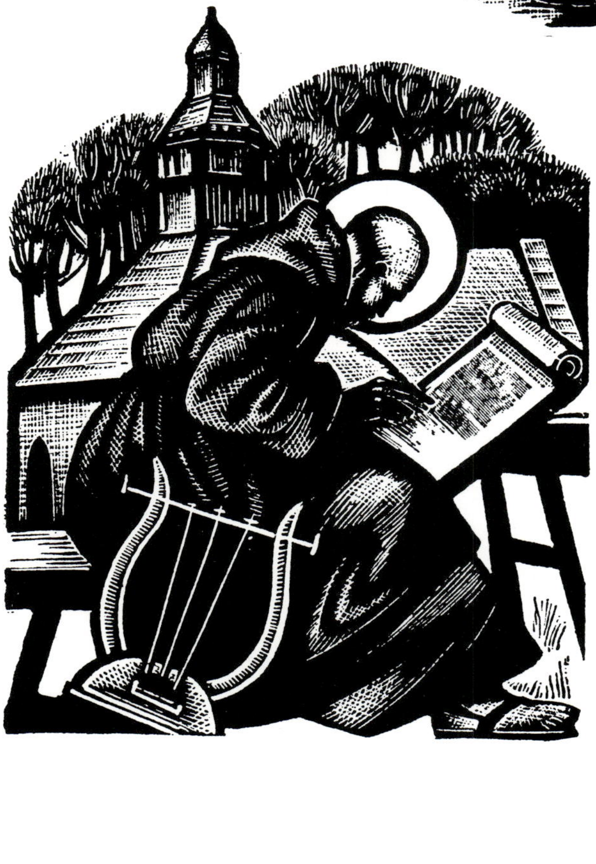

131a. *Sir Bedivere committing King Arthur's Sword Excalibur to the lake*, 1960
10.2 × 7.6 cms.: 4 × 3 ins., p. 61 in Hugh Ross Williamson, *The Flowering Hawthorn*, London: Peter Davies; New York: Hawthorn Books, 1962

131b. *St. Dunstan composing the music which he himself played on the harp*, 1960
9.5 × 7.6 cms.: 3¾ × 3 ins., p. 74 in Hugh Ross Williamson, *The Flowering Hawthorn*, London: Peter Davies; New York: Hawthorn Books, 1962

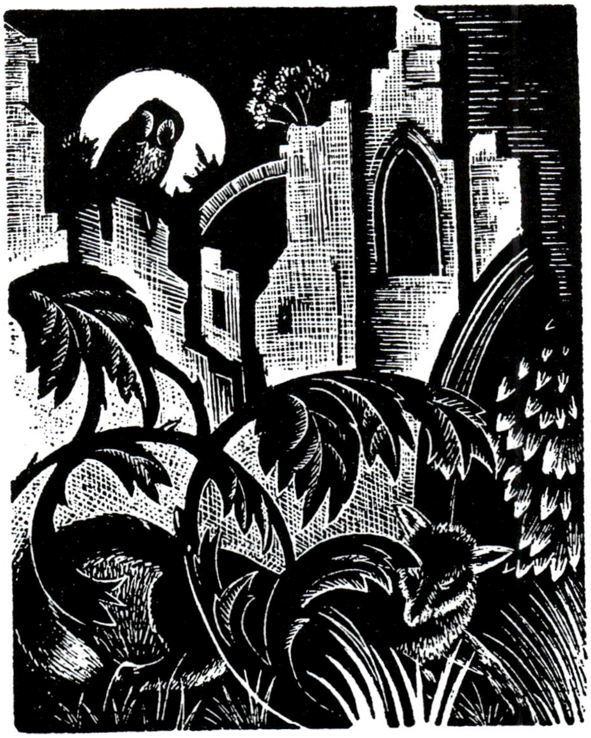

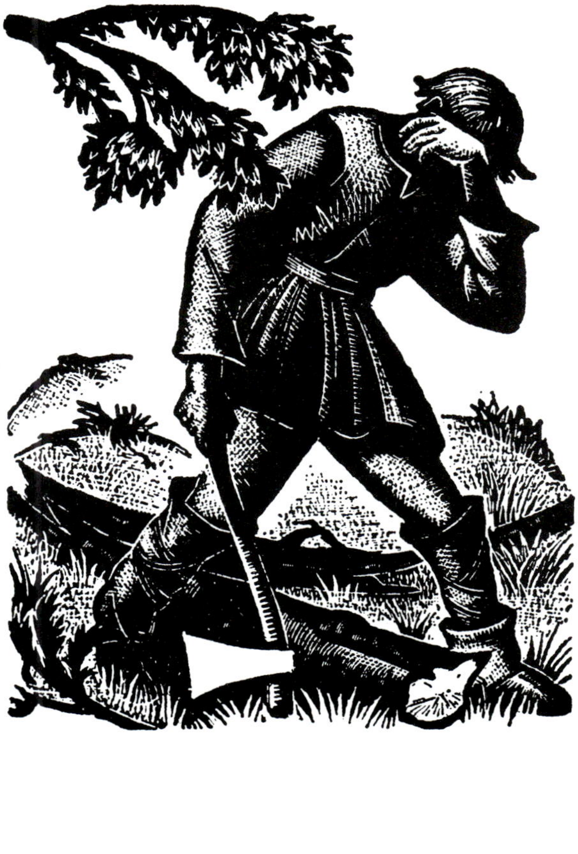

132a. *The ruins of Glastonbury at night, with the Wordsworth poem in mind*, 1960 7.5 × 9.5 cms.: 2¹⁵⁄₁₆ × 3¾ ins., p. 89 in Hugh Ross Williamson, *The Flowering Hawthorn*, London: Peter Davies: New York: Hawthorn Books, 1962

132b. *A local zealot blinded by a chip whilst attempting to cut down the hawthorn tree on Weary-all Hill*, 1960 9.5 × 7.5 cms.: 3¾ × 2¹⁵⁄₁₆ ins., p. 109 in Hugh Ross Williamson, *The Flowering Hawthorn*, London: Peter Davies: New York: Hawthorn Books, 1962

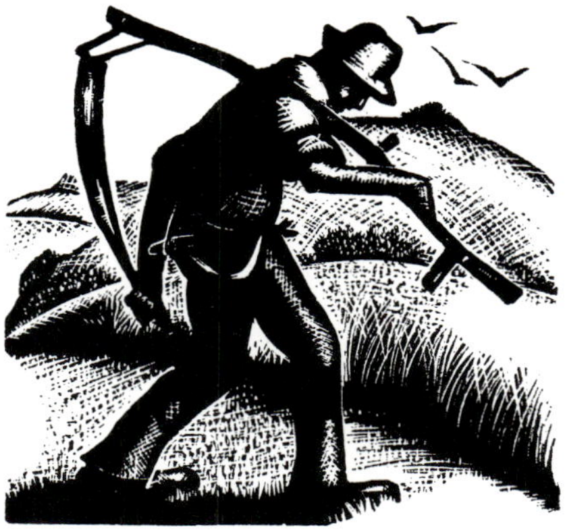

133a. *Farmer*, 1975 5.1 × 5.4 cms.: 2 × 2⅛ ins., title page in Clare Leighton, *Growing New Roots*, San Francisco: The Book Club of California, 1976

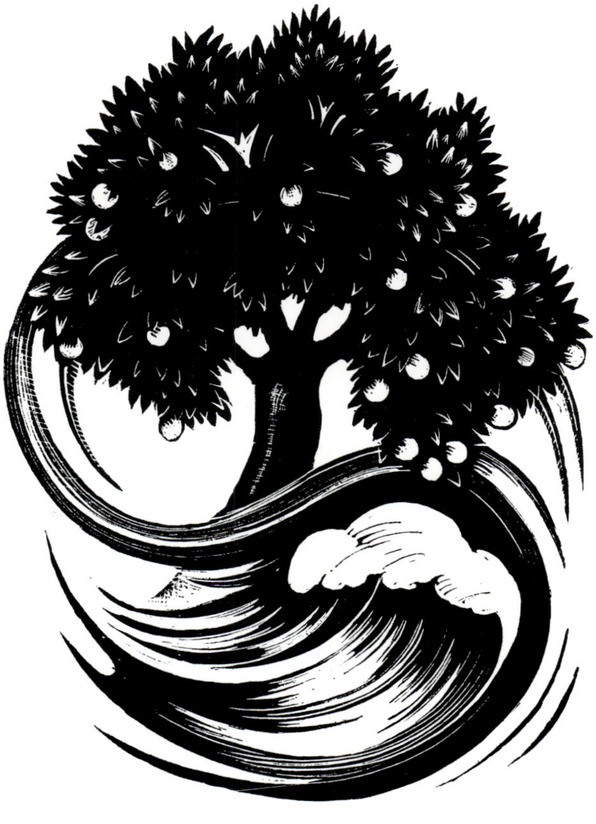

133b. *Growing New Roots, Safe and Firm*, 1975 10.5 × 7.9 cms.: 4⅛ × 3⅛ ins., frontispiece in Clare Leighton, *Growing New Roots*, San Francisco: The Book Club of California, 1976

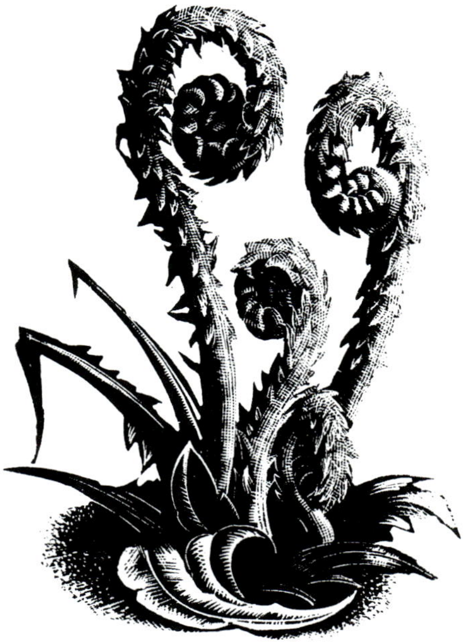

134a. *The Fern*, 1975 7.9 × 5.9 cms.: 3⅛ × 2$\frac{5}{16}$ ins. (p. 17) in Clare Leighton, *Growing New Roots*, San Francisco: The Book Club of California, 1976

134b. *Homespun are we, Fashioned from Yarns, Legends, Forebearers* (sic), *Heroes*, 1975 10.2 × 8.6 cms.: 4 × 3⅜ ins. (p. 25) in Clare Leighton, *Growing New Roots*, San Francisco: The Book Club of California, 1976

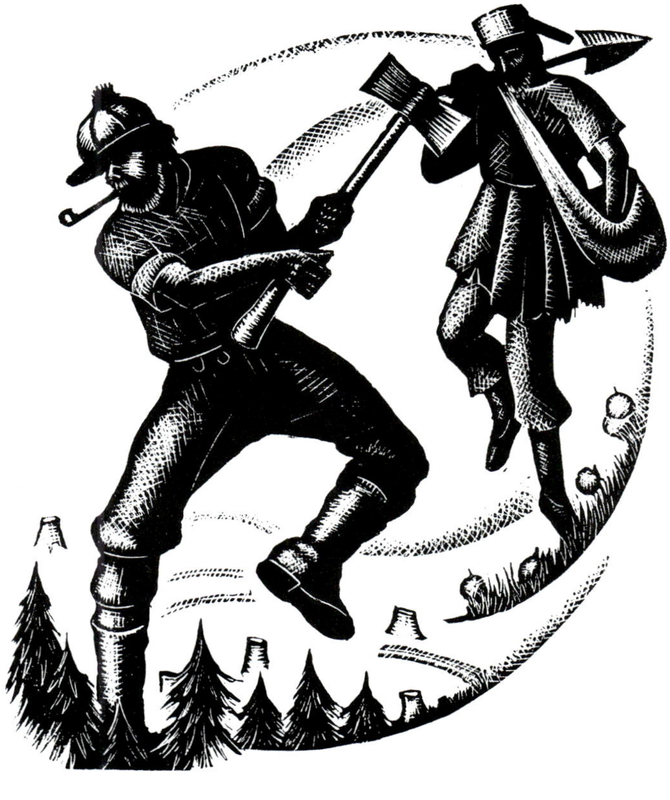

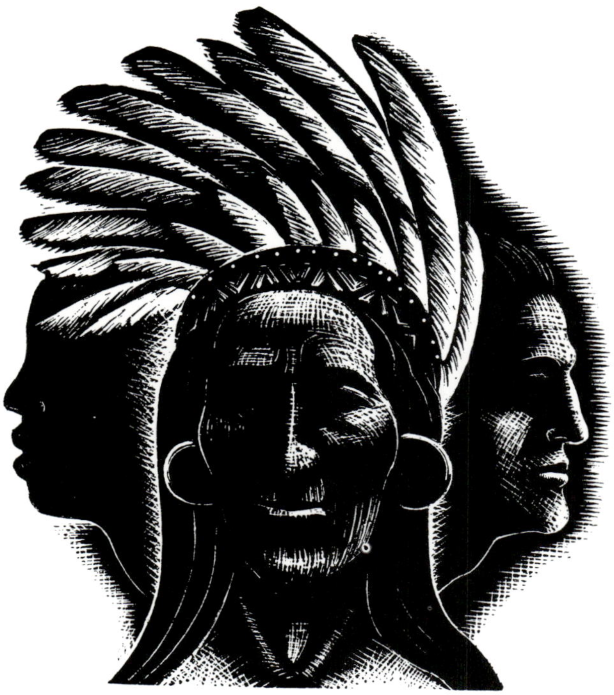

135a. *Nations Many, One People, One Country*, 1975 9.1 × 8.1 cms.: 3⁹⁄₁₆ × 3³⁄₁₆ ins. (p. 21) in Clare Leighton, *Growing New Roots*, San Francisco: The Book Club of California, 1976

135b. *The American Genius, Change, Diversity, Stability*, 1975 10 × 8.3 cms.: 3¹⁵⁄₁₆ × 3¼ ins. (p. 27) in Clare Leighton, *Growing New Roots*, San Francisco: The Book Club of California, 1976

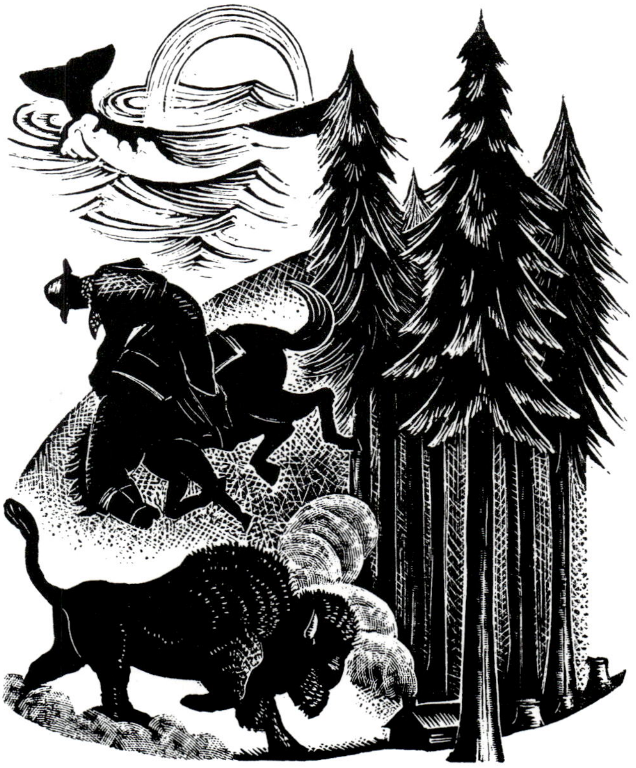

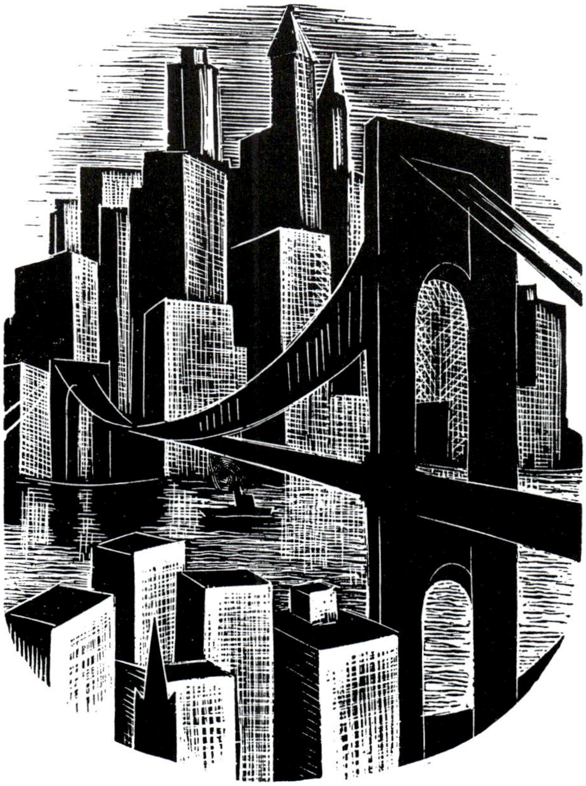

136a. *A Common Lot, Villages, Towns, Cities*, 1975 10.5 × 7.6 cms.: 4⅛ × 3 ins. (p. 31) in Clare Leighton, *Growing New Roots*, San Francisco: The Book Club of California, 1976

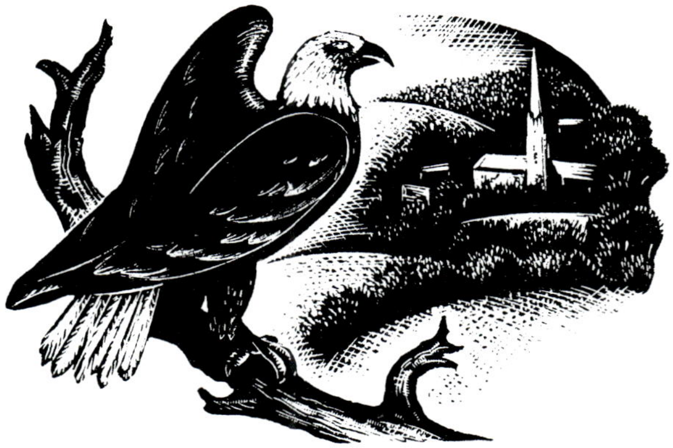

136b. *The American Vista, A Heritage rich, A Future open*, 1975 5.1 × 7.6 cms.: 2 × 3 ins. (p. 49) in Clare Leighton, *Growing New Roots*, San Francisco: The Book Club of California, 1976

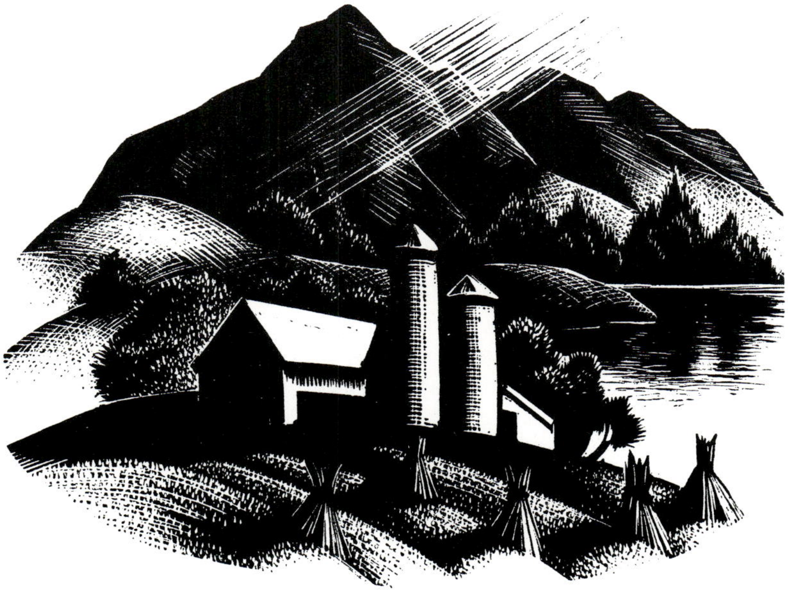

137a. *America, Now Mine, Yours too,* 1975 7.9 × 10.3 cms.: 3⅛ × 4¹⁄₁₆ ins. (p. 37) in Clare Leighton, *Growing New Roots*, San Francisco: The Book Club of California, 1976

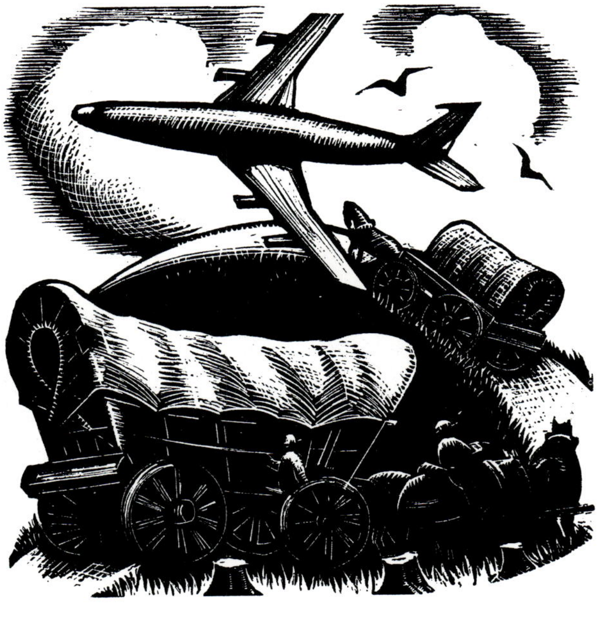

137b. *A People ever moving on, Frontiers to Fathom,* 1975 7.8 × 7.8 cms.: 3¹⁄₁₆ × 3¹⁄₁₆ ins. (p. 33) in Clare Leighton, *Growing New Roots*, San Francisco: The Book Club of California, 1976

BIBLIOGRAPHY

The writings of Clare Leighton

Wood-engraving and Woodcuts: How to do it series, No. 2, London: The Studio, October 1932; 2nd impression October 1932; new edition 1944; 3rd edition 1948

The Farmer's Year: A Calendar of English Husbandry. London: Collins, November 1933; 2nd impression January 1934; 3rd impression February 1934; American edition, New York: Longmans, Green and Co., 1933 (in slip-case)

Four Hedges: A Gardener's Chronicle. London: Gollancz, October 1935; 2nd impression November 1935; 3rd impression November 1935; 4th impression December 1935; 1st cheap edition autumn 1936; 2nd edition 1946; 3rd edition 1970; 4th English edition St. Albans: The Sumach Press, 1991; American edition, New York: Macmillan Co., 1935

Wood Engravings of the 1930s. London: The Studio Ltd., 1936 (cloth and paper editions); New York: The Studio Publications Inc., 1936

Country Matters. London: Gollancz, 1937; New York: Macmillan Co., 1937 (with the addition of a *Preface* dated September 1937); 2nd American impression 1939

Southern Harvest. New York: Macmillan Co., 1942; London: Gollancz, 1943 (size reduced and text and blocks, though entire, occupy less pages. There is a special *Introduction* for the English edition).

Where Land meets Sea: The Tide Line of Cape Cod. New York: Rinehart and Co., 1954; Riverside, Connecticut: The Chatham Press, 1973 (with new sub-title: *The Enduring Cape Cod*, and a new *Introduction*); Boston, Massachusetts: Godine, 1984 (paperback).

Growing New Roots: An Essay with Fourteen Wood Engravings. San Francisco: The Book Club of California, 1976 (edition limited to 500 copies, signed by the artist).

Books with illustrations by Clare Leighton

HOLTBY, Winifred. *Lovers' Meeting*. London: *The New Leader Book*, The Blackfriars Press, 1925

MACKENZIE, A. Muir. *The Half Loaf*. London: Heinemann Ltd., 1925

BODEN, F.C. *In Normandy*. London: *The New Leader Book*, Blackfriars Press, 1926.

FELIX-JONES, Ivor. *The Walking Voice*. London: Duckworth, 1926

WILDER, Thornton. *The Angel that Troubled the Waters, and other Plays*. New York, London, Toronto: Longmans, Green and Co., 1927 (edition limited to 260 copies, signed by the author. The one illustration is the only Leighton engraving in colour).

MULGAN, Alan. *Home: A New Zealander's Adventure*. London: Longmans, Green and Co., 1927

NATHAN, Robert. *The Fiddler in Barly*. London: Heinemann Ltd., 1927

AUSLANDER, Joseph. *Letters to Women*. New York, London: Harper & Brothers, 1929 (trade edition, plus edition limited to 125 copies, signed by the author, and slip-cased).

HARDY, Thomas. *The Return of the Native.* London: Macmillan and Co., Ltd., 1929; New York: Harper & Brothers, 1929 (this was a joint Macmillan/Harper & Brothers edition limited to 1500 copies, 500 for sale in England, 1000 for sale in the U.S.A., all signed by the artist, the American copies slip-cased).

WILDER, Thornton. *The Bridge of San Luis Rey.* London, New York, Toronto: Longmans, Green and Co., October 1929; new impressions November 1929 and February 1930

BELLOC, Hilaire. *Woodcuts: Examples of the work of Clare Leighton.* London, New York, Toronto: Longmans, Green and Co., 1930 (edition limited to 450 copies, signed by the artist).

BRAILSFORD, Mabel. *The Making of William Penn.* London, New York, Toronto: Longmans, Green and Co., 1930

WILDER, Thornton, *The Woman of Andros.* London, New York, Toronto: Longmans, Green and Co., 1930 (edition limited to 260 copies, signed by the author, engraving tipped in as frontispiece, artist not credited).

TOMLINSON, H.C. *The Sea and the Jungle.* London: Duckworth, 1930 (trade edition, and an edition limited to 515 copies printed on handmade paper, numbered and signed by the author); New York: Harper & Brothers, 1930 (trade edition, and an edition limited to 325 copies, signed by the author, and slip-cased).

BRONTE, Emily. *Wuthering Heights.* London: Duckworth, 1931; New York: Random House, 1931 (trade edition, and edition limited to 450 copies, signed by the artist).

BENSON, Stella. *Christmas Formula and other Stories.* London: William Jackson, Ltd., 1932 (edition limited to 550 copies, signed by the author. The whole edition was taken over, after printing, by Joiner and Steele, Ltd., London).

FARJEON, Eleanor. *Pannychis.* Shaftesbury: The High House Press, 1933 (edition limited to 225 copies, signed by the author).

ADAMIC, Louis. *The Native's Return.* New York: Harper & Brothers, 1934

HOLME, Constance. *The Trumpet in the Dust.* London: Ivor Nicholson and Watson, 1934

DOUGLAS-IRVINE, Helen. *Fray Mario.* London, New York, Toronto: Longmans, Green and Co., 1939

HARDY, Thomas. *Under the Greenwood Tree or The Mellstock Quire: A Rural Painting of the Dutch School.* London: Macmillan and Co. Ltd., 1940; New York: Macmillan Col., 1940

SYMINGTON, Elsie. *By Light of Sun.* New York: G.P. Putnam's Sons, 1941

WHITE, Gilbert. *The Natural History of Selborne.* London: John Lane, Penguin paperback No. 296, 1941

ROBERTS, Elizabeth Madox. *The Time of Man.* New York: The Viking Press, 1945 (slip-cased); New York: Compass Book, 1963 (paperback with *Introduction* by Robert Penn Warren).

SASSOON, Siegfried. *Siegfried's Journey, 1916–1920.* New York: The Viking Press, 1946

CASE, Josephine. *Freedom's Farm.* Boston, Massachusetts: Houghton Mifflin and Co., 1946

The Book of Psalms and the first Psalm of David, The Book of Proverbs, the Book of Ecclesiastes, King James Version. Garden City, N.Y.: Doubleday, 1952

The Frank C. Brown Collection of North Carolina Folklore. Durham, N.C.: Duke University Press, 1952–64 (7 volumes).

PLOTZ, Helen, ed., *Imagination's Other Place: Poems of Science and Mathematics.* New York: Thomas Y. Crowell Co., 1955

PLOTZ, Helen, ed., *Untune the Sky: Poems of Music and the Dance.* New York: Thomas Y. Crowell Co., 1957

BELLOWS, Henry Adams, ed. *The Poetica Edda.* New York: The Scandinavian Foundation, 1957

ABBE, George. *The Winter House: A Novel about the Rebellion of a New England Minister's Son.* Garden City, N.Y.: Doubleday, 1957

PARKER, Elinor, ed. *I was Just Thinking: A Book of Essays.* New York: Thomas Y. Crowell Co., 1959

THOREAU, Henry David. *The Works of Henry David Thoreau.* New York: Thomas Y. Crowell Co., 1961 (cloth and paper editions, 4 volumes, slip-cased).

PARKER, Elinor, ed., *The Singing and the Gold: Poems translated from World Literature.* New York: Thomas Y. Crowell Co., 1962

WILLIAMSON, Hugh Ross. *The Flowering Hawthorn.* London: Peter Davies, 1962; New York: Hawthorn Books, 1962

PLOTZ, Helen, ed., *The Earth is the Lord's: Poems of the Spirit.* New York: Thomas Y. Crowell Co., 1965

ELLIOTT, Norman K. *The Lord Your Shepherd: The Twenty-third Psalm for Modern Man.* Garden City, N.Y.: Doubleday, 1969

BUTCHER, S.H. – LANG, Andrew. *The Odyssey of Homer.* New York: Franklin Watts Inc., Keith Jennison Books, 1969 (edition in large type).

THOREAU, Henry David. *Walden.* New York: Franklin Watts Inc., Keith Jennison Books, 1969 (edition in large type).

PLOTZ, Helen, ed., *The Pinnacled Tower: Selected Poems by Thomas Hardy.* New York: Macmillan Publishing Co., 1975

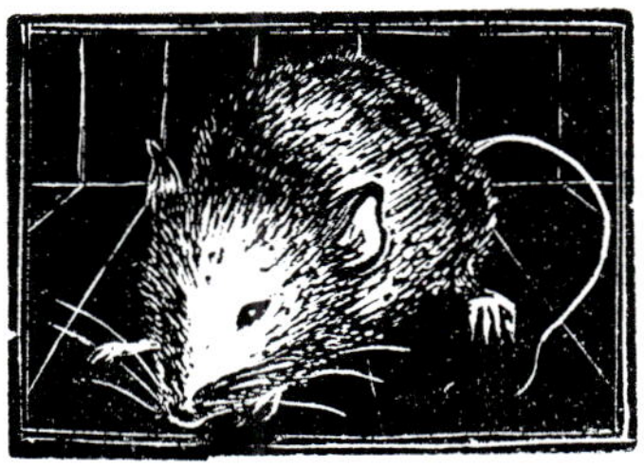

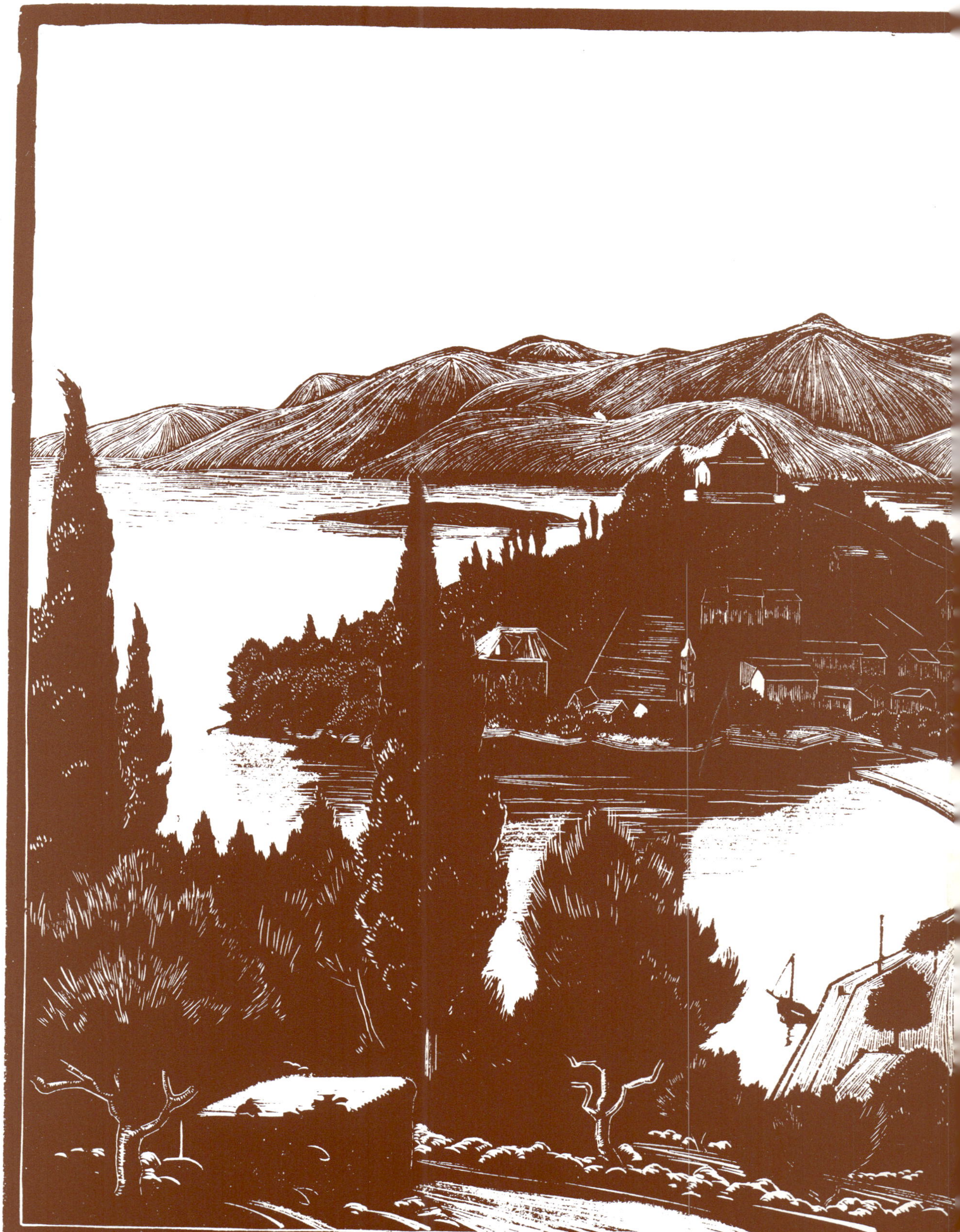